THE CORRESPONDENCE BETWEEN
PRINCESS ELISABETH OF BOHEMIA
AND RENÉ DESCARTES

THE OTHER VOICE IN EARLY MODERN EUROPE

A Series Edited by Margaret L. King and Albert Rabil Jr.

RECENT BOOKS IN THE SERIES

Princess Elisabeth of Bohemia
and
René Descartes

THE CORRESPONDENCE BETWEEN PRINCESS ELISABETH OF BOHEMIA AND RENÉ DESCARTES

ぷ

Edited and Translated
by Lisa Shapiro

THE UNIVERSITY OF CHICAGO PRESS
Chicago & London

Elisabeth of Bohemia, Princess Palatine, 1618–1680
René Descartes, 1596–1650

Lisa Shapiro is associate professor of philosophy
at Simon Fraser University.

The University of Chicago Press, Chicago 60637
The University of Chicago Press, Ltd., London
© 2007 by The University of Chicago
All rights reserved. Published 2007
Printed in the United States of America

16 15 14 13 12 11 10 09 08 07   1 2 3 4 5

ISBN-13: 978-0-226-20441-3 (cloth)
ISBN-13: 978-0-226-20442-0 (paper)
ISBN-10: 0-226-20441-3 (cloth)
ISBN-10: 0-226-20442-1 (paper)

The University of Chicago Press gratefully acknowledges the generous support of
James E. Rabil, in memory of Scottie W. Rabil, toward the publication of this book.

Library of Congress Cataloging-in-Publication Data

Elisabeth, Countess Palatine, 1618–1680.
   [Correspondence. English. Selections]
   The correspondence between Princess Elisabeth of Bohemia and René Descartes / edited
and translated by Lisa Shapiro.
      p.   cm. — (The other voice in early modern Europe)
   Includes bibliographical references and index.
   ISBN-13: 978-0-226-20441-3 (cloth : alk. paper)
   ISBN-10: 0-226-20441-3 (cloth : alk. paper)
   ISBN-13: 978-0-226-20442-0 (pbk. : alk. paper)
   ISBN-10: 0-226-20442-1 (pbk. : alk. paper)
   1. Descartes, Reni, 1596–1650—Correspondence.   2. Elisabeth, Countess Palatine,
1618–1680—Correspondence.   3. Philosophy, Modern—17th century.   I. Shapiro, Lisa.
II. Descartes, Reni, 1596–1650. Correspondence. English. Selections.   III. Title.
B1873.E55   2007
193—dc22

                                                                                    2006039657

CONTENTS

ACKNOWLEDGMENTS

This edition of Princess Elisabeth of Bohemia's correspondence with Descartes and with others has been a long time in the making, and so there are many thanks due to those who have provided assistance, advice, and encouragement along the way. I thank the Other Voice series editors for their interest in this volume, their patience as it awaited completion, and their comments on it. The enthusiasm of Annette Baier and Stephen Engstrom when I first began thinking about the project provided the impetus to get started on it. Daniel Garber and Eileen O'Neill provided significant encouragement and advice that carried through to the completion of the project. Their generosity of spirit has been remarkable. The conference on women philosophers of the seventeenth century at the University of Massachusetts–Amherst organized in 1998 by Eileen O'Neill, with Vere Chappell and Robert Sleigh, provided an occasion for me to begin thinking about Elisabeth's metaphysics. Another conference on seventeenth-century women philosophers organized by Dan Kaufman at the University of Florida gave me occasion to work out Elisabeth's position in moral philosophy. I was able to try out my translation and my reading of Elisabeth on students in a Nordic graduate course at Uppsala University. I thank them for their patience and comments. Lilli Alanen, Annette Baier, Robert D'Amico, and Charles Pidgen provided helpful feedback on parts of the introduction. Karen Detlefsen provided thoughtful comments on the whole of it. Several have alerted me to and helped me access archival material. I thank Carol Pal for drawing my attention to mentions of Elisabeth in the Pell and Coventry papers. Theo Verbeek and Erik-Jan Bos facilitated my accessing the newly rediscovered manuscripts of Elisabeth's letters and, with Jeroen van de Ven, provided answers to questions of historical context. Dr. Jorien Jas, of the Geldersch Landschap/Geldersche Kasteelen, made my examination of those manuscripts seem effortless. Thanks to Susanne Fader, Jennifer Liderth, and Patrick Monaghan for help in the mechanics of preparing the manuscript. Thanks to Randy Petilos for help in securing permission for the portraits of Elisabeth and for his general editorial assistance. Susan Tarcov's fine copy-editing improved the translation immensely. The errors remain all my own. Eileen's work on the women philosophers of the early modern period deserves special mention. Her efforts to rehabilitate and methods in reading these women are inspirational. Her own work provides a model that mine can only attempt to emulate. Support from the National Endowment for the Humanities, the American Council of Learned Societies, and Simon Fraser University facilitated the completion of this edition.

Lisa Shapiro

THE OTHER VOICE IN
EARLY MODERN EUROPE:
INTRODUCTION TO THE SERIES

Margaret L. King and Albert Rabil Jr.

THE OLD VOICE AND THE OTHER VOICE

In western Europe and the United States, women are nearing equality in the professions, in business, and in politics. Most enjoy access to education, reproductive rights, and autonomy in financial affairs. Issues vital to women are on the public agenda: equal pay, child care, domestic abuse, breast cancer research, and curricular revision with an eye to the inclusion of women.

These recent achievements have their origins in things women (and some male supporters) said for the first time about six hundred years ago. Theirs is the "other voice," in contradistinction to the "first voice," the voice of the educated men who created Western culture. Coincident with a general reshaping of European culture in the period 1300–1700 (called the Renaissance or early modern period), questions of female equality and opportunity were raised that still resound and are still unresolved.

The other voice emerged against the backdrop of a three-thousand-year history of the derogation of women rooted in the civilizations related to Western culture: Hebrew, Greek, Roman, and Christian. Negative attitudes toward women inherited from these traditions pervaded the intellectual, medical, legal, religious, and social systems that developed during the European Middle Ages.

The following pages describe the traditional, overwhelmingly male views of women's nature inherited by early modern Europeans and the new tradition that the "other voice" called into being to begin to challenge reigning assumptions. This review should serve as a framework for understanding the texts published in the series The Other Voice in Early Modern Europe. Introductions specific to each text and author follow this essay in all the volumes of the series.

TRADITIONAL VIEWS OF WOMEN, 500 B.C.E.–1500 C.E.

Embedded in the philosophical and medical theories of the ancient Greeks were perceptions of the female as inferior to the male in both mind and body. Similarly, the structure of civil legislation inherited from the ancient Romans was biased against women, and the views on women developed by Christian thinkers out of the Hebrew Bible and the Christian New Testament were negative and disabling. Literary works composed in the vernacular of ordinary people, and widely recited or read, conveyed these negative assumptions. The social networks within which most women lived—those of the family and the institutions of the Roman Catholic Church—were shaped by this negative tradition and sharply limited the areas in which women might act in and upon the world.

GREEK PHILOSOPHY AND FEMALE NATURE. Greek biology assumed that women were inferior to men and defined them as merely childbearers and housekeepers. This view was authoritatively expressed in the works of the philosopher Aristotle.

Aristotle thought in dualities. He considered action superior to inaction, form (the inner design or structure of any object) superior to matter, completion to incompletion, possession to deprivation. In each of these dualities, he associated the male principle with the superior quality and the female with the inferior. "The male principle in nature," he argued, "is associated with active, formative and perfected characteristics, while the female is passive, material and deprived, desiring the male in order to become complete."[1] Men are always identified with virile qualities, such as judgment, courage, and stamina, and women with their opposites—irrationality, cowardice, and weakness.

The masculine principle was considered superior even in the womb. The man's semen, Aristotle believed, created the form of a new human creature, while the female body contributed only matter. (The existence of the ovum, and with it the other facts of human embryology, was not established until the seventeenth century.) Although the later Greek physician Galen believed there was a female component in generation, contributed by "female semen," the followers of both Aristotle and Galen saw the male role in human generation as more active and more important.

In the Aristotelian view, the male principle sought always to reproduce

---

1. Aristotle, *Physics* 1.9.192a20–24, in *The Complete Works of Aristotle,* ed. Jonathan Barnes, rev. Oxford trans., 2 vols. (Princeton, 1984), 1:328.

itself. The creation of a female was always a mistake, therefore, resulting from an imperfect act of generation. Every female born was considered a "defective" or "mutilated" male (as Aristotle's terminology has variously been translated), a "monstrosity" of nature.[2]

For Greek theorists, the biology of males and females was the key to their psychology. The female was softer and more docile, more apt to be despondent, querulous, and deceitful. Being incomplete, moreover, she craved sexual fulfillment in intercourse with a male. The male was intellectual, active, and in control of his passions.

These psychological polarities derived from the theory that the universe consisted of four elements (earth, fire, air, and water), expressed in human bodies as four "humors" (black bile, yellow bile, blood, and phlegm) considered, respectively, dry, hot, damp, and cold and corresponding to mental states ("melancholic," "choleric," "sanguine," "phlegmatic"). In this scheme the male, sharing the principles of earth and fire, was dry and hot; the female, sharing the principles of air and water, was cold and damp.

Female psychology was further affected by her dominant organ, the uterus (womb), *hystera* in Greek. The passions generated by the womb made women lustful, deceitful, talkative, irrational, indeed—when these affects were in excess—"hysterical."

Aristotle's biology also had social and political consequences. If the male principle was superior and the female inferior, then in the household, as in the state, men should rule and women must be subordinate. That hierarchy did not rule out the companionship of husband and wife, whose cooperation was necessary for the welfare of children and the preservation of property. Such mutuality supported male preeminence.

Aristotle's teacher Plato suggested a different possibility: that men and women might possess the same virtues. The setting for this proposal is the imaginary and ideal Republic that Plato sketches in a dialogue of that name. Here, for a privileged elite capable of leading wisely, all distinctions of class and wealth dissolve, as, consequently, do those of gender. Without households or property, as Plato constructs his ideal society, there is no need for the subordination of women. Women may therefore be educated to the same level as men to assume leadership. Plato's Republic remained imaginary, however. In real societies, the subordination of women remained the norm and the prescription.

The views of women inherited from the Greek philosophical tradition became the basis for medieval thought. In the thirteenth century, the su-

---

2. Aristotle, *Generation of Animals* 2.3.737a27–28, in *The Complete Works*, 1: 1144.

preme Scholastic philosopher Thomas Aquinas, among others, still echoed Aristotle's views of human reproduction, of male and female personalities, and of the preeminent male role in the social hierarchy.

ROMAN LAW AND THE FEMALE CONDITION. Roman law, like Greek philosophy, underlay medieval thought and shaped medieval society. The ancient belief that adult property-owning men should administer households and make decisions affecting the community at large is the very fulcrum of Roman law.

About 450 B.C.E., during Rome's republican era, the community's customary law was recorded (legendarily) on twelve tablets erected in the city's central forum. It was later elaborated by professional jurists whose activity increased in the imperial era, when much new legislation was passed, especially on issues affecting family and inheritance. This growing, changing body of laws was eventually codified in the *Corpus of Civil Law* under the direction of the emperor Justinian, generations after the empire ceased to be ruled from Rome. That *Corpus,* read and commented on by medieval scholars from the eleventh century on, inspired the legal systems of most of the cities and kingdoms of Europe.

Laws regarding dowries, divorce, and inheritance pertain primarily to women. Since those laws aimed to maintain and preserve property, the women concerned were those from the property-owning minority. Their subordination to male family members points to the even greater subordination of lower-class and slave women, about whom the laws speak little.

In the early republic, the *paterfamilias,* or "father of the family," possessed *patria potestas,* "paternal power." The term *pater,* "father," in both these cases does not necessarily mean biological father but denotes the head of a household. The father was the person who owned the household's property and, indeed, its human members. The *paterfamilias* had absolute power — including the power, rarely exercised, of life or death — over his wife, his children, and his slaves, as much as his cattle.

Male children could be "emancipated," an act that granted legal autonomy and the right to own property. Those over fourteen could be emancipated by a special grant from the father or automatically by their father's death. But females could never be emancipated; instead, they passed from the authority of their father to that of a husband or, if widowed or orphaned while still unmarried, to a guardian or tutor.

Marriage in its traditional form placed the woman under her husband's authority, or *manus.* He could divorce her on grounds of adultery, drinking wine, or stealing from the household, but she could not divorce him. She could neither possess property in her own right nor bequeath any to her children upon her death. When her husband died, the household property passed not to her but to his male heirs. And when her father died, she had no claim to any family inheritance, which was directed to her brothers or more remote male relatives. The effect of these laws was to exclude women from civil society, itself based on property ownership.

In the later republican and imperial periods, these rules were significantly modified. Women rarely married according to the traditional form. The practice of "free" marriage allowed a woman to remain under her father's authority, to possess property given her by her father (most frequently the "dowry," recoverable from the husband's household on his death), and to inherit from her father. She could also bequeath property to her own children and divorce her husband, just as he could divorce her.

Despite this greater freedom, women still suffered enormous disability under Roman law. Heirs could belong only to the father's side, never the mother's. Moreover, although she could bequeath her property to her children, she could not establish a line of succession in doing so. A woman was "the beginning and end of her own family," said the jurist Ulpian. Moreover, women could play no public role. They could not hold public office, represent anyone in a legal case, or even witness a will. Women had only a private existence and no public personality.

The dowry system, the guardian, women's limited ability to transmit wealth, and total political disability are all features of Roman law adopted by the medieval communities of western Europe, although modified according to local customary laws..

CHRISTIAN DOCTRINE AND WOMEN'S PLACE. The Hebrew Bible and the Christian New Testament authorized later writers to limit women to the realm of the family and to burden them with the guilt of original sin. The passages most fruitful for this purpose were the creation narratives in Genesis and sentences from the Epistles defining women's role within the Christian family and community.

Each of the first two chapters of Genesis contains a creation narrative. In the first "God created man in his own image, in the image of God he created him; male and female he created them" (Gn 1:27). In the second, God created Eve from Adam's rib (2:21–23). Christian theologians relied principally on Genesis 2 for their understanding of the relation between man and woman, interpreting the creation of Eve from Adam as proof of her subordination to him.

The creation story in Genesis 2 leads to that of the temptations in Genesis 3: of Eve by the wily serpent and of Adam by Eve. As read by Christian theologians from Tertullian to Thomas Aquinas, the narrative made Eve responsible for the Fall and its consequences. She instigated the act; she deceived her husband; she suffered the greater punishment. Her disobedience made it necessary for Jesus to be incarnated and to die on the cross. From the pulpit, moralists and preachers for centuries conveyed to women the guilt that they bore for original sin.

The Epistles offered advice to early Christians on building communities of the faithful. Among the matters to be regulated was the place of women. Paul offered views favorable to women in Galatians 3:28: "There is neither Jew nor Greek, there is neither slave nor free, there is neither male nor female; for you are all one in Christ Jesus." Paul also referred to women as his coworkers and placed them on a par with himself and his male coworkers (Phlm 4:2–3; Rom 16:1–3; 1 Cor 16:19). Elsewhere, Paul limited women's possibilities: "But I want you to understand that the head of every man is Christ, the head of a woman is her husband, and the head of Christ is God" (1 Cor 11:3).

Biblical passages by later writers (although attributed to Paul) enjoined women to forgo jewels, expensive clothes, and elaborate coiffures; and they forbade women to "teach or have authority over men," telling them to "learn in silence with all submissiveness" as is proper for one responsible for sin, consoling them, however, with the thought that they will be saved through childbearing (1 Tm 2:9–15). Other texts among the later Epistles defined women as the weaker sex and emphasized their subordination to their husbands (1 Pt 3:7; Col 3:18; Eph 5:22–23).

These passages from the New Testament became the arsenal employed by theologians of the early church to transmit negative attitudes toward women to medieval Christian culture—above all, Tertullian (*On the Apparel of Women*), Jerome (*Against Jovinian*), and Augustine (*The Literal Meaning of Genesis*).

THE IMAGE OF WOMEN IN MEDIEVAL LITERATURE. The philosophical, legal, and religious traditions born in antiquity formed the basis of the medieval intellectual synthesis wrought by trained thinkers, mostly clerics, writing in Latin and based largely in universities. The vernacular literary tradition that developed alongside the learned tradition also spoke about female nature and women's roles. Medieval stories, poems, and epics also portrayed women negatively—as lustful and deceitful—while praising good housekeepers and loyal wives as replicas of the Virgin Mary or the female saints and martyrs.

There is an exception in the movement of "courtly love" that evolved in southern France from the twelfth century. Courtly love was the erotic love between a nobleman and noblewoman, the latter usually superior in social rank. It was always adulterous. From the conventions of courtly love derive modern Western notions of romantic love. The tradition has had an impact disproportionate to its size, for it affected only a tiny elite, and very few women. The exaltation of the female lover probably does not reflect a higher evaluation of women or a step toward their sexual liberation. More likely it gives expression to the social and sexual tensions besetting the knightly class at a specific historical juncture.

The literary fashion of courtly love was on the wane by the thirteenth century, when the widely read *Romance of the Rose* was composed in French by two authors of significantly different dispositions. Guillaume de Lorris composed the initial four thousand verses about 1235, and Jean de Meun added about seventeen thousand verses — more than four times the original — about 1265.

The fragment composed by Guillaume de Lorris stands squarely in the tradition of courtly love. Here the poet, in a dream, is admitted into a walled garden where he finds a magic fountain in which a rosebush is reflected. He longs to pick one rose, but the thorns prevent his doing so, even as he is wounded by arrows from the god of love, whose commands he agrees to obey. The rest of this part of the poem recounts the poet's unsuccessful efforts to pluck the rose.

The longer part of the *Romance* by Jean de Meun also describes a dream. But here allegorical characters give long didactic speeches, providing a social satire on a variety of themes, some pertaining to women. Love is an anxious and tormented state, the poem explains: women are greedy and manipulative, marriage is miserable, beautiful women are lustful, ugly ones cease to please, and a chaste woman is as rare as a black swan.

Shortly after Jean de Meun completed *The Romance of the Rose*, Mathéolus penned his *Lamentations*, a long Latin diatribe against marriage translated into French about a century later. The *Lamentations* sum up medieval attitudes toward women and provoked the important response by Christine de Pizan in her *Book of the City of Ladies*.

In 1355, Giovanni Boccaccio wrote *Il Corbaccio*, another antifeminist manifesto, although ironically by an author whose other works pioneered new directions in Renaissance thought. The former husband of his lover appears to Boccaccio, condemning his unmoderated lust and detailing the defects of women. Boccaccio concedes at the end "how much men naturally surpass women in nobility" and is cured of his desires.[3]

WOMEN'S ROLES: THE FAMILY. The negative perceptions of women expressed in the intellectual tradition are also implicit in the actual roles that

---

3. Giovanni Boccaccio, *The Corbaccio, or The Labyrinth of Love,* trans. and ed. Anthony K. Cassell, rev. ed. (Binghamton, N.Y., 1993), 71.

women played in European society. Assigned to subordinate positions in the household and the church, they were barred from significant participation in public life.

Medieval European households, like those in antiquity and in non-Western civilizations, were headed by males. It was the male serf (or peasant), feudal lord, town merchant, or citizen who was polled or taxed or succeeded to an inheritance or had any acknowledged public role, although his wife or widow could stand as a temporary surrogate. From about 1100, the position of property-holding males was further enhanced: inheritance was confined to the male, or agnate, line—with depressing consequences for women.

A wife never fully belonged to her husband's family, nor was she a daughter to her father's family. She left her father's house young to marry whomever her parents chose. Her dowry was managed by her husband, and at her death it normally passed to her children by him.

A married woman's life was occupied nearly constantly with cycles of pregnancy, childbearing, and lactation. Women bore children through all the years of their fertility, and many died in childbirth. They were also responsible for raising young children up to six or seven. In the propertied classes that responsibility was shared, since it was common for a wet nurse to take over breast-feeding and for servants to perform other chores.

Women trained their daughters in the household duties appropriate to their status, nearly always tasks associated with textiles: spinning, weaving, sewing, embroidering. Their sons were sent out of the house as apprentices or students, or their training was assumed by fathers in later childhood and adolescence. On the death of her husband, a woman's children became the responsibility of his family. She generally did not take "his" children with her to a new marriage or back to her father's house, except sometimes in the artisan classes.

Women also worked. Rural peasants performed farm chores, merchant wives often practiced their husbands' trades, the unmarried daughters of the urban poor worked as servants or prostitutes. All wives produced or embellished textiles and did the housekeeping, while wealthy ones managed servants. These labors were unpaid or poorly paid but often contributed substantially to family wealth.

WOMEN'S ROLES: THE CHURCH. Membership in a household, whether a father's or a husband's, meant for women a lifelong subordination to others. In western Europe, the Roman Catholic Church offered an alternative to the career of wife and mother. A woman could enter a convent, parallel in function to the monasteries for men that evolved in the early Christian centuries.

In the convent, a woman pledged herself to a celibate life, lived according to strict community rules, and worshiped daily. Often the convent offered training in Latin, allowing some women to become considerable scholars and authors as well as scribes, artists, and musicians. For women who chose the conventual life, the benefits could be enormous, but for numerous others placed in convents by paternal choice, the life could be restrictive and burdensome.

The conventual life declined as an alternative for women as the modern age approached. Reformed monastic institutions resisted responsibility for related female orders. The church increasingly restricted female institutional life by insisting on closer male supervision.

Women often sought other options. Some joined the communities of laywomen that sprang up spontaneously in the thirteenth century in the urban zones of western Europe, especially in Flanders and Italy. Some joined the heretical movements that flourished in late medieval Christendom, whose anticlerical and often antifamily positions particularly appealed to women. In these communities, some women were acclaimed as "holy women" or "saints," whereas others often were condemned as frauds or heretics.

In all, although the options offered to women by the church were sometimes less than satisfactory, they were sometimes richly rewarding. After 1520, the convent remained an option only in Roman Catholic territories. Protestantism engendered an ideal of marriage as a heroic endeavor and appeared to place husband and wife on a more equal footing. Sermons and treatises, however, still called for female subordination and obedience.

THE OTHER VOICE, 1300–1700

When the modern era opened, European culture was so firmly structured by a framework of negative attitudes toward women that to dismantle it was a monumental labor. The process began as part of a larger cultural movement that entailed the critical reexamination of ideas inherited from the ancient and medieval past. The humanists launched that critical reexamination.

THE HUMANIST FOUNDATION. Originating in Italy in the fourteenth century, humanism quickly became the dominant intellectual movement in Europe. Spreading in the sixteenth century from Italy to the rest of Europe, it fueled the literary, scientific, and philosophical movements of the era and laid the basis for the eighteenth-century Enlightenment.

Humanists regarded the Scholastic philosophy of medieval universities as out of touch with the realities of urban life. They found in the rhetorical discourse of classical Rome a language adapted to civic life and public speech. They learned to read, speak, and write classical Latin and, eventually, classical Greek. They founded schools to teach others to do so, establishing the pattern for elementary and secondary education for the next three hundred years.

In the service of complex government bureaucracies, humanists employed their skills to write eloquent letters, deliver public orations, and formulate public policy. They developed new scripts for copying manuscripts and used the new printing press to disseminate texts, for which they created methods of critical editing.

Humanism was a movement led by males who accepted the evaluation of women in ancient texts and generally shared the misogynist perceptions of their culture. (Female humanists, as we will see, did not.) Yet humanism also opened the door to a reevaluation of the nature and capacity of women. By calling authors, texts, and ideas into question, it made possible the fundamental rereading of the whole intellectual tradition that was required in order to free women from cultural prejudice and social subordination.

A DIFFERENT CITY. The other voice first appeared when, after so many centuries, the accumulation of misogynist concepts evoked a response from a capable female defender: Christine de Pizan (1365–1431). Introducing her *Book of the City of Ladies* (1405), she described how she was affected by reading Mathéolus's *Lamentations:* "Just the sight of this book . . . made me wonder how it happened that so many different men . . . are so inclined to express both in speaking and in their treatises and writings so many wicked insults about women and their behavior."[4] These statements impelled her to detest herself "and the entire feminine sex, as though we were monstrosities in nature."[5]

The rest of *The Book of the City of Ladies* presents a justification of the female sex and a vision of an ideal community of women. A pioneer, she has received the message of female inferiority and rejected it. From the fourteenth to the seventeenth century, a huge body of literature accumulated that responded to the dominant tradition.

---

4. Christine de Pizan, *The Book of the City of Ladies,* trans. Earl Jeffrey Richards, foreword by Marina Warner (New York, 1982), 1.1.1, pp. 3–4.

5. Ibid., 1.1.1–2, p. 5.

The result was a literary explosion consisting of works by both men and women, in Latin and in the vernaculars: works enumerating the achievements of notable women; works rebutting the main accusations made against women; works arguing for the equal education of men and women; works defining and redefining women's proper role in the family, at court, in public; works describing women's lives and experiences. Recent monographs and articles have begun to hint at the great range of this movement, involving probably several thousand titles. The protofeminism of these "other voices" constitutes a significant fraction of the literary product of the early modern era.

THE CATALOGS. About 1365, the same Boccaccio whose *Corbaccio* rehearses the usual charges against female nature wrote another work, *Concerning Famous Women*. A humanist treatise drawing on classical texts, it praised 106 notable women: ninety-eight of them from pagan Greek and Roman antiquity, one (Eve) from the Bible, and seven from the medieval religious and cultural tradition; his book helped make all readers aware of a sex normally condemned or forgotten. Boccaccio's outlook nevertheless was unfriendly to women, for it singled out for praise those women who possessed the traditional virtues of chastity, silence, and obedience. Women who were active in the public realm—for example, rulers and warriors—were depicted as usually being lascivious and as suffering terrible punishments for entering the masculine sphere. Women were his subject, but Boccaccio's standard remained male.

Christine de Pizan's *Book of the City of Ladies* contains a second catalog, one responding specifically to Boccaccio's. Whereas Boccaccio portrays female virtue as exceptional, she depicts it as universal. Many women in history were leaders, or remained chaste despite the lascivious approaches of men, or were visionaries and brave martyrs.

The work of Boccaccio inspired a series of catalogs of illustrious women of the biblical, classical, Christian, and local pasts, among them Filippo da Bergamo's *Of Illustrious Women*, Pierre de Brantôme's *Lives of Illustrious Women*, Pierre Le Moyne's *Gallerie of Heroic Women*, and Pietro Paolo de Ribera's *Immortal Triumphs and Heroic Enterprises of 845 Women*. Whatever their embedded prejudices, these works drove home to the public the possibility of female excellence.

THE DEBATE. At the same time, many questions remained: Could a woman be virtuous? Could she perform noteworthy deeds? Was she even, strictly speaking, of the same human species as men? These questions were debated over four centuries, in French, German, Italian, Spanish, and English, by authors male and female, among Catholics, Protestants, and Jews, in ponderous volumes and breezy pamphlets. The whole literary genre has been called the *querelle des femmes*, the "woman question."

The opening volley of this battle occurred in the first years of the fifteenth century, in a literary debate sparked by Christine de Pizan. She exchanged letters critical of Jean de Meun's contribution to *The Romance of the Rose* with two French royal secretaries, Jean de Montreuil and Gontier Col. When the matter became public, Jean Gerson, one of Europe's leading theologians, supported de Pizan's arguments against de Meun, for the moment silencing the opposition.

The debate resurfaced repeatedly over the next two hundred years. *The Triumph of Women* (1438) by Juan Rodríguez de la Camara (or Juan Rodríguez del Padron) struck a new note by presenting arguments for the superiority of women to men. *The Champion of Women* (1440–42) by Martin Le Franc addresses once again the negative views of women presented in *The Romance of the Rose* and offers counterevidence of female virtue and achievement.

A cameo of the debate on women is included in *The Courtier*, one of the most widely read books of the era, published by the Italian Baldassare Castiglione in 1528 and immediately translated into other European vernaculars. *The Courtier* depicts a series of evenings at the court of the duke of Urbino in which many men and some women of the highest social stratum amuse themselves by discussing a range of literary and social issues. The "woman question" is a pervasive theme throughout, and the third of its four books is devoted entirely to that issue.

In a verbal duel, Gasparo Pallavicino and Giuliano de' Medici present the main claims of the two traditions. Gasparo argues the innate inferiority of women and their inclination to vice. Only in bearing children do they profit the world. Giuliano counters that women share the same spiritual and mental capacities as men and may excel in wisdom and action. Men and women are of the same essence: just as no stone can be more perfectly a stone than another, so no human being can be more perfectly human than others, whether male or female. It was an astonishing assertion, boldly made to an audience as large as all Europe.

THE TREATISES. Humanism provided the materials for a positive counterconcept to the misogyny embedded in Scholastic philosophy and law and inherited from the Greek, Roman, and Christian pasts. A series of humanist treatises on marriage and family, on education and deportment, and on the nature of women helped construct these new perspectives.

The works by Francesco Barbaro and Leon Battista Alberti—*On Marriage* (1415) and *On the Family* (1434–37)—far from defending female equality, reasserted women's responsibility for rearing children and managing the housekeeping while being obedient, chaste, and silent. Nevertheless, they served the cause of reexamining the issue of women's nature by placing domestic issues at the center of scholarly concern and reopening the pertinent classical texts. In addition, Barbaro emphasized the companionate nature of marriage and the importance of a wife's spiritual and mental qualities for the well-being of the family.

These themes reappear in later humanist works on marriage and the education of women by Juan Luis Vives and Erasmus. Both were moderately sympathetic to the condition of women without reaching beyond the usual masculine prescriptions for female behavior.

An outlook more favorable to women characterizes the nearly unknown work *In Praise of Women* (ca. 1487) by the Italian humanist Bartolommeo Goggio. In addition to providing a catalog of illustrious women, Goggio argued that male and female are the same in essence, but that women (reworking the Adam and Eve narrative from quite a new angle) are actually superior. In the same vein, the Italian humanist Mario Equicola asserted the spiritual equality of men and women in *On Women* (1501). In 1525, Galeazzo Flavio Capra (or Capella) published his work *On the Excellence and Dignity of Women*. This humanist tradition of treatises defending the worthiness of women culminates in the work of Henricus Cornelius Agrippa *On the Nobility and Preeminence of the Female Sex*. No work by a male humanist more succinctly or explicitly presents the case for female dignity.

THE WITCH BOOKS. While humanists grappled with the issues pertaining to women and family, other learned men turned their attention to what they perceived as a very great problem: witches. Witch-hunting manuals, explorations of the witch phenomenon, and even defenses of witches are not at first glance pertinent to the tradition of the other voice. But they do relate in this way: most accused witches were women. The hostility aroused by supposed witch activity is comparable to the hostility aroused by women. The evil deeds the victims of the hunt were charged with were exaggerations of the vices to which, many believed, all women were prone.

The connection between the witch accusation and the hatred of women is explicit in the notorious witch-hunting manual *The Hammer of Witches* (1486) by two Dominican inquisitors, Heinrich Krämer and Jacob Sprenger. Here the inconstancy, deceitfulness, and lustfulness traditionally associated with women are depicted in exaggerated form as the core features of witch behavior. These traits inclined women to make a bargain with the devil—sealed by sexual intercourse—by which they acquired unholy powers. Such bizarre claims, far from being rejected by rational men, were broadcast by intellectuals. The German Ulrich Molitur, the Frenchman Nicolas Rémy, and the Italian Stefano Guazzo all coolly informed the public of sinister orgies and midnight pacts with the devil. The celebrated French jurist, historian, and political philosopher Jean Bodin argued that because women were especially prone to diabolism, regular legal procedures could properly be suspended in order to try those accused of this "exceptional crime."

A few experts such as the physician Johann Weyer, a student of Agrippa's, raised their voices in protest. In 1563, he explained the witch phenomenon thus, without discarding belief in diabolism: the devil deluded foolish old women afflicted by melancholia, causing them to believe they had magical powers. Weyer's rational skepticism, which had good credibility in the community of the learned, worked to revise the conventional views of women and witchcraft.

WOMEN'S WORKS. To the many categories of works produced on the question of women's worth must be added nearly all works written by women. A woman writing was in herself a statement of women's claim to dignity.

Only a few women wrote anything before the dawn of the modern era, for three reasons. First, they rarely received the education that would enable them to write. Second, they were not admitted to the public roles—as administrator, bureaucrat, lawyer or notary, or university professor—in which they might gain knowledge of the kinds of things the literate public thought worth writing about. Third, the culture imposed silence on women, considering speaking out a form of unchastity. Given these conditions, it is remarkable that any women wrote. Those who did before the fourteenth century were almost always nuns or religious women whose isolation made their pronouncements more acceptable.

From the fourteenth century on, the volume of women's writings rose. Women continued to write devotional literature, although not always as cloistered nuns. They also wrote diaries, often intended as keepsakes for their children; books of advice to their sons and daughters; letters to family members and friends; and family memoirs, in a few cases elaborate enough to be considered histories.

A few women wrote works directly concerning the "woman question," and some of these, such as the humanists Isotta Nogarola, Cassandra Fedele, Laura Cereta, and Olympia Morata, were highly trained. A few were professional writers, living by the income of their pens; the very first among them was Christine de Pizan, noteworthy in this context as in so many others. In addition to *The Book of the City of Ladies* and her critiques of *The Romance of the*

Rose, she wrote *The Treasure of the City of Ladies* (a guide to social decorum for women), an advice book for her son, much courtly verse, and a full-scale history of the reign of King Charles V of France.

WOMEN PATRONS. Women who did not themselves write but encouraged others to do so boosted the development of an alternative tradition. Highly placed women patrons supported authors, artists, musicians, poets, and learned men. Such patrons, drawn mostly from the Italian elites and the courts of northern Europe, figure disproportionately as the dedicatees of the important works of early feminism.

For a start, it might be noted that the catalogs of Boccaccio and Alvaro de Luna were dedicated to the Florentine noblewoman Andrea Acciaiuoli and to Doña María, first wife of King Juan II of Castile, while the French translation of Boccaccio's work was commissioned by Anne of Brittany, wife of King Charles VIII of France. The humanist treatises of Goggio, Equicola, Vives, and Agrippa were dedicated, respectively, to Eleanora of Aragon, wife of Ercole I d'Este, duke of Ferrara; to Margherita Cantelma of Mantua; to Catherine of Aragon, wife of King Henry VIII of England; and to Margaret, Duchess of Austria and regent of the Netherlands. As late as 1696, Mary Astell's *Serious Proposal to the Ladies, for the Advancement of Their True and Greatest Interest* was dedicated to Princess Anne of Denmark.

These authors presumed that their efforts would be welcome to female patrons, or they may have written at the bidding of those patrons. Silent themselves, perhaps even unresponsive, these loftily placed women helped shape the tradition of the other voice.

THE ISSUES. The literary forms and patterns in which the tradition of the other voice presented itself have now been sketched. It remains to highlight the major issues around which this tradition crystallizes. In brief, there are four problems to which our authors return again and again, in plays and catalogs, in verse and letters, in treatises and dialogues, in every language: the problem of chastity, the problem of power, the problem of speech, and the problem of knowledge. Of these the greatest, preconditioning the others, is the problem of chastity.

THE PROBLEM OF CHASTITY. In traditional European culture, as in those of antiquity and others around the globe, chastity was perceived as woman's quintessential virtue—in contrast to courage, or generosity, or leadership, or rationality, seen as virtues characteristic of men. Opponents of women charged them with insatiable lust. Women themselves and their defenders—

without disputing the validity of the standard—responded that women were capable of chastity.

The requirement of chastity kept women at home, silenced them, isolated them, left them in ignorance. It was the source of all other impediments. Why was it so important to the society of men, of whom chastity was not required, and who more often than not considered it their right to violate the chastity of any woman they encountered?

Female chastity ensured the continuity of the male-headed household. If a man's wife was not chaste, he could not be sure of the legitimacy of his offspring. If they were not his and they acquired his property, it was not his household, but some other man's, that had endured. If his daughter was not chaste, she could not be transferred to another man's household as his wife, and he was dishonored.

The whole system of the integrity of the household and the transmission of property was bound up in female chastity. Such a requirement pertained only to property-owning classes, of course. Poor women could not expect to maintain their chastity, least of all if they were in contact with high-status men to whom all women but those of their own household were prey.

In Catholic Europe, the requirement of chastity was further buttressed by moral and religious imperatives. Original sin was inextricably linked with the sexual act. Virginity was seen as heroic virtue, far more impressive than, say, the avoidance of idleness or greed. Monasticism, the cultural institution that dominated medieval Europe for centuries, was grounded in the renunciation of the flesh. The Catholic reform of the eleventh century imposed a similar standard on all the clergy and a heightened awareness of sexual requirements on all the laity. Although men were asked to be chaste, female unchastity was much worse: it led to the devil, as Eve had led mankind to sin.

To such requirements, women and their defenders protested their innocence. Furthermore, following the example of holy women who had escaped the requirements of family and sought the religious life, some women began to conceive of female communities as alternatives both to family and to the cloister. Christine de Pizan's city of ladies was such a community. Moderata Fonte and Mary Astell envisioned others. The luxurious salons of the French *précieuses* of the seventeenth century, or the comfortable English drawing rooms of the next, may have been born of the same impulse. Here women not only might escape, if briefly, the subordinate position that life in the family entailed but might also make claims to power, exercise their capacity for speech, and display their knowledge.

THE PROBLEM OF POWER. Women were excluded from power: the whole cultural tradition insisted on it. Only men were citizens, only men bore arms, only men could be chiefs or lords or kings. There were exceptions that did not disprove the rule, when wives or widows or mothers took the place of men, awaiting their return or the maturation of a male heir. A woman who attempted to rule in her own right was perceived as an anomaly, a monster, at once a deformed woman and an insufficient male, sexually confused and consequently unsafe.

The association of such images with women who held or sought power explains some otherwise odd features of early modern culture. Queen Elizabeth I of England, one of the few women to hold full regal authority in European history, played with such male/female images—positive ones, of course—in representing herself to her subjects. She was a prince, and manly, even though she was female. She was also (she claimed) virginal, a condition absolutely essential if she was to avoid the attacks of her opponents. Catherine de' Medici, who ruled France as widow and regent for her sons, also adopted such imagery in defining her position. She chose as one symbol the figure of Artemisia, an androgynous ancient warrior-heroine who combined a female persona with masculine powers.

Power in a woman, without such sexual imagery, seems to have been indigestible by the culture. A rare note was struck by the Englishman Sir Thomas Elyot in his *Defence of Good Women* (1540), justifying both women's participation in civic life and their prowess in arms. The old tune was sung by the Scots reformer John Knox in his *First Blast of the Trumpet against the Monstrous Regiment of Women* (1558); for him rule by women, defects in nature, was a hideous contradiction in terms.

The confused sexuality of the imagery of female potency was not reserved for rulers. Any woman who excelled was likely to be called an Amazon, recalling the self-mutilated warrior women of antiquity who repudiated all men, gave up their sons, and raised only their daughters. She was often said to have "exceeded her sex" or to have possessed "masculine virtue"—as the very fact of conspicuous excellence conferred masculinity even on the female subject. The catalogs of notable women often showed those female heroes dressed in armor, armed to the teeth, like men. Amazonian heroines romp through the epics of the age—Ariosto's *Orlando Furioso* (1532) and Spenser's *Faerie Queene* (1590–1609). Excellence in a woman was perceived as a claim for power, and power was reserved for the masculine realm. A woman who possessed either one was masculinized and lost title to her own female identity.

THE PROBLEM OF SPEECH. Just as power had a sexual dimension when it was claimed by women, so did speech. A good woman spoke little. Excessive speech was an indication of unchastity. By speech, women seduced men. Eve had lured Adam into sin by her speech. Accused witches were commonly accused of having spoken abusively, or irrationally, or simply too much. As enlightened a figure as Francesco Barbaro insisted on silence in a woman, which he linked to her perfect unanimity with her husband's will and her unblemished virtue (her chastity). Another Italian humanist, Leonardo Bruni, in advising a noblewoman on her studies, barred her not from speech but from public speaking. That was reserved for men.

Related to the problem of speech was that of costume—another, if silent, form of self-expression. Assigned the task of pleasing men as their primary occupation, elite women often tended toward elaborate costume, hairdressing, and the use of cosmetics. Clergy and secular moralists alike condemned these practices. The appropriate function of costume and adornment was to announce the status of a woman's husband or father. Any further indulgence in adornment was akin to unchastity.

THE PROBLEM OF KNOWLEDGE. When the Italian noblewoman Isotta Nogarola had begun to attain a reputation as a humanist, she was accused of incest—a telling instance of the association of learning in women with unchastity. That chilling association inclined any woman who was educated to deny that she was or to make exaggerated claims of heroic chastity.

If educated women were pursued with suspicions of sexual misconduct, women seeking an education faced an even more daunting obstacle: the assumption that women were by nature incapable of learning, that reasoning was a particularly masculine ability. Just as they proclaimed their chastity, women and their defenders insisted on their capacity for learning. The major work by a male writer on female education—that by Juan Luis Vives, *On the Education of a Christian Woman* (1523)—granted female capacity for intellection but still argued that a woman's whole education was to be shaped around the requirement of chastity and a future within the household. Female writers of the following generations—Marie de Gournay in France, Anna Maria van Schurman in Holland, and Mary Astell in England—began to envision other possibilities.

The pioneers of female education were the Italian women humanists who managed to attain a literacy in Latin and a knowledge of classical and Christian literature equivalent to that of prominent men. Their works implicitly and explicitly raise questions about women's social roles, defining problems that beset women attempting to break out of the cultural limits that had bound them. Like Christine de Pizan, who achieved an advanced education through her father's tutoring and her own devices, their bold questioning makes clear the importance of training. Only when women were educated to the same standard as male leaders would they be able to raise that other voice and insist on their dignity as human beings morally, intellectually, and legally equal to men.

THE OTHER VOICE. The other voice, a voice of protest, was mostly female, but it was also male. It spoke in the vernaculars and in Latin, in treatises and dialogues, in plays and poetry, in letters and diaries, and in pamphlets. It battered at the wall of prejudice that encircled women and raised a banner announcing its claims. The female was equal (or even superior) to the male in essential nature—moral, spiritual, and intellectual. Women were capable of higher education, of holding positions of power and influence in the public realm, and of speaking and writing persuasively. The last bastion of masculine supremacy, centered on the notions of a woman's primary domestic responsibility and the requirement of female chastity, was not as yet assaulted—although visions of productive female communities as alternatives to the family indicated an awareness of the problem.

During the period 1300–1700, the other voice remained only a voice, and one only dimly heard. It did not result—yet—in an alteration of social patterns. Indeed, to this day they have not entirely been altered. Yet the call for justice issued as long as six centuries ago by those writing in the tradition of the other voice must be recognized as the source and origin of the mature feminist tradition and of the realignment of social institutions accomplished in the modern age.

We thank the volume editors in this series, who responded with many suggestions to an earlier draft of this introduction, making it a collaborative enterprise. Many of their suggestions and criticisms have resulted in revisions of this introduction, although we remain responsible for the final product.

PROJECTED TITLES IN THE SERIES

Ana de San Bartolomé, *Autobiography and Other Writings*, edited and translated by Darcy Donahue

Catharina Regina von Greiffenberg, *Meditations on the Life of Christ*, edited and translated by Lynne Tatlock

Emilie du Châtelet, *Selected Writings of an Enlightenment Philosophe*, edited by Judith Zinsser, translated by Isabelle Bour

Christine de Pizan, *Debate over the "Romance of the Rose,"* edited and translated David Hult

Christine de Pizan, *Early Defense of Women Poems*, edited and translated by Thelma Fenster

Christine de Pizan, *Life of Charles V*, edited and translated by Nadia Margolis

Christine de Pizan, *The Long Road of Learning*, edited and translated by Andrea Tarnowski

Vittoria Colonna, Chiari Matraini, and Lucrezia Marinella, *Who is Mary? Three Early Modern Women on the Idea of the Virgin Mary*, edited and translated by Susan Haskins

Pernette du Guillet, *Complete Poems*, edited with an introduction by Karen James, translated by Marta Finch Koslowsky

Sister Margaret of the Mother of God, *Autobiography*, edited with an introduction by Cordula van Wyhe, translated by Paul Arblaster and Susan Smith

Hortense and Marie Mancini, *Memoirs of Hortense and Marie Mancini*, edited and translated by Sarah Nelson

Marguerite de Navarre, *Selected Writing*, edited and translated by Rouben Cholakian and Mary Skemp

Lucrezia Marinella, *Enrico, or Byzantium Conquered*, edited and translated by Maria Galli Stampino

Valeria Miani, *Celinda: A Tragedy*, edited with an introduction by Valeria Finucci, translated by Julia Kisacky

Cecilia del Nacimiento, *Autobiography and Poetry*, edited with an introduction by Sandra Sider, translated by Kevin Donnelly and Sandra Sider

Sister Giustina Niccolini, *Chronicle of Le Murate*, edited and translated by Saundra Weddle

Antonia Tanini Pulci, *Saints' Lives and Biblical Stories for the State (1483–1492)*, edited by Elissa Weaver, translated by James Cook (a new edition of *Florentine Drama for Convent and Festival*, published in the series in 1997)

Gaspara Stampa, *Complete Poems*, edited and translated by Jane Tylus

Sara Copio Sullam, *Jewish Poet and Intellectual in Early Seventeenth-Century Venice*, edited and translated by Don Harrán

Maria Vela y Cueto, *Autobiography*, edited with an introduction by Susan Laningham, translated by Jane Tar

Women Religious in Late Medieval and Early Modern Italy: Selected Writings, edited and translated by Lance Lazar

Maria de Zayas y Sotomayor, *Exemplary Tales of Love and Tales of Undeceiving*, edited and translated by Margaret Greer and Elizabeth Rhodes

VOLUME EDITOR'S
INTRODUCTION

THE OTHER VOICE

While the correspondence between Princess Elisabeth of Bohemia (1618–80) and René Descartes covers topics spanning the range of philosophical inquiry, still it was not written for the public. Early on in the correspondence, Elisabeth is quite insistent that their exchanges be kept private. In concluding her letter of 6 May 1643, she charges Descartes to refrain from making their exchange public,[1] and her letter of 10 October 1646 demonstrates that they considered communicating in code. Yet later on, without Elisabeth's permission, Descartes, through his envoy Pierre Chanut,[2] sent Queen Christina of Sweden a copy of both sides of their exchange on the sovereign good. Chanut, in a letter to Elisabeth of 19 February 1650 informing her of Descartes' death, asked for permission to make her letters to Descartes public, suggesting that it might be to her advantage to have their correspondence more widely known.[3] Elisabeth, however, re-

---

1. In concluding her letter of 6 May 1643, the first that we have, she charges Descartes, as "the best doctor for my soul," to observe the Hippocratic oath.

2. Descartes attaches these letters to his letter to Chanut of 20 November 1647, *Oeuvres de Descartes*, ed. Charles Adam and Paul Tannery, 11 vols. (Paris: Cerf, 1897–1913; new ed., Paris: Vrin, 1964–7; reprint, Paris: Vrin, 1996), 5:86–88 (cited hereafter as AT); *The Philosophical Writings of Descartes*, ed. John Cottingham, Robert Stoothoff, and Dugald Murdoch, and for vol. 3, Anthony Kenny, 3 vols. (Cambridge: Cambridge University Press, 1984–1991), 3:326–27 (cited hereafter as CSM or CSMK, respectively). He advises Elisabeth that he has done so in his letter to her of the same date. Chanut (1601–62) was the French resident in Stockholm from 1645 to 1649 and was appointed French ambassador to Sweden in 1649. As a close friend to Descartes, he served as intermediary between Descartes and Queen Christina and was largely responsible for Descartes' accepting her invitation to Sweden. For how Chanut figures in the correspondence with Elisabeth, see Descartes to Elisabeth, 20 November 1647, October 1648, and June 1649, and Elisabeth to Descartes, 23 August 1648.

3. AT 5:471.

Willem van Honthorst, *Elisabeth as Diana* (c. 1640). Oil on wood. Verwaltung der Staatlichen, Schlösser und Gärten, Germany.

fused permission and requested that the letters be returned to her.[4] It is quite clear that, at least from Elisabeth's point of view, the correspondence was not intended for any audience. While Descartes did see things somewhat differently, Elisabeth's wishes were respected. While Descartes' literary executor, Claude Clerselier, published many of Descartes' letters to Elisabeth

4. While we do not have Elisabeth's reply, Chanut's second letter indicates her desire to keep their correspondence private. Chanut pressed her to allow at least some of her letters to be made public "to serve as a geometrical demonstration of what he [Descartes] wrote" in his

in his edition of Descartes' correspondence,[5] Elisabeth's side of the correspondence remained unpublished.

Its privacy marks the exchange as different from other canonical instances of philosophical correspondence—for example, Plato's, Seneca's, and Cicero's letters—which were quite public. Indeed, Descartes' other correspondence seems to have been widely circulated, in accord with common practice. Not much later in the seventeenth century, women thinkers made public the private thoughts contained in correspondence. Mary Astell's letters to John Norris on the love of God were published,[6] and though Margaret Cavendish's *Philosophical Letters* involved an imagined correspondence,[7] it was premised on blurring this distinction between the public and private in intellectual life.

The privacy of this correspondence need not compromise its status as a work with regard to Descartes. Not only did he share portions of the correspondence, but also philosophical exchanges were simply part of his work. While readers look first to Descartes' published works to glean the philosophical theses he put forward, in order to understand those theses we turn to his correspondence. A full five of the eleven volumes of Descartes' *Oeuvres* are devoted to correspondence, and the proportion of his corpus devoted to exchanges with others only increases if we include the Objections to his *Meditations* along with his Replies to Objections, both of which were originally published with that work. Indeed, this is the framework within which readers of the correspondence between Descartes and Elisabeth have usually read their exchange. In trying better to understand central issues in Descartes' philosophical program—his account of the union of mind and body, his ethics, his account of the passions, his political philosophy—scholars turn to the correspondence with Elisabeth for further insight, historical background, or in the case of his idea of the sovereign good and his political philosophy, the most well-considered formulation of his views.

It is harder to know how to treat the correspondence with regard to Elisabeth, for there are no other extant philosophical writings by her. Her

---

dedicatory letter to the *Principles of Philosophy*. Elisabeth does not seem to have bended. See AT 5:472–74.

5 *Lettres de Monsieur Descartes*, ed. Claude Clerselier, 3 vols. (Paris: Angot, 1657–67). For a thorough account of the provenance of these letters, as well as others of Descartes, see the introduction to *The Correspondence of René Descartes 1643*, ed. Theo Verbeek, Erik-Jan Bos, and Jeroen van de Ven (Utrecht: Zeno Institute for Philosophy, 2003).

6. John Norris, *Letters concerning the Love of God* (London: Samuel Manship and Richard Wilkin, 1695).

7. Margaret Cavendish, *Philosophical Letters, or Modest Reflections on some Opinions in Natural Philosophy* (London, 1664).

letters to Descartes *are* her philosophical writings. Her letters are thus different from standard philosophical correspondence in at least two ways.
They are not written with a wider audience in mind, nor do they supplement other written work. Complicating matters is the fact that so little is
known about the place women held in mid-seventeenth-century intellectual
life. Elisabeth's engagement in public affairs, from lobbying universities on
behalf of professorial candidates to keeping abreast of peace negotiations to
arranging marriages for her siblings, makes her something much more than
the learned maid defended by her acquaintance Anna Maria van Schurman.
For learned maids, according to van Schurman, should study the fine arts,
letters, and the sciences, but they should consider military, legal, and political matters only theoretically, for they are "less fitting or necessary." For her,
women's learning is to be conducted in private and its effects are to be seen
in private. Its aim is to perfect their knowledge of God and assure salvation.[8]
While Elisabeth was educated in private by tutors, this education was clearly
put to public use and was meant to have served her well in governing, should
she have married appropriately or the family have regained its fortunes.
Moreover, Elisabeth's exchange with Descartes predates the *salons* of the latter part of the century, and she does not seem to fit the category of *salonière*.
Elisabeth certainly corresponded with Descartes and sought out intellectual
contact with others, but her goal does not seem to have been to form a social
circle premised on intellectual discussions. Perhaps Elisabeth stands in an
intellectual category all her own—her peculiar position as exiled royalty
would allow for that—or perhaps she conforms to a role available to women
of a certain class in the mid-seventeenth century, one that proved to be
short-lived. Without more study of women intellectuals of the middle part
of that century we cannot decide the question.

Without a clearly defined category into which we might fit Elisabeth, I
propose to read her side of the correspondence just as we would any other
philosophical work. Elisabeth's writings here are substantial, and they afford
us a clear sense of her intellect. Moreover, even though she does not put
forward theses, as she might have in a treatise, essay, discourse, or other
genre of published work, with proper attention we gain a clear sense of
her philosophical commitments. Her remarks to Descartes, including her
objections to his own positions, are internally consistent. She does not raise
objections simply because it is possible to do so. That is, she does not simply
press Descartes along certain lines in an effort to help him clarify his posi-

8. Anna Maria van Schurman, *Whether a Christian Woman Should Be Educated*, ed. and trans. Joyce L.
Irwin (Chicago: University of Chicago Press, 1998), 27.

tion against dissenters, although sometimes her positions do take this form. Her more central objections derive from a set of commitments she holds consistently throughout the correspondence.

Focusing on Elisabeth's philosophical contribution was, of course, almost impossible without any written record of her thought. However, with the revival of interest in Descartes by Victor Cousin in the early nineteenth century, scholars wanted to hear more of what Elisabeth had to say. By then, her letters had gone missing, and all that could be heard of Elisabeth's voice was its echo in Descartes' replies to her. Elisabeth's letters reappeared in the mid-1870s, when Frederick Muller, an antiquarian bookseller, found them amid uncatalogued papers at Rosendael castle outside Arnhem in the Netherlands.[9] Muller notified the philosopher A. Foucher de Careil, who published the letters in 1879, along with two letters of Queen Christina of Sweden.[10] Both sides of the correspondence were then published in the *Oeuvres* of Descartes, edited by Charles Adam and Paul Tannery, who consulted the manuscripts.[11] Jacques Chevalier also consulted the manuscripts in his edition of Descartes' letters on moral philosophy.[12] But then the manuscripts went missing once again. They have only just been recovered, once again in the collection of the van Pallandt family, the former owners of Rosendael.[13] The manuscripts are not in Elisabeth's own hand but are copies. The provenance of the copies is mysterious.[14]

The mystery of the origin of the letters can divert us from what Elisabeth has to say, even though we now have her letters. Moreover, the correspondence itself contains additional diversions. For one, there are gaps in the correspondence that raise an array of questions about how it fits together. Why is the exchange over the interaction and union of mind and

9. Rosendael then belonged to Baron Reinhardt J. C. van Pallandt (1826–99). Frederick Muller (1817–81) published his finding in a short article, "27 onuitgegeven brieven aan Descartes," *De Nederlandsche Spectator* (1876): 336–39.

10. A. Foucher de Careil, *Descartes, la Princesse Elisabeth, et la Reine Christine, d'après des lettres inédites* (Paris and Amsterdam: Germer-Baillière/Muller, 1879).

11. See note 2 above.

12. René Descartes, *Lettres sur la morale*, ed. Jacques Chevalier (Paris: Boivin, 1935).

13. Professor Theo Verbeek and his coresearchers, persistent in their development of a new edition of Descartes' correspondence, finally succeeded in retrieving these manuscripts in 2003. Through the efforts of Verbeek's research team, and in particular Jan-Erik Bos, the manuscripts have been digitally photographed, though at the time of this writing they have yet to be professionally microfilmed.

14. Verbeek speculates that they are a copy of a copy made surreptitiously by Chanut at the time of Descartes' death, even though Chanut assured Elisabeth he would do no such thing. Further details can be found in the note on texts and translation.

body abruptly suspended before the problem at hand has been satisfactorily resolved? How do Elisabeth and Descartes make the transition from discussing the vagueness of Descartes' account of the union of mind and body to the methods of algebraic geometry? Why does Elisabeth feel she can turn to Descartes with her medical problems in the summer of 1644? Why does the exchange pick up again only when he once again deigns to serve as her physician? Were letters exchanged which are now lost? Or did Descartes and Elisabeth continue their conversations in person?

Historically, there has been another diversion from Elisabeth's philosophical position. Many have been moved to wonder about just what sort of relationship existed between Elisabeth and Descartes. Was it simply an intellectual relation? Did Elisabeth take Descartes as a kind of father figure, standing in the stead of her own father, who died in 1632 when she was thirteen? Did Descartes take Elisabeth as an adopted daughter, standing in the stead of his own daughter Francine who died at age six in 1640? Was there a romantic liaison between the two? Readers have a penchant for profiling the personalities of the two correspondents, and so perhaps it is unsurprising that they have spun from these letters elaborate historical narratives meant to answer one or another of these questions.[15] In this introduction I shall try to resist the temptation to extrapolate from the letters we have to the drama that might underlie them. Telling such a story for oneself is, after all, one of the great sources of pleasure in reading this correspondence.

This pleasure should not detract from that of working through philosophical topics being discussed. Much ink has been spilled trying to sort out Descartes' views as presented in this correspondence. I will not add to that discussion here. Interested readers should consult the bibliography for further direction on this point. I shall, however, outline the central philosophical issues addressed in the correspondence and move on to suggest a particular interpretation of Elisabeth's writings. Readers have only just begun to take Elisabeth's side of the correspondence as representing a positive philosophical view rather than simply a reaction to Descartes' own program. The interpretation I suggest here is meant to be a starting point, to help readers think carefully about Elisabeth's side of the correspon-

---

15. See, for instance, Samuel Sorbière's entry on Elisabeth in his *Sorberiana, ou bons mots, rencontres agreables, pensées judicieuse et observations curieuses de M. Sorbiere* (Amsterdam: George Gallet, 1694); Marie Blaze de Bury, *Memoirs of the Princess Palatine, princess of Bohemia, including her correspondence with the great men of her day* (London: Richard Bentley, 1853); Léon Petit, *Descartes et la Princesse Elisabeth: roman d'amour vécu* (Paris: Editions A-G Nizet, 1969); Andrea Nye, *The Princess and the Philosopher: Letters of Elisabeth of the Palatine to René Descartes* (Lanham, MD: Rowman and Littlefield, 1999).

dence and so to hear her voice. Before turning to the philosophical content, I provide some biographical notes on both Elisabeth and Descartes.

BIOGRAPHICAL NOTES: PRINCESS ELISABETH OF BOHEMIA

Elisabeth Simmern van Pallandt was born in Heidelberg on 26 December 1618, the third child and eldest daughter of Frederick V, Elector Palatine and later king of Bohemia, and Elizabeth Stuart, daughter of James I of England and sister of Charles I. Elisabeth was one of thirteen children, two of whom, Louis and Charlotte, died in infancy. She died on 8 February 1680 as abbess of the Lutheran convent at Herford in the Rhine valley. Relatively little is known about her life outside of her family relations. These relations, however, not only provide a context for some of the comments Elisabeth makes to Descartes but also help situate Elisabeth in the politics of the early and mid-seventeenth century.

Elisabeth's parents' marriage in 1613 was touted as the union of English and continental Protestantism and so was taken as promise of the new strength of the Protestant movement in Catholic Europe. Shortly after their marriage, the Protestant electors of Bohemia, of which Frederick was one, revolted against the emperor of the Holy Roman Empire, Ferdinand II. This revolt culminated in the Defenestration of Prague, the event usually taken as the start of the Thirty Years' War. The electors persuaded Frederick V, as president of the Protestant Union, to assume the crown, and in August 1620 he departed Heidelberg for Prague with his wife and eldest son, Frederick Henry. Elisabeth and her older brother Charles Louis (also known as Karl Ludwig) were entrusted to the care of their paternal grandmother, Juliana of Nassau, and aunt, Catherine.

Frederick's reign was short-lived. It did not take him very long to lose the support of the electors, nor did it take Ferdinand long to regain his forces. On 8 November 1620 Frederick, no longer supported by his fellow electors, lost his new kingdom at the Battle of White Mountain. Shortly thereafter, Spanish forces took the other lands of the Palatinate, and Frederick earned for himself the title of Winter King. Frederick V and his wife, Elizabeth, along with their eldest child, Frederick Henry, and their infant son, Rupert, fled to Brandenburg, where his sister Charlotte and her husband, the elector of Brandenburg, sheltered them. With the enemy forces approaching Heidelberg, Juliana fled to Brandenburg as well, joined by her daughter Catherine, Elisabeth, and Charles Louis. In 1621, Frederick and Elizabeth moved on to The Hague, sheltered by his maternal uncle, Maurice of Nassau. Princess Elisabeth, along with several of her siblings, stayed at

Brandenburg with her grandmother and aunts until the late 1620s, when they were sent for to The Hague.

The events in Bohemia exacerbated already existing tensions in continental Europe and developed into the Thirty Years' War. Not only did the struggle between Frederick V and Ferdinand reflect and deepen divisions between German Protestant princes and German Catholic princes, but it also served as a touchstone for worries about Hapsburg hegemony in Europe. The Spanish king intervened to help Ferdinand because both were of the Hapsburg family. War erupted in southern Germany and ignited a conflict between Denmark and Sweden that spread into northern Germany. As part of this conflict, in 1632, Elisabeth's father died as a result of wounds suffered battling on behalf of King Gustav of Sweden. Gustav was the father of Queen Christina. Eventually, the Dutch and French forces entered the war as well. Peace negotiations did not begin in earnest until 1640 and were quite protracted, even while French and Swedish forces conquered Germany. Negotiations concluded finally with the Peace of Westphalia in 1648. The Hapsburg empire was in decline, and the German economy, countryside, and population were left ravaged.

Elisabeth's siblings seemed to have figured quite prominently in her life, either through the course of events or through their rather distinctive characters. Frederick Henry, the eldest child, was born in 1614 and died at fifteen as the result of a boating accident during a tour he and his father made of the Spanish fleet at harbor in the Netherlands. Charles Louis was born second, in 1617. At the end of the Thirty Years' War he gained control of what remained of the Palatinate. During his reign he restored and rejuvenated the University of Heidelberg.[16] Rupert, born in 1619, gained fame on two fronts: for his chemical experiments and pioneering use of the engraving technique of mezzotint; and for his soldiering in defense of the crown during the English Civil War. He was instrumental in the founding of the Hudson's Bay Company.[17] Maurice, born in 1620, was also known for his soldiering, though he died in battle in 1654. Elisabeth's sister, Louise Hollandine, was born in 1622 and gained fame as an accomplished painter, taught by Gerritt van Honthorst. She converted to Catholicism and con-

---

16. Elisabeth's later correspondence with him, published in Alexandre Foucher de Careil, *Descartes et la Princesse Palatine, ou de l'influence du Cartésianisme sur les femmes au XVIIe siècle* (Paris: Auguste Durand, 1862), reveals a relationship fraught with disputes over money.

17. Rupert has worked his way into common parlance in surprising ways. Prince Rupert's Exploding Drops were introduced in Britain by him in the 1640s, providing his uncle Charles I with great pleasure. Melted glass dripped into cold ice water solidifies into a drop with a thin tail. While the bulbous end is tremendously hard, when the tail is snapped, the body explodes into a glass powder—hence, their name "exploding drops." In addition, the British Columbia logging town of Prince Rupert is named after him.

cluded her life as abbess of the convent at Maubisson. Louis, the next born, died at sixteen months. Edward was born in 1624. In this correspondence with Descartes, Elisabeth shows herself to be appalled at the transparency of his bad faith in converting to Catholicism to marry Anne of Gonzaga.[18] Apparently, Louise Hollandine converted in good faith. The sisters remained close until Elisabeth's death.[19] The next sister, Henrietta, was born in 1626 and married a Hungarian nobleman, Sigismund Rakoczy. She died in 1651, just a few months after her marriage. Charlotte, the next sibling, died at age two. Philip, born in 1629, and Sophie, born in 1630, both figure in the correspondence. Sophie served as intermediary for Descartes' letters to Elisabeth while Elisabeth was in Berlin. Later, Sophie, through her marriage to Ernst Augustus, became electress of Hanover. Her son became George I of England, but she is also renowned for her intellectual patronage, most particularly of Leibniz,[20] who tutored her daughter Sophie-Charlotte. Philip's appearance in these letters is not so distinguished. He is the source of some difficulty on Elisabeth's part, having challenged a suitor of his mother's (and perhaps of his sister Louise as well) to a duel, only to stab him to death in a public square instead. Elisabeth, for defending her brother's actions, was sent away from The Hague by her mother.[21] Philip died battling for Spain in 1650.

In 1633, Elisabeth received a proposal of marriage from King Wladislav of Poland, a Catholic. The marriage would have been beneficial to the Palatine fortunes, and negotiations proceeded. The marriage was agreed to, provided that Elisabeth could retain her Protestant faith. The king of Poland himself consented, but in order to undertake the marriage he needed the approval of the estates of Poland. They refused to consent to the marriage of their Catholic king to a Protestant. The arrangements could have gone forward had Elisabeth been willing to convert to Catholicism, but she was

18. See Elisabeth's letter of 30 November 1645 and Descartes' reply of January 1646.

19. Some later correspondence between Louise Hollandine and Elisabeth can be found in Foucher de Careil, *Descartes et la Princesse Palatine, ou de l'influence du Cartésianisme sur les femmes au XVIIe siècle.*

20. Gottfried Wilhelm von Leibniz (1646–1716) was a German philosopher and mathematician. Philosophically, he is known for his theory of monads and doctrine of preestablished harmony, as well as his articulation of basic logical principles concerning necessary and contingent truths, the principle of sufficient reason, the principle of noncontradiction, and the principle of identity of indiscernibles. He is often credited with inventing the differential and integral calculus, though there is a dispute about whether he or Isaac Newton arrived at the calculus first.

21. These events are taken to have precipitated Elisabeth's visit to Germany (see Elisabeth to Descartes, July 1646), though they might well be connected to the sadness Descartes remarks on in his letter of 18 May 1645, a year earlier.

Louise Hollandine, *Elisabeth, Princess Palatine* (seventeenth century). Oil on canvas, 28 × 23 in. Courtesy Mallett, Inc., New York.

unwilling to do so. By the end of 1635 or early 1636, it was clear that the marriage would not happen. While there were other rumors of potential matches for Elisabeth, none came to pass, and she remained unmarried.

In part because of her unsettled childhood, it is hard to know how Elisabeth was educated. It is clear that she was schooled in painting, music, and dancing, as well as in languages, which certainly included Latin, Greek, French, English, and German, and perhaps others. We can also infer that she was taught logic, mathematics, politics, philosophy, and the sciences. She is consistently represented as studious and intellectual, so much so that

Louise Hollandine, *Henrietta, Princess Palatine* (seventeenth century). Oil on canvas, 28 × 23 in. Courtesy Mallett, Inc., New York.

she earned the nickname "La Grecque" from her siblings. At The Hague, she may well have been tutored by Constantijn Huygens, as he was present at court, and Elisabeth did correspond with him.[22] A remark she made to Descartes suggests that she read Machiavelli's *The Prince* around 1640, that is,

22. Constantijn Huygens (1596–1687) was a humanist scholar and poet and the father of mathematician and physicist Christian Huygens. For the correspondence see *De Briefwisseling van Constantijn Huygens (1608–1687)*, ed. J. A. Worp, Rijks Geschiedkundige Publicatien, 24 The Hague: Martinus Nijhoff, 1915).

when she was twenty-two.[23] She learned her mathematics, and in particular algebra, from Stampioen's textbook,[24] which is particularly interesting since Descartes and Stampioen had several public disputes over solutions to problems. Elisabeth interacted with the celebrated Anna Maria van Schurman,[25] whom, much later in life, she came to shelter at the convent at Herford, along with the Labadists,[26] whom van Schurman had joined. There is some suggestion that she attended lectures at the University of Leiden, but it is unclear what evidence there is for this claim.

The first written record of Elisabeth's intellectual interests predates her correspondence with Descartes by several years. In 1640, Edward Reynolds, an English preacher, schooled at Merton College, Oxford, known for his eloquent sermons, dedicated his *A Treatise of the Passions and Faculties of the Soule of Man* to Elisabeth.[27] His dedicatory letter suggests that Elisabeth had seen a draft manuscript and approved of it, so there must have been some correspondence between them. This correspondence has not as yet been found. The dedication is included in the appendix to this volume.

Elisabeth's correspondence with Descartes constitutes by far the most substantial record of her philosophical thought. The correspondence begins in 1643, after Elisabeth had read Descartes' *Meditations on First Philosophy* and requested the Frenchman Alfonse Pollot[28] to query its author. The correspondence continues until 1649, shortly before Descartes' death. I discuss the substance of the correspondence in more detail below. The correspondence does reveal a few more details of Elisabeth's intellectual life. Her letter to Descartes concerning her efforts to support his disciple Frans van Schooten suggests that she had some connection to the university at Leiden and was well regarded as a mathematician, given that van Schooten was being considered

23. See Elisabeth to Descartes, 10 October 1646.

24. Johan Stampioen, *Algebra ofte Nieuwe Stel-Regel,* (The Hague: by the author, 1639). Stampioen also tutored Christiaan Huygens.

25. Anna Maria van Schurman (1607–79). Two letters of Elisabeth to van Schurman appear in the Other Voice volume of van Schurman's writings, *On Whether a Christian Woman Should be Educated,* 57–60, 66–67.

26. Labadists were followers of Jean de Labadie (1610–74), a French mystic who turned to Protestantism after having been a Catholic priest. Labadie's followers formed a religious community that lived simply and held goods and children in common. In part because of their living practices, they courted controversy wherever they went.

27. Edward Reynolds (1599–1676) was a Caroline prelate whose sermons were recognized for their style and later collected and published. His *Treatise of the Passions and Faculties of the Soule of Man* (London: Robert Bostock, 1640) has been reissued in facsimile, edited by Margaret Lee Wiley (Gainesville, FL: Scholars' Facsimiles and Reprints, 1971). I have not been able to locate any correspondence between Elisabeth and Reynolds.

28. Alphonse Pollot (1602–68) was a gentleman in waiting to the prince of Orange.

for a mathematical post.[29] Indeed, there are at least two letters from John Pell referring to Elisabeth's mathematical talent as adduced from her relation to Descartes.[30]

Because of her family, both its rank and its precarious position, Elisabeth was also quite involved in politics. As early as 1639 she played a state role, representing the queen, her mother, in sending letters of condolence. In the early 1640s she corresponded with Thomas Roe regarding Roe's efforts to negotiate her brother Rupert's release from prison, as well as other political matters.[31] This latter incident formed part of the English Civil War, as Rupert as well as another brother, Maurice, fought in defense of their uncle, Charles I. Elisabeth's correspondence suggests she kept abreast of developments in that matter.

The English Civil War, really a series of three wars, and involving Ireland, Scotland, and Wales as well as England, was, in essence, a battle between the royalist Cavaliers and the parliamentarian Roundheads. The Cavaliers followed Charles I in defending the divine right of kings and were taken to be supporters of the episcopacy of the Anglican church. The Roundheads insisted that Parliament had rights and privileges independent of the crown and were aligned with Puritanism. The war was characterized not only by military campaigns but also by economic maneuvering. Charles I's income rested on his ability to collect taxes. Taxes, however, were set and collected through parliamentary acts, and initially with the king's dissolution of Parliament in 1640 and later with Parliament's opposition to the king, his income was compromised. In an effort to raise more funds both for himself and for his

29. See Elisabeth to Descartes, 27 December 1645.

30. John Pell (1610–85), an English mathematician, is most famous for his work in algebra, and in particular for Pell's equation, $y^2 = ax^2 + 1$ (where a is a nonsquared integer). From 1643 to 1646 Pell taught mathematics in Amsterdam, and Elisabeth might well have met him there. The first letter, from 1657, testifies to Elisabeth's expertise in Cartesian philosophy (British Library, additional MSS 4364, letter book of John Pell; 1655–58.f.150). The second letter, from 1665, also from Pell's letter book, directed a Mr. Haak to ask Elisabeth for her solution to the problem of the three circles (British Library, additional MSS 4365.f.198). Mr. Haak is no doubt Theodore Haak (1605–90). Haak was part of the Hartlib Circle, serving as a link between it and the continent. He later played a similar role with the Royal Society. He is also known for his translation of the Dutch Bible Annotations into English and *Paradise Lost* into German. I am greatly indebted to Carol Pal for drawing these letters to my attention.

31. See Anna Creese, "The Letters of Elisabeth, Princess Palatine: A Seventeenth Century Correspondence" (Ph.D. diss., Princeton University, 1993), 51–54; and *Calendar of State Papers, Domestic Series, of the reign of Charles I,* 23 vols. (London: Longmans, 1856–1924), in particular vol. 18 (Great Britain, 1641–43), 4, 91, 183. Additional letters of Elisabeth regarding matters of state and family can be found in *Calendar of State Papers. Domestic and Calendar of State Papers and Manuscripts, Relating to English Affairs, existing in the archives and collections of Venice, and in other libraries of Northern Italy,* 24 vols. (London: HMSO, 1864–1923).

campaign in the Civil War, Charles imposed taxes himself, a move that did not garner support for his cause. As the English crown was largely responsible for supporting Elisabeth's mother and her family, Charles I's precarious position weighed heavily not only on the family's political fortunes but also on their immediate economic status. The struggle between the two sides continued until the royalists suffered heavy losses against the Roundhead New Model Army at the Battle of Naseby in 1645. From there the tide turned against Charles I. He surrendered to the Scots in May 1646, and the Scots surrendered him to Parliament in early 1647. At this point, however, conflict escalated again. Charles escaped to the Isle of Wight and agreed with the Scots to impose Presbyterianism in exchange for their support. On the other side, the New Model Army under Oliver Cromwell became increasingly politicized. The Royalist cause collapsed in late 1648, and Charles I was tried and then beheaded on 30 January 1649. His son, crowned Charles II shortly thereafter in Scotland, attempted to carry on the battle with the help of Scottish forces, but he was defeated soundly by Cromwell. In 1651 he fled to France. England was ruled as a commonwealth under the protectorate of Cromwell. With Cromwell's death in 1658, opportunity for a restoration of monarchy arose, and in 1660 Charles II was restored to the English throne.

In her correspondence with Descartes, we see Elisabeth fully apprised of her brothers' efforts at securing their own political positions, Philip in signing a treaty with the prince of Venice, and Charles Louis in securing a small portion of the Palatine lands in the Treaty of Westphalia.[32] Indeed, one gathers from her later letters to Descartes that she herself may have attempted a trip to Sweden to broker a further concession in that treaty by Sweden.[33] From 1649–50 Elisabeth played a principal role in negotiating her sister Henrietta's marriage to Ragoczy. And there is additional correspondence with Henry Coventry, the Secretary of State for Northern Lands in England, indicating her involvement in political matters.[34]

In 1660, Elisabeth entered the Lutheran convent at Herford as coadjutrix, where her cousin Elizabeth Louise was abbess. Her dowry was negotiated and ultimately financed by her uncle the elector of Brandenburg. In 1667, when Elizabeth Louise died, Elisabeth herself became abbess. Just as in other parts of Elisabeth's life, there is relatively little information available

---

32. See Elisabeth to Descartes, 25 April 1646 and May 1647.

33. See Elisabeth to Descartes, 30 June 1648, July 1648, and 23 August 1648.

34. See *Correspondence and Papers of Henry Coventry, Secretary Of State, 1672–1680, and His Brother, Sir William Coventry, Secretary to the Duke of York As Lord High Admiral*, Coventry Papers, Archives of the Marquess of Bath, Longleat, England. Thanks to Carol Pal for alerting me to these letters.

about her life at the convent. She seems to have remained active intellectually, as Pell suggests that Theodore Haak[35] contact her during this period. Her response indicates a familiarity with Henry More, the Cambridge Platonist.[36] She also seems to have been a very effective manager of the convent's lands, as its estates prospered and recovered from the ravages of the Thirty Years' War. As abbess, she also was particularly welcoming to marginal religious sects. At the request of her old acquaintance, Anna Maria van Schurman, she extended the convent's hospitality to the followers of Jean Labadie, managing to convince her benefactor, the elector of Brandenburg, that all would turn out well. The group's communitarian spirit, however, led to conflicts with the townspeople, who requested that the convent ask the Labadists to leave. Given the pressure from both the elector and the locals, Elisabeth obliged. This episode, however, did not prevent her from hosting the Quakers. Robert Barclay[37] visited the convent in 1676, William Penn[38] stopped in Herford for several days during his journey to the Rhineland in 1677, and other Quakers, such as George Fox,[39] may also have visited. The Quakers were clearly trying to convince Elisabeth to join their sect, and while she was always gracious in correspondence, she remained skeptical that she was capable of the enthusiastic intuition of God they required. Elisabeth's exchanges with Penn and Barclay are included in the appendix to this volume.

Further evidence of Elisabeth's continued intellectual engagement includes a very short exchange with the Cartesian philosopher Nicholas Malebranche, concerning his *La Recherche de la vérité*,[40] and a report that Francis

---

35. See above, note 30.

36. Henry More (1614–87) was committed to proving the existence and providential nature of God by proving the existence of an immaterial spirit. While More was a dualist, he rejected the mechanist explanation of the natural world, preferring to account for the motions of bodies by the activity of spiritual substance.

37. Robert Barclay (1648–90) was a Scottish Quaker theologian, known for his writings on Quakerism. His correspondence with Elisabeth can be found in *Reliquiae Barclaianae. Correspondence of Colonel David Barclay and Robert Barclay of Urie and his son Robert, including letters from Princess Elisabeth of the Rhine, William Penn, George Fox and others, etc.* (London: Winter and Bailey, 1870 [Lithograph]).

38. William Penn (1644–1718) was a leading figure among English Quakers and the founder of the American colony of Pennsylvania. His exchange with Elisabeth is found in his *An Account of W. Penn's travails in Holland and Germany Anno MDCLXXVII*, 2nd corrected ed. (London: T. Sowle, 1695).

39. George Fox (1624–91) was a founder of the Society of Friends, which became the Quakers.

40. Nicholas Malebranche (1638–1715), an Oratorian priest, was a principal figure in the development of Cartesianism. See his *Oeuvres Complètes*, ed. André Robinet (Paris: Vrin, 1958–84). His major works include *La recherche de la vérité* (1674–75), *Traité de la nature et de la grace* (1680), and *Entretiens sur la métaphysique et sur la religion* (1688), as well as *Traité de la morale* (1683). According to

Mercury van Helmont[41] and Leibniz were at her bedside near her death. It should be clear that we have only fragments of an intellectual life. One cannot help but wonder what else Elisabeth may have written. Admittedly, because of her public responsibilities and, later, those of governing the convent at Herford as its abbess, it is unlikely that she ever produced a full treatise. Doing so requires a stretch of free time, after all. But might there not be other correspondence that has gone missing, correspondence that reveals again the range of her philosophical interests and that might reveal more of her own positive intellectual positions?

Elisabeth's epitaph reads: "Most Serene Princess and Abbess of Herford, born of Palatine Electors and Kings of Great Britain, unconquered and in all fortune full of constancy and fortitude, singularly capable and prudent in affairs and of an erudition worthy of wonder, celebrated beyond the condition of her sex, friend of learned men and of princes."[42]

BIOGRAPHICAL NOTES: RENÉ DESCARTES

René Descartes was born in La Haye, near Tours, France, on 31 March 1596. His mother died when he was fourteen months old, and though he appeals to his mother's untimely death in his correspondence with Elisabeth, he is somewhat liberal with the facts there.[43] His grandmother raised him along with his brother. His father was a member of the Brittany parliament. What follows is a biographical sketch. There are a number of very good recent biographies of Descartes, cited in the bibliography, which interested readers may consult for further detail.

Descartes received his education at the flagship Jesuit Collège de La Flèche in Anjou, roughly during the period 1606–14. After La Flèche, Descartes obtained a baccalauréat and license in law at the University of Poitiers in 1616. In 1618, Descartes traveled to Holland where he joined the army of

---

Robinet, these letters are no longer available. In his edition of Malebranche's *Oeuvres,* he summarizes their content based on Père André's biography of Malebranche.

41. Francis Mercury van Helmont (1614–98) was a son of the alchemist Jan Baptiste van Helmont. His study of Kabbalah was influential on Anne Conway. The senior van Helmont's alchemical vitalism was influential on Margaret Cavendish.

42. Serenissima Princeps, et Antista Herfordiensis Elisabeth Electoribus Palatinis et Magnae Brittaniae Regibus orta Regii prorsus animi virgo invicta in omni fortuna constantia et gravitate singulari in rebus gerendis prudentia ac dexteritatae admirabili eruditione atque doctrina supra sexus et aevi conditionem celeberrima regum studiis, principum amicitiis doctorum virorum literis et monumentis omnium christianorum gentium linguis et plausibus sed maxime propria virtute sui nominis immortalitatem adepta.

43. See Descartes to Elisabeth, May or June 1645.

Maurice of Nassau and as a soldier traveled around Europe, fighting in the Thirty Years' War.[44] While some have speculated that Descartes was a part of the forces that defeated Elisabeth's father, Frederick V, at the Battle of White Mountain, this does not seem to have been the case. During his foray as a soldier, Descartes composed his *Compendium Musicae*, a work of music theory, in which he also suggests a naturalist account of music's capacity to affect us emotionally. In 1622 Descartes returned to France and spent some time in Paris as well as more time traveling in Europe.

In 1628 Descartes finished composing what he wrote of *Rules for the Direction of the Mind*. In this work, which remained incomplete, he began to develop an account of human knowledge that took as inspiration the methods of mathematics and geometrical construction. Central to this account is the proper ordering of our thoughts. Achieving this order involves first reducing complicated propositions to simpler ones and then reconstructing them through intuition of the relations between the simple thoughts. In this same year, Descartes left for Holland, a country in which he was to make his home until 1649, when he departed for Sweden at the invitation of Queen Christina. During this time, he made occasional trips back to France to conduct various business matters.

While Descartes lived in Holland throughout this period, he changed his address rather frequently. These moves have no easy explanation, though they may well have been due to a justified caution on his part. While he no doubt found Dutch culture somewhat more tolerant than that of Jesuit-dominated France, even in the Netherlands the new mechanical science and its associated worldview were far from widely accepted. Indeed, though in 1629 Descartes began working on *Le Monde*, a mechanist treatment of physics, he abandoned his plans to publish it upon the condemnation of Galileo in 1633. He did, however, circulate it, and it is almost certain that he shared a copy with Elisabeth. He adverts to it in complaining about Henricus Regius' misguided appropriation of his work.[45]

In 1635, Descartes' daughter Francine was born. Her mother was a servant in Descartes' household. While Descartes did not marry this woman, he did recognize the child as his own, as his name appears in the church baptismal records. Francine died in 1640, and her death seems to have made an

---

44. For Descartes' own account of this part of his life, see part 1 of his *Discourse on the Method*.

45. See Descartes to Elisabeth, December 1646, and the letters following it. He also adverts to an unpublished treatise on animals, possibly his *Treatise of Man*, in his letter to Elisabeth of 6 October 1646.

impact on him.[46] It was around this time that Descartes was first introduced at the court of the exiled queen of Bohemia in The Hague.

In 1637, Descartes published his *Discourse on the Method for Rightly Conducting Reason.* There he sets out the basic tenets of his philosophical position: the method of simplifying problems and then ordering these simple thoughts into more complex objects of knowledge; the claim that mind is essentially a thinking thing and not corporeal; that we can avoid error by assenting only to those things we perceive clearly and distinctly; that God exists and is a perfect being; that the material world is extended and nonthinking and that its workings are to be understood mechanistically as a chain of efficient causes; and that the human being is a union of mind and body. The *Discourse* was published with three essays, *Optics, Meteorology,* and *Geometry,* which are meant to realize the fruits of the method in the sciences. The work was published in French, in part to signal its break with the philosophy of the Schools, where the language of choice was Latin and the disputation was the standard form. It was also written in the vernacular to reach as many readers as possible. In 1641 Descartes offered a more rigorous presentation of his philosophical program in his *Meditations on First Philosophy,* defending his dualist metaphysics and his epistemology. The *Meditations* was originally published together with six sets of objections and replies. A seventh set was included in the 1642 edition, along with a letter to Father Dinet, in which Descartes addressed additional concerns about the work. While it is likely that Descartes and Elisabeth met in the Bohemian court at The Hague prior to the publication of the *Meditations,* their correspondence began in 1643 with Elisabeth's querying Descartes about the coherence of his account of the human being presented in the Sixth Meditation.

In that same year, Cartesian philosophy was condemned at the University of Utrecht at the instigation of Gisbertus Voëtius. There are different ways of understanding the battle between Voëtius and Descartes. On the one hand, it can be read simply as a battle between a theologian and a philosopher. This reading, however, imposes a division between disciplines that was not at all in place until the late seventeenth century, if by then. As theologians such as Voëtius were proponents of the philosophical doctrines of Aristotelianism, a more plausible explanation of the controversy is the challenge that the new mechanist natural philosophy posed to Aristotelianism and the hegemony of its disciples. While the new science began developing long before Descartes, Cartesianism set it on a philosophical foundation,

---

46. In a letter of mid-January 1641, thought to be to Pollot, Descartes speaks of his sadness at her death. See AT 3:278–79, CSMK 167–68.

which gave it both roots and a certain legitimacy. Its tractability made it more threatening to the status quo.[47] Exacerbating matters, Henricus Regius, a professor of medicine at Utrecht, was promulgating Cartesianism and the new science. After initially proceeding indirectly to censor the new science, Voëtius started a pamphlet war against Descartes directly. Descartes responded in a letter to Voëtius and was summoned before the magistrates to answer to charges of irreligion. Around the same time, Voëtius's associate, Martin Schoock, was called before the University of Groningen to defend the charges he had made against Descartes. That matter was resolved, in Descartes' favor, in mid-1645.[48]

In 1644, Descartes published his *Principles of Philosophy*, written in Latin and designed to serve as a textbook for the new mechanist philosophy, replacing Scholastic textbooks such as that of Eustachius.[49] The work was dedicated to Elisabeth, and in that dedicatory letter Descartes characterizes his pupil and correspondent as follows:

> The outstanding and incomparable sharpness of your intelligence is obvious from the penetrating examination you have made of all the secrets of these sciences, and from the fact that you have acquired an exact knowledge of them in so short a time. I have even greater evidence of your powers—and this is special to myself—in the fact that you are the only person I have so far found who has completely understood all my previously published works. Many other people, even those of the utmost acumen and learning, find them very obscure; and it generally happens with almost everyone else that if they are accomplished in metaphysics they hate geometry, while if they have mastered geometry they do not grasp what I have written on first philosophy. Your intellect is, to my knowledge, unique in finding everything equally clear; and this is why my use of the term "incomparable" is quite deserved.[50]

47. More detail on the differences between Aristotelian and mechanist accounts of the natural world can be found in the Philosophical Background section of this introduction.

48. See Elisabeth to Descartes, 22 June 1645. For further detail about the controversy, see Theo Verbeek, *Descartes and the Dutch: Early Reactions to Cartesian Philosophy (1637–1650)* (Carbondale: Southern Illinois University Press, 1992), and *La querelle d'Utrecht: René Descartes et Martin Schoock*, ed. Verbeek and Jean-Luc Marion (Paris: Les Impressions Nouvelles, 1988). See also E. J. Dijksterhuis et al., *Descartes et le cartésianisme hollandaise* (Paris and Amsterdam: PUF and Editions Français d'Amsterdam, 1950).

49. Eustachius a Sancto Paulo, *Summa Theologica tripartite* (Paris, 1613–16) and *Summa philosophiae quadripartite* (Cologne, 1629 [1609]). See Roger Ariew, *Descartes and the Last Scholastics* (Ithaca: Cornell University Press, 1999).

50. AT 8A:3–4, CSM 1:192.

While it is tempting to read the high praise Descartes sings of the princess here as typical of the exaggerations and embellishments of these sorts of dedications, the consistent sophistication of the discussion in the correspondence would indicate that Descartes' praise is sincere, even if couched in the flowery prose of courtly manners. In Elisabeth's letter of 1 August 1644, we see her surprise at this dedication.

The *Principles* begins with an exposition of the metaphysical principles arrived at through the *Meditations* and then goes on in parts 2, 3, and 4 to develop a physics consistent with the view that the material world is extended and nonthinking. In particular, Cartesian physics is divested of the substantial forms of Aristotelian Scholastic philosophy. Instead, natural phenomena are explained by natural laws, derived from the nature of material substance and the nature of God as creator of that substance. From these laws follow rules of impact, which in turn are meant to explain basic physical phenomena, as well as such problematic phenomena as magnetic attraction and heaviness, by the collisions of bodies. At the end of part 4, Descartes makes a further effort to explain human nature as a union of mind and body, and in particular human capacity for sensation, from his first principles, but his account of the living world is left unfinished.

The French translation of the *Principles*, published in 1647, includes a preface in which Descartes explicates his conception of philosophy. Here, he compares "the whole of philosophy" to a tree:

> The roots are metaphysics, the trunk is physics, and the branches emerging from the trunk are all the other sciences, which may be reduced to three principal ones, namely, medicine, mechanics, and morals. By "morals" I understand the highest and most perfect moral system, which presupposes a complete knowledge of the other sciences and is the ultimate level of wisdom.[51]

This metaphor proves helpful not only for understanding Descartes' physics but also for making sense of his moral psychology and ethics presented in the correspondence with Elisabeth and his last work, *The Passions of the Soul*.

Descartes continued to work on developing an account of the living world founded on mechanist principles, beginning work in 1647 on *Description of the Human Body and the Formation of the Fetus*, which remained unpublished in his lifetime.

He also continued his correspondence with Elisabeth, and in the correspondence from 1645–47 we find the development of his moral philosophy,

51. AT 9B:14, CSM 1:186

and in particular his account of the sovereign good. That Descartes took his letters to constitute part of his philosophical program is clear, as this is the exchange he forwarded to Queen Christina. In addition, as a result of this later correspondence, Descartes' last work, *The Passions of the Soul*, was published in French in November 1649.[52] The passions, for Descartes, while modes of thought, have a physiological cause, and with that cause a physiological manifestation. Descartes approaches this subject *en physicien*, that is, from the point of view of the natural scientist interested in the causes of the phenomenon. At the same time, insofar as our passions do represent the ways in which things are important to us, they figure importantly in our moral psychology, and Descartes punctuates his discussions of the way the passions figure in the causal economy of the human being with accounts of how we might regulate the passions to achieve as much contentment as we can in this life. These accounts resonate with what he had written earlier to Elisabeth.

In August 1649 Descartes traveled to Sweden at the request of Queen Christina to serve as her tutor. There, the climate and schedule at court were not at all conducive to his health. He contracted what is thought to have been pneumonia and died in Stockholm on 11 February 1650. Descartes' papers and possessions were returned to Paris by his friend Chanut, then the French ambassador to Sweden. His correspondence was originally published posthumously in three volumes by Claude Clerselier, his literary executor.

PHILOSOPHICAL BACKGROUND

The correspondence between Elisabeth and Descartes is an unusual philosophical correspondence in that the two manage to address the full scope of philosophical inquiry. Their discussions range from what has become one of the most central issues in contemporary philosophy—the mind-body problem—to topics in natural philosophy from physics and geometry to medicine, as well as to moral psychology, ethics, and political philosophy. Indeed, working through the correspondence serves as an exemplary introduction to philosophy. I first provide an overview of the philosophical issues engaged in the correspondence, along with some essential background for understanding those issues. In the bibliography, readers can find direction

---

52. Elisabeth commissions Descartes to define the passions in her letter to him of 30 September 1645.

to select secondary literature on these topics. I then move on to consider in greater depth Elisabeth's own philosophical position.

Metaphysics

With her letter of 6 May 1643, Elisabeth initiates the correspondence by posing to Descartes a very pointed question about his *Meditations on First Philosophy*: "I ask you please to tell me how the soul of a human being (it being only a thinking substance) can determine the bodily spirits, in order to bring about voluntary actions." In order to understand the exchange that follows, one has to understand something of the dualist metaphysics that structures the question of how the mind can move the body.

Descartes subscribes to a substance-mode ontology. In his philosophical system, there are infinite and finite things. God is the only infinite thing, and for finite things there are two ways of existing or being: as a substance or as a mode. A substance, or a thing, properly speaking, is capable of existing independently of anything other than God. Finite substances have modes, sometimes considered as properties or as ways of being a substance. The existence of these modes depends on the substance of which they are modes. In the Sixth Meditation Descartes defends the position that mind and body are *really distinct* entities, that mind is thinking and nonextended, and body is extended and nonthinking, and that mind and body are capable of existing apart. That is, he maintains that there are two substances: mind, or a thinking thing, and body, an extended (and so a material) thing.[53] Each substance has its own modes. We can think of modes of mind as particular thoughts and modes of body as particular ways of being extended in space.

Though mind and body are really distinct entities for Descartes, in the case of a human being they join together to form a true unit. Our sensations of the world around us and of the condition of our bodies are evidence of this union. But the fact that mind and body are united in the case of the human being, the fact that we have the sensations we do, raises a constellation of questions. First, there are questions about the possibility and nature of mind-body interaction: How do mind and body causally interact with one another? How can an extended thing affect a nonextended thing? And how can a nonextended thing affect an extended thing? Or alternatively, how can

---

53. There is disagreement among commentators about what the "real distinction" consists in. Margaret Wilson, in her *Descartes* (New York: Routledge, 1978), defends the view that the real distinction consists in the separability of mind and body. Their being two distinct substances follows from their separability. Marleen Rozemond, in her *Descartes's Dualism* (Cambridge: Harvard University Press, 1998), argues that the real distinction follows from mind and body being two distinct substances.

modes of a nonextended thing affect modes of an extended thing, and vice versa? What kind of causation is at work? These issues are at the heart of Elisabeth's initial question. But other questions arise as well. There are questions about the metaphysical status of the union: What is the nature of the union of mind and body? Is a human being a third substance, in Descartes' sense of substance? If not, in what sense do mind and body form a true unit? And finally, there are questions of representationality: How does the mind represent the material world? That is, how, through the union, are we able to have knowledge of the world? Collectively, this constellation of questions has come to be known as the mind-body problem, and contemporary metaphysics and philosophy of mind have come to be dominated by answers to these questions. While Descartes is asked about the possibility of mind-body interaction by Pierre Gassendi in the Fifth Objections, as well as in the Sixth Objections compiled by Marin Mersenne, he offers only cursory answers in his replies there.[54] Elisabeth presses Descartes more pointedly than anyone else on this matter. In this way, she can be viewed as the first person to pose the mind-body problem.

Elisabeth's main concern is with the nature of mind-body interaction, for she does not see how an immaterial substance can affect, or cause some change in, a material substance. The accounts of causation she is willing to entertain tie causal efficacy to being extended, and since mind is not extended on Descartes' view, it is not clear how it can cause anything to happen in the body.[55] As she frames the problem, there are two alternatives open to Descartes. Either he can articulate a notion of causation that has the resources to explain mind-body interaction or he can further articulate the way in which mind is substance such that an available notion of causation could explain the way our thoughts effect actions in our body. Some contemporary commentators have claimed that any causal interaction between mind and body violates the causal principle—that any cause must have at least as much reality as its effect—articulated in Descartes' Third Meditation. Others have defended the metaphysical possibility of such interaction, arguing that since mind and body are both substances, they are of comparable reality, and their modes, as modes, are also of comparable reality.[56] It is

54. For Gassendi's objection see AT 7:339ff., CSM 2:235ff., and for that in the Sixth Objections see AT 7:420, CSM 2:283 and for Descartes' replies see AT 7:587–88, CSM 2:265ff. and AT 7:444–45, CSM 2:299–300, respectively.

55. It is significant that Elisabeth's question presupposes one or another mechanist account of causation. I discuss the significance of this in more detail below.

56. For a critic of Descartes on mind-body interaction, see Daisie Radner, "Descartes' Notion of the Union of Mind and Body," *Journal of the History of Philosophy* 9 (1971): 159–71; for

worth noting that Elisabeth does not frame the problem in these metaphysical terms; she is simply looking for an acceptable account of causation.

Descartes' response to Elisabeth's initial query exacerbates the mind-body problem as expressed here.[57] First, he appeals to the "primitive notions" through which we understand the world and claims that while the primitive notion of thought explains the nature of mind and that of extension explains body, the primitive notion of the union of mind and body explains their interaction. Descartes' appeal to these primitive notions feeds questions about the metaphysical status of the mind-body union, for it is unclear whether the primitive notions are meant to correspond to the kinds of substances that exist, or whether they are epistemic primitives—the basis for our understanding. Moreover, it is not clear how the primitive notion of the union answers the question about mind-body interaction. Descartes, just as he did in his Replies to the Sixth Objections, appeals to the Scholastic notion of a real quality, and in particular to the Scholastic account of heaviness. In the same way that, for Scholastics, the real quality of heaviness is to explain why a lead ball, say, falls to the ground, so too are we to explain how the mind moves the body. The problem is that Descartes wants to maintain that the Scholastics are misguided in their account of the heaviness of bodies but that the explanatory framework is properly employed in the context of mind-body interaction. Elisabeth is quick to point out that it is not clear how the two explanatory contexts are to be distinguished from one another. It is far from clear to her why what is mistaken in the case of the heaviness of bodies should not also be mistaken in thinking about the mind-body union.[58] Descartes' reply here is weak, for his appeal to a primitive notion of the union is rooted simply in our incontrovertible knowledge *that* mind and body are united and able to affect one another. But as Elisabeth reminds him, this was not the initial problem. She never denied an ability to experience the union of mind and body. Rather she (with us) still demands an understanding of *how* mind and body interact in properly mechanist terms.

In addition to the mind-body problem, Elisabeth and Descartes engage with the problem of free will later in the correspondence—in the letters from 30 September 1645 to January 1646. The problem as it arises in this context derives from a commitment to the two apparently contradic-

a defender, see Eileen O'Neill, "Mind-Body Interaction and Metaphysical Consistency: A Defense of Descartes," *Journal of the History of Philosophy* 25, no. 2 (1987): 227–45.

57. See Descartes to Elisabeth, 21 May 1643 and 28 June 1643.

58. Daniel Garber, in his "Understanding Interaction: What Descartes Should Have Told Elisabeth," *Southern Journal of Philosophy*, supp. 21 (1983): 15–37, argues that Descartes, though he did not, could have consistently responded to Elisabeth.

tory claims of (a) divine providence, or the view that God both has foreknowledge of all that will occur in the world and determines everything to happen in this way and is beneficent, wanting what is good for each creature,[59] and (b) human freedom. Descartes asserts a compatibilist position, or the view that human freedom is compatible with divine providence, but Elisabeth is at pains to see how this freedom, understood as a positive power to do otherwise, as Descartes seems to understand it, does not violate God's determination of human action. Elisabeth herself does not seem to reject the doctrine of freedom of will, though her Calvinist background might suggest she would. Rather she is seeking a truly viable compatibilist position.[60]

In its contemporary version, the problem of free will aims to reconcile human freedom with physical determinism rather than divine providence. Neither Elisabeth nor Descartes is moved by the problem framed in this way, even though they do take the physical world to be deterministic. For them, the determinism of the physical world is explained by God's role in creating and sustaining that world.

Natural Philosophy and Medicine

Elisabeth's questions about mind-body interaction presuppose a commitment to a mechanist account of the natural world, a commitment shared by Descartes. Indeed, Descartes' metaphysics, seen in its intellectual and historical context, aims to set the mechanist science, which by the mid-seventeenth century had gained momentum, on a firm philosophical foundation.[61] In this way, Cartesian philosophy was instrumental in the development of mechanism as a real alternative to Aristotelian accounts of the natural world.

While the positions of the late Scholastics had already begun to complicate the model, it is perhaps most helpful to begin to situate Descartes' view

59. In this correspondence, divine foreknowledge and divine beneficence seem to be conflated. Both within Scholastic philosophy and later with Leibniz these two divine attributes are distinguished and in turn generate very different metaphysical problems. Divine foreknowledge raises issues for our freedom understood as an ability to do otherwise. Divine beneficence raises issues about our freedom to act contrary to our good (or a problem of weakness of the will) as well as the problem of evil, the need to explain how things can happen in the world that do not seem in the least conducive to our good.

60. In her letters of 30 September 1645 and 28 October 1645.

61. "Mechanism" is not a univocal term. As J. E. Maguire points out:

It is obvious that the term "mechanical" meant many different things to thinkers of the seventeenth century: nature is governed by immutable geometric laws; contact action is the only mode of change; first principles are to be integrated with experimental investigations; regularities are to be explained in mathematical form; that all phenomena arise from matter in motion, or matter and motion; that compound bodies against the standard Aristotelian one.[62] On the Aristotelian view, particular substances, or things, in nature are hylomorphic combinations of matter and form. Matter, though composed of four elements (earth, air, fire, and water), is not in and of itself distinguishable into the variety of things found in nature. This inchoate matter is quite literally informed, or given shape, in being united with forms. The form of a thing serves to define it as the thing it is, or constitutes its nature. For Aristotle natural phenomena are to be explained in terms of four causes: material, efficient, formal, and final.[63] A house, though an artifact, provides a standard example for illustrating the explanatory role of each of these causes: the wood, straw, mud, or other materials that go into building the house are the material cause of the house; the workmen who build the house, and whose actions effect the house, are the efficient cause of the house; the blueprints, which determine the structure of the house, are the formal cause of the house; and the purpose of providing shelter is the final cause of the house. On the Aristotelian model, what is true of artifacts, such as houses, is also true of things in the natural world. Every thing in nature has a material, efficient, formal, and final cause: the material cause of quartz, say, is the matter (or proportion of the four elements) of the quartz; the efficient cause is the geological process that brings the quartz crystal into being; the formal cause is the crystal structure of the quartz; and the final cause is the purpose the quartz serves in the natural world. On this view, physical properties taken

---

are composed of vortices (Descartes), centers of force (Leibniz), or tiny bits of matter conceived as atoms or corpuscles; that changes in phenomena result from the way in which internal particles alter their configurations; that the "new science" conceives nature dynamically in terms of motion rather than statically in terms solely of the size and shape of internal particles; that occult qualities are to be banished from explanations which must be based on sensory experience in terms of clear and distinct ideas; or that nature is to be conceived in analogy to the operations of mechanical activities. . . . [W]hile they [mechanists] all agreed that contact action was a necessary condition for a mechanical explanation, there was no settled agreement as to sufficient conditions.

From "Boyle's Conception of Nature," *Journal of the History of Ideas* 33, no. 4 (1972): 523 n. 2. The discussion that follows here is greatly simplified. For a more full account of Descartes' place in the development of mechanism, see Daniel Garber, *Descartes' Metaphysical Physics* (Chicago: University of Chicago Press, 1992), and Alan Gabbey, "The Case of Mechanics: One Revolution or Many?" in *Reappraisals of the Scientific Revolution*, ed. David C. Lindberg and Robert S. Westman (Cambridge: Cambridge University Press, 1990), 493–528.

62. For a fuller, richer account of the complexity of late Scholasticism and its relation to Cartesianism, see Ariew, *Descartes and the Last Scholastics*, and Dennis Des Chene, *Physiologia: Natural Philosophy in Late Aristotelian and Cartesian Thought* (Ithaca: Cornell University Press, 1996).

63. See Aristotle, *Physics* 2.1–3 (192b–194b). For a helpful overview of Aristotle's philosophy, see J. L. Ackrill, *Aristotle the Philosopher* (Oxford: Oxford University Press, 1980); for a more detailed discussion see Sarah Waterlow, *Nature, Change and Agency in Aristotle's "Physics"* (Oxford: Oxford University Press, 1982).

to be essential to a particular sort of thing, for instance, magnetic affinity, are explained by appeal to the form or nature of the thing with those properties.

This account of the natural world came more and more under pressure with the observations of phenomena that were not easily subsumed under the Aristotelian system—most famously, those of Copernicus and Galileo. At the same time, the development of mechanical devices—some designed for practical purposes, such as assisting in construction or keeping time, others, such as hydraulic fountains, to serve a more ornamental function—provided a model for an alternative view of the workings of the natural world.[64] The world was conceived as working just like a machine. This alternative account came to be dubbed, appropriately enough, mechanist.

To understand what is distinctive about the mechanist model of nature it is useful to work through the metaphor of the world as machine. First, just as a machine is composed of parts that can be separated from one another, and even put together in a wide variety of ways, the world is conceived as composed of parts or atoms. These atoms then fit together in ways as varied as are the kinds of things in the world. Things are thus differentiated not by their form, conceived as something distinct from matter, but rather simply by the configuration of matter. Furthermore, the workings of a machine can be explained wholly in terms of efficient causes, without appeal to the machine's purpose or even its design. The motion of one part of the machine, say, a lead ball moving downward, effects a motion of another part of a machine, say, a rope moving around a pulley, which in turn effects the motion of another part of a machine, say, a plank of wood lifting, which in turn effects the motion of another part, and so on. We do not need to know the purpose of the machine to understand how it works. In a similar way, on the mechanist view, we are to understand the motion of one part of the matter composing the natural world (i.e., one atom or set of atoms) as effecting the motion of another part of matter, and so on. All physical phenomena, from the impact of one body on another, to plant life, to digestion, are to be accounted for by appeal to efficient causes alone. More specifically, a mechanist explanation of natural phenomena eschews both formal and final causes.[65] Since things in nature are composed wholly of matter, on the mechanist view there is no conceptual space for Aristotelian-style formal explanation. Final causal explanations, insofar as they involve an appeal to divine purposes in creating the world as it is, are not the proper province of philosophy, at least as far as Descartes is concerned.

---

64. See Dennis Des Chene, *Spirits and Clocks: Mechanism and Organism in Descartes* (Ithaca: Cornell University Press, 2001), for a good discussion of the development of machines.

65. Some, such as Gary Hatfield in "Descartes' Physiology and Its Relation to His Psychology," in *The Cambridge Companion to Descartes*, ed. John Cottingham (Cambridge: Cambridge University

The new mechanist model of scientific explanation faced several challenges. First, a mechanist needed to develop more fully the notion of efficient causation. Though a mechanist might well claim that natural phenomena are brought about by other natural phenomena, much more needed to be said about the mechanism through which they do so. And there was much debate about what the proper account of efficient causation should be. On one common view, causal efficacy consisted in the transfer of impulse from one thing to another, though there was some disagreement about what might be required for such impulse to be transmitted: Do the bodies need to be in contact? If so, is it sufficient that their surfaces touch, or do they need to fit more closely together? On another view, bodies were inert matter, and their causal role was to serve as an occasion for a third, intrinsically powerful, entity to bring about the effect.[66] Second, there were at least two phenomena that the Aristotelian model seemed to account for better: heaviness and magnetic attraction. A mechanist needed to offer an explanation of both these phenomena. And third, there was the problem of understanding human nature, and in particular accounting for the human capacity for thought and the immortality of the human soul in terms consistent with mechanism. As Elisabeth pointed out to Descartes, it was a somewhat ad hoc solution to fall back into Aristotelianism in the case of the human being.

Descartes' mechanism was already well documented in his published works. In parts 5 and 6 of the *Discourse on the Method*, Descartes lays out a mechanist account of the beating of the heart and extends a call for research into the new science. In two of the accompanying essays, *Optics* and *Meteorology*, he begins the project of offering mechanist accounts of vision and of select natural phenomena. In the third essay, *Geometry*, he illustrates his method of solving problems using algebraic geometry, a method that was supposed to bear fruit in understanding the geometrical structure of the material world. Descartes' dualism, in particular, his insistence that the mind is an immaterial substance, can be understood as a strategy for addressing the mechanist problem of understanding human nature.

Elisabeth's initial questions to Descartes about mind-body interaction reflect that she too is committed to the new mechanism. The accounts of causation she adverts to are all positions defended by those who endorse

---

Press, 1992), 335–70, have argued that conceiving the world as a machine in and of itself does not preclude formal causal explanations, though conceiving of natural phenomena as explainable by parts of matter in motion does do so.

66. For a good overview of the discussion, see Kenneth Clatterbaugh, *The Causation Debate in Modern Philosophy, 1637–1739* (New York: Routledge, 1999); and the essays in Steven Nadler, ed., *Causation in Early Modern Philosophy* (University Park: Pennsylvania State University Press, 1993).

the new science, and she is unwilling to admit a species of formal causation to explain the way mind can move the body. Moreover, she suggests to him that mind, or the capacity for thought, might well be best understood as the motion of matter of a particular sort. In understanding mind as material in this way, a mechanist would be able to account straightforwardly for intentional action and sensation by appeal to the same notion of causation that explains other natural phenomena.

Both Descartes and Elisabeth also reveal their mechanist commitments in the brief discussion of Descartes' *Principles,* as well as in that concerning the physiology of the passions.[67] As noted above, in parts 2–4 of the *Principles,* Descartes develops his mechanist physics, not only justifying the theoretical framework of the laws of nature and rules of impact governing the motion of bodies, but also explaining a range of physical phenomena within that framework. In her response to his dedication of the *Principles* to her, Elisabeth focuses on the explanations of magnetism and the density of mercury, and while she raises objections to these accounts, her worries are about the details and presuppose that she accepts the basic framework in which they are offered. The same is true of the discussion of the physiology of the passions. Descartes' account is thoroughly mechanistic, and Elisabeth's objections are not to this framework of explanation but rather to the plausibility of the details of the motions of the animals' spirits that the explanation involves.

In addition, this correspondence offers us insight into mechanist medicine. While works such as the *Discourse on the Method* and, later, parts of the *Passions of the Soul* and the posthumously published *Treatise of Man* present Descartes' mechanist physiology, in this correspondence we can get a glimpse of how that physiology gets translated into a therapeutics. In 1644 and 1645 Elisabeth seems to have been quite ill, and she turns to Descartes for counsel. Her own physicians subscribed to the Galenic medicine of the Schools, aiming to rebalance the four humors—blood or the sanguine humor, phlegm or the sluggish humor, black bile or the melancholic humor, and yellow bile or the choleric humor—in the body. They prescribed remedies, or taking the waters at Spa, or bloodletting, but they could explain how these prescriptions caused the illness to abate only by appeal to formal causes, the nature of the humors. Descartes counsels Elisabeth to follow some of the doctors' recommendations and suggests his own prescription of diet and exercise, and his advice does retain a certain aspect of the Galenic

67. See Elisabeth to Descartes, 1 August 1644 and 25 April 1646, and Descartes to Elisabeth, August 1644, 6 October 1645, and May 1646 (A).

system. Just like Galenic medicine, mechanist therapeutics models the body as a hydraulic system. However, Descartes' mechanist model differs from the Galenic model in that the fluids of the body are all of one kind of matter—the only kind—and the parts of the blood are distinguished only by their size. Moreover, the health of the body requires that the matter constituting the blood, in particular the animal spirits, move in such a way that the body will maintain itself. Our health and the cure for illness are to be explained according to the same laws and rules of motion governing all bodies in nature, that is, simply in terms of efficient causation.

Moral Psychology

The insights into mechanist medicine in the correspondence come not as a result of a theoretical discussion but rather in the very real context of Elisabeth's illness. While Descartes' prescriptions are consistent with mechanist principles, he diagnoses Elisabeth as suffering the ill effects of a disorder of the passions. This intersection of medicine and moral psychology reflects well the seventeenth-century context. In the early seventeenth century, the passions figured in two different sorts of intellectual pursuits. Medical writings concerned with therapeutics reserved a place for the disorders of the passions—excessive sadness or melancholy and lovesickness were two favorites—and typically offered an assortment of remedies, ranging from dietary recommendations and exercise to specific herbal prescriptions.[68] In parallel, the early seventeenth century also found a renewed interest in Stoic moral philosophy, which generated a breed of moralists who argued for the elimination of the passions.[69] With Descartes' diagnosis of Elisabeth, and in the discussion that follows, we can see the intersection and balancing of these two approaches to the passions.

Neither Descartes nor Elisabeth is wholly aligned with the neo-Stoic moralists, for neither wants to do away with the passions altogether. Descartes certainly acknowledges the reasonableness of what is probably best described as Elisabeth's depression, for he admits that the pressures of exile and money problems, as well as of other family and political misfortunes, can well take their toll.[70] And Elisabeth, for her part, asserts the legitimacy

---

68. See, for instance, Robert Burton, *The Anatomy of Melancholy* (Oxford: Henry Cripps, 1628); Nicholas Abraham de La Framboisière, *Oeuvres* (Lyon: Jean Antoine Huguetan, 1644), in particular *Le Gouvernement nécessaire a chacun pour vivre longuement en santé*. La Framboisière's works were first published in 1613.

69. Guillaume Du Vair was the most prominent of these moralists. See his *De la sainte philosophie* and *La philosophie morale des Stoïques* in his *Oeuvres* (Lyon: B. Nugo, 1641; rpt., Geneva: Slatkine, 1970).

70. See Descartes to Elisabeth, 18 May 1645, in which he distances himself from "those cruel philosophers who want their sage to be insensible."

of her own feelings against Descartes' oversimplification of her troubles.[71] Nonetheless, the problem of the regulation of the passions lies at the heart of their discussion. While, as Descartes comes to maintain in the *Passions of the Soul,* the passions are in their nature good, they do often misrepresent the value of things, making them seem better or worse than they actually are. The task is to feel things to the appropriate degree.

The model of the regulation of the passions we are given in this correspondence is at heart a cognitive one. The passions represent the value of things to us, and the regulation of excessive or disordered passions involves our reassessing those evaluations. While at the outset of this portion of the correspondence, Descartes seems to think that this reevaluation is simply a matter of directing our attention to the reasons to see things differently, the view is refined to meet Elisabeth's concerns. For, she points out, keeping our attention focused on the reason to think otherwise is not as easy as it might seem. I may well know that I ought to feel joy at the philosophical conversations I am able to engage in, and so not feel the despair I do at my family's fortunes, but that awareness of reasons for joy does not entail that I will be able to see my family situation in proper relation to the other parts of my life. While both acknowledge that there is a cognitive dimension to the passions, they also come to acknowledge that the passions have a staying power that other thoughts need not have. Part of the explanation for this sort of intransigence of the passions lies in a lack of complete understanding of the relative value of things, but that cannot be all. We often have difficulty properly assessing the value of things precisely because our passions come with a bodily affect that hinders our seeing things otherwise than the way we do. Regulating the passions thus involves also regulating their bodily aspect. It is here that the tie with medicine comes in. For through medicine we can temper the bodily motions sustaining our disordered passions and so achieve a physical calm that facilitates our turning our attention to other thoughts.

These discussions of human moral psychology complicate the Cartesian account of the workings of the mind and of reasoning. Most of our thoughts, like our passions, are caused by our bodily states.[72] While we can consider the reasons that argue against the excesses of our passionate evaluations, those reasons can gain sway only if the physiological force keeping those passions before our mind subsides. However, our considering reasons to feel otherwise than we do is not without its own physiological affect. In entertaining countervailing thoughts, we affect the physiological forces at

---

71. See Elisabeth to Descartes, 24 May 1645.

72. Our sensations are also caused by bodily states. For Descartes, we do have purely intellectual ideas, caused by the mind alone. They include our idea of ourselves as thinking things, the idea

work in our body, and with sustained attention the excesses of the passions can be tempered. The goal of the regulation of the passions here is thus not for reason to triumph over the passions but rather for our reasoning to restore a proper balance both to our physiological feelings and to the order of our thoughts. Indeed, reason is not dispassionate on this view but rather a matter of feeling things appropriately.

Regulating the passions effectively involves, as Elisabeth puts it, "know[ing] exactly all the passions we feel,"[73] that is, having a catalogue of the ways in which things are important to us, and equally, of the physiology particular to each of these passions. In charging Descartes to define the passions in this way, Elisabeth insists that Descartes follow his own method in this investigation of the passions. In following her charge, Descartes drafts the treatise that will form the *Passions of the Soul*.

Ethics

It is appropriate that the correspondence moves from a discussion of the regulation of the passions to a consideration of one of the central questions of ethics: the nature of the sovereign good. The discussion is framed as a distraction for Elisabeth—it comes out of a reading of Seneca's *De vita beata*. However, in order to regulate the passions properly, we need to have a proper sense of the value of things, which, for Descartes, comes along with clarity about the highest good.

Philosophical discussions of the sovereign good typically engage with two issues: the nature of the sovereign good and its relation to happiness. For Descartes, the sovereign good consists simply in virtue, which he defines as having "a firm and constant will to execute all that we judge to be the best and to employ all the force of our understanding to judge well."[74] Some philosophers would maintain that the sovereign good is just human happiness, though it would still remain to spell out an account of happiness. For Descartes, while the sovereign good is certainly necessary for happiness, which is for him a true contentment or satisfaction of mind, it is not identical with it. At times, Descartes does suggest that achieving the sovereign good is also sufficient for happiness—that we cannot fail to be happy if we achieve virtue[75]—but nonetheless he insists that striving for virtue and striving for

---

of God, the idea of body or extended substance, as well as other innate ideas. Some ideas, such as what he calls the intellectual passions, may not fit so clearly into this framework of analysis.

73. Elisabeth to Descartes, 30 September 1645.

74. Descartes to Elisabeth, 18 August 1645.

75. See, for instance, Descartes to Elisabeth, 4 August 1645.

contentment of mind are two different aims, though they may well achieve the same result.

For Descartes, virtue is a form of self-perfection. On his view, we are virtuous just in proportion to our own self-mastery. We are able to achieve self-mastery through self-understanding and a determination to act in accord with that understanding. In understanding ourselves and our place in nature as a whole, we also understand the proper value of things. Thereby we not only reason well about what we should do but also determine ourselves to act in accordance with that understanding. This clear perception of value, along with a resoluteness of will, results in the tempering of the passions and the dispositions to act well.

Descartes' account of virtue is somewhat peculiar, as Elisabeth herself remarks. For, on his view, to be virtuous we do not need the cooperation of fortune. While being well-born may afford one material goods that make achieving virtue easier, having that good fortune is not essential to virtue in any way. To be virtuous one simply needs to judge well and to be resolute in acting on those judgments. In a similar way, judging well need not involve judging correctly about what will come to pass as a result of one's actions. Rather, judging well, on Descartes' view, is a matter of reasoning well about what is to be done, given the information available, limited though it may be, and given the limited time one has available to make a decision. This view thus would seem to have the rather odd consequence that one can be virtuous even though one acts in a way that turns out to be bad. Part of this consequence might be avoided if the Cartesian account of virtue placed moral weight on an agent's understanding of the situation, but the view still places self-mastery at the center of virtue and the sovereign good.

That Descartes conceives of the sovereign good in this perfectionist way, and focuses in particular on the role of this good in regulating the passions, marks this discussion as one in virtue ethics. As noted earlier, Descartes figures in the revival of Stoicism in the seventeenth century, and his virtue ethics approach makes that connection tighter. Beginning with the more scholarly Justus Lipsius, Stoic moral philosophy provided inspiration for an alternative to the natural law tradition that dominated the Schools.[76] While the natural law tradition founded morality on divine prescription, a command external to the agent, the neo-Stoics sought to ground morality in human reason, demands deriving from the nature of the agent. Descartes' position is also to be distinguished from the emerging contractarian model,

---

76. Justus Lipsius (1547–1606). His most influential works were *De Constantia* (1584) and *Phys-iologia Stoicorum* (1604). His *Manductio ad Stoicam Philosophiam* (1604) provided an overview of

most famously developed by Hobbes in his *Leviathan*,[77] which grounds morality in the agreements forged by individuals in their efforts at self-preservation. The Hobbesian framework has provided the basis for contemporary rational choice theory. For Hobbes, a self-interested agent will choose to enter into a contract with another self-interested agent, thereby constraining his ability to act in some way, just when each agent recognizes that doing so is in his interest.

Within contemporary philosophy, virtue ethics is distinguished from deontological ethics and consequentialism. Deontologists explain why a particular action is good by appeal to duties or rules of morality. Consequentialists focus on the outcomes of actions, explaining why it is good to act in a particular way, say, to help a stranger in need, by appeal to the degree to which the outcomes promote human well-being. Contractarian ethics is, in a certain sense, a species of consequentialism. For it understands self-interested agents to choose to cooperate or contract with one another based on the outcome of that cooperation. Insofar as these contractual arrangements fix what is good or bad, the contractarian model roots value in outcomes of actions. Virtue ethicists, on the other hand, appeal to character and dispositions to act, along with the reasons for which an agent will act: a virtuous person has the character that disposes her to act in the right way for the right reasons. For Descartes, the outcomes of our actions bear little relation to whether we have acted well. Indeed, he maintains that we can be virtuous even when we prove to be mistaken in doing what we did, so long as our intentions were well-founded. Similarly, he systematically avoids offering any rules or duties that circumscribe morality. The maxims he offers are simply reminders that we must strive to cultivate within ourselves a virtuous character: to reason carefully about what is to be done, to be resolute in acting in accordance with reason, and to distinguish what is within one's power from what is not.[78]

That Descartes presents a virtue ethics in this correspondence can seem somewhat surprising. In part 3 of his *Discourse on the Method*, Descartes puts forward a *morale par provision* of "just three or four maxims" [79] in which he seems to conceive of morality as the following of a set of rules: we act well just insofar as we follow those maxims of morality in our actions. The

---

Stoic thought. Guillaume Du Vair (see above, note 69) and Pierre Charron were also important figures in this movement. For further insight see Anthony Levi, *French Moralists: The Theory of the Passions, 1585–1649* (Oxford: Clarendon Press, 1964).

77. Thomas Hobbes, *Leviathan* (London: Andrew Crooke, 1651).

78. Descartes to Elisabeth, 4 August 1645.

79. See AT 6:22–23, CSM 1:122–23.

maxims Descartes offers here do echo those of the *Discourse on the Method,* but his focus has shifted. He is concerned here less with the importance of following them as rules and more with the conception of the human good they contain. We might well understand Descartes here to be clarifying for himself in just what way morals follow from metaphysics and physics as suggested by the metaphor of the tree of philosophy in the *Principles*.

Descartes' individualist account of the sovereign good, and in particular his lending primacy to self-mastery in his account of virtue, invites questions about how each individual relates to other individuals and about how each individual is to measure her own good in relation to that of others.

Descartes and Elisabeth address the question of how the individual relates to the community of which she is a part in conjunction with their extended exchange on the regulation of the passions. Regulating the passions requires the proper evaluation of the value of things to us, and so the question of the appropriate measure of value naturally arises. One might well subscribe to an individualist account of value, that is, one that would have things be more or less valuable to the degree to which they benefit or harm each of us individually. Such an account could seem to fit with Descartes' account of virtue as self-mastery. However, one might also have a more tempered individualism. On this view, Descartes' own, I am not to measure what is beneficial to me in isolation from my relations to others. Rather, in assigning things their proper value, I must understand that

> even though each of us is a separate person from others and, by consequence, with interests that are in some manner distinct from those of the rest of the world, . . . one does not know how to subsist alone and . . . is, in effect, one part of the universe and, more particularly even, one part of this earth, one part of this state, and this society, and this family, to which one is joined by his home, by his oath, by his birth.[80]

Value for Descartes thus has a social if not a political dimension.

Political Philosophy

Political philosophy is centrally concerned with matters of the public good, including the question of how to govern well, as well as with the more general question of how individuals are, and ought to be, related to others through institutions of various kinds. Elisabeth directs Descartes to turn his attention away from the private matter of regulating the passions and guiding individual actions and to those of public life: "Since you have already

---

80. Descartes to Elisabeth, 15 September 1645.

told me the principal maxims concerning private life, I will content myself with now hearing those concerning civil life."[81] The view we receive from both is filtered through a reading of Machiavelli's *The Prince*.

Machiavelli's work, written in 1513 but first published in 1532, aims to lay out a set of strategies to secure and maintain political power. In focusing on political power, Machiavelli effectively separates political theory from ethics, and in particular from notions of right and wrong, just and unjust action. Descartes and Elisabeth do not address this particular methodological move directly, however. Rather, at the center of their discussion is a disagreement about the proper framework in which to lay out maxims for governing well. Descartes takes *The Prince* to be flawed methodologically, insofar as it presupposes that the prince has usurped power and offers guidelines for governing well under those conditions. Descartes asserts that the proper maxims for governing follow rather from considering a good ruler who has arrived in power through just means. Elisabeth, on the other hand, appreciates the methodology of *The Prince* insofar as it confronts directly the difficulties of governing by considering the hardest case. She does, however, find fault with the brutality of some of Machiavelli's implicit recommendations. Elisabeth's interest in political philosophy is driven by the real pragmatic considerations of her own family's position.

ELISABETH AS PHILOSOPHER

With a clear view of the philosophical issues in place, I now turn to consider Elisabeth's own philosophical position. Doing so is unavoidably speculative. As noted earlier, these letters are all we have of her philosophical writings. Adducing her views involves a close and sympathetic reading, one that of necessity must attend to other historical clues. Additional research on the intellectual historical context might well influence how we choose to read Elisabeth's remarks.

Natural Science and Mathematics

Before elucidating Elisabeth's own philosophical commitments, it is worth remarking on the high degree of both her interest and her competence in natural science and mathematics. That she was so engaged controverts many assumptions about women's place within natural philosophy and helps to chart a history of women scientists. Before her, Moderata Fonte, in *The Worth of Women*, devotes the second half of the work to an extensive exploration

---

81. Elisabeth to Descartes, 25 April 1646.

of natural history.[82] After her, we see Margaret Cavendish and Emilie du Châtelet and others fully engaged in scientific enterprise.[83]

While Elisabeth is perhaps best known for her challenges to the consistency of Descartes' dualist metaphysics and account of human nature, to which I shall turn in more detail presently, those challenges are grounded in a clear grasp of a range of accounts of causation. As noted above, the way Elisabeth frames her question reveals two things. First, she demonstrates a keen interest in alternatives to Aristotelian philosophy, and in particular the new mechanist science. Second, she shows herself to be more than a mere disciple, keeping well abreast of the debates on the proper account of causation in a natural world described mechanistically. For she entertains three different possible accounts of causal interaction—causation by transfer of impulse, causation by the manner of contact of cause and effect, and causation by the conformity of the surfaces of cause and effect—and argues that none can do the work required to explain the way the soul, an immaterial thing, can move the body. This interest in natural philosophy is not isolated; it permeates her letters to Descartes. Equally, she demonstrates herself to be quite a talented mathematician.

Shortly, after her initial exchange with Descartes, they turn their attention to mathematics, and in particular to the new method of algebraic geometry pioneered by Descartes. Descartes sets Elisabeth the problem of the three circles, or Apollonius's problem, to solve. The problem assumes three circles on a plane and requires one to find a fourth that touches each of the given circles.[84] Though Descartes worries that he has assigned Elisabeth too difficult a problem, she provides a solution with an elegance that clearly surprises Descartes. While Elisabeth's solution no longer exists, we do have Descartes' comments on it.

From those comments, we learn, first, that Elisabeth used algebraic geometry to try to arrive at a general solution—a theorem. She thus demonstrated

---

82. Moderata Fonte, *The Worth of Women*, ed. and trans. Virginia Cox (Chicago: University of Chicago Press, 1997).

83. See, for instance, Margaret Cavendish, *Observations upon Experimental Philosophy*, ed. Eileen O'Neill, (Cambridge: Cambridge University Press, 2001). Emilie du Châtelet (1706–49) was an accomplished mathematician, published *Institutions de la physique* (1740), and translated Newton's *Principia* into French and introduced the work. See also Londa Schiebinger, *The Mind Has No Sex? Women in the Origins of Modern Science* (Cambridge: Harvard University Press, 1989).

84. Pappus, in his *Collection* 7.11, mentions the problem and attributes it to Apollonius but does not give his solution, which was to be effected with ruler and compass. The first known solution to the problem using this method was by François Viète in 1600. Thus, in 1643, the problem was well known, and recognized to be difficult. No algebraic solution had been published.

a very advanced mathematical skill, as algebraic geometry was a relatively new technique. Moreover, Elisabeth's approach to the problem differed from Descartes' own, and significantly, her strategy seems to have had a symmetry and a transparency that Descartes' lacked. Descartes uses three unknowns, chosen not because they are intuitive but so he can avail himself of the Pythagorean theorem, and then substitution equations, to show that one can arrive at a second-degree equation for a single remaining unknown variable. Descartes does not perform the "laborious calculations," but his success in showing that there is a second-degree equation solution also demonstrates that there is a rule and compass solution to the problem.[85] Practically speaking, however, Descartes' solution would not help very much in arriving at an actual solution to Apollonius's problem. The equation one would arrive at if one did the substitutions would be difficult to translate into an actual construction. Elisabeth, on the other hand, used only one unknown in her solution to the problem—the radius of the tangent circle to be found. Her choice of unknown thus preserved the original problem and so left the structure of the solution transparent. She aimed to express this unknown in terms of the radii of the three given circles and sides of the triangle formed by the centers of the three circles. Like Descartes, she ended up with computational difficulties and so did not succeed in arriving at a theorem solution. Descartes, in his initial letter, before he has seen Elisabeth's solution, explains that he chose to use several unknowns in part to simplify the algebra involved. Elisabeth's solution, using only one variable, did prove to be dauntingly complicated. However, her choice of fixed quantities, and in particular the sides of the triangle formed by the centers of the three circles, had been dismissed by him. In working through Elisabeth's solution, then, Descartes seems to learn something about algebraic geometry.[86]

That Descartes, as well as others, recognized Elisabeth as an accomplished mathematician is also evidenced by her advocacy of the appointment of Frans van Schooten to the faculty of mathematics at the University of Leiden. Her support was a favor to Descartes, but she was clearly in contact with the mathematicians on whom van Schooten's appointment turned.[87] In addition, later in Elisabeth's life, the English mathematician John Pell, having come across these letters concerning the problem of the three circles, wrote to Elisabeth asking to see her solution. While Elisabeth refused this request

---

85. Descartes had shown in his *Geometry* how to derive rule-and-compass solutions from second-degree equations. See AT 6:374–76.

86. For an excellent discussion of this exchange, from which this account has benefited, see Descartes, *Correspondence of René Descartes 1643*, appendix 3.

87. See Elisabeth to Descartes, 27 December 1645.

on the grounds that all one needed to know in order to do what she had done was a little geometry and algebra, it is clear that Pell held her in high regard as a mathematician and proponent of Cartesian science.[88]

Elisabeth's interest in natural philosophy, and in particular physics and medicine, is also evidenced throughout her correspondence with Descartes. As remarked upon earlier, in her response to his dedication to her of his *Principles of Philosophy*, Elisabeth focuses her attention not on his metaphysics but on the plausibility and consistency of his accounts of magnetic attraction and of the heaviness of mercury. She also shows herself to be keeping abreast of developments in the sciences in the English-speaking world. She offers a pointed criticism of Kenelm Digby's objections to Cartesian philosophy, taking him to task for not properly understanding Descartes' account of collisions, and offers to have Digby's work translated so that Descartes may engage with it himself.[89] In her stay in Germany, she aims to circulate and discuss Descartes' *Principles*, though she has a hard time finding scholars willing to entertain this new physics. That she is so starved for people with whom to discuss the new science is evidenced by her glee at finding one person to discuss things with, only to be frustrated by his reticence, as well as by her impatience as she awaits the arrival of copies of the latest books by the likes of Hogelande and Regius. In their correspondence of 1645–46 regarding the passions, Elisabeth shows her interest in medicine, and in particular the explanation for the action of remedies for various illnesses. In her letter of 25 April 1646, she asks Descartes for a fuller account of the physiological causes of the passions, skeptical of what seems to be invention on his part.

This interest in causes of natural phenomena, along with a keen faculty of observation of the phenomena themselves, runs through the letters she writes Descartes from her stay with her aunt at Crossen. There she gathers information about the curative powers of the spring at Hornhausen, striving to find the proper explanation of these powers. She equally observes the way her party comes down with a feverish rash after a walk in the woods, an infestation of mosquitoes, and the medical treatment she herself receives for abscesses and impetigo. Though we do get more observation of natural phenomena than a detailed explanation, it is important to see here that

---

88. British Library, additional MSS 4365, f.198 and 196. Thanks very much to Carol Pal for drawing these letters to my attention (see above, note 30). The intermediary for this exchange was Theodore Haak, and interestingly, Elisabeth's response to Pell's request is directed to a M. More, presumably Henry More, who had requested copies of Descartes' letters as well as her own solution.

89. See Elisabeth to Descartes, 24 May 1645.

Elisabeth's interest was not merely that of a natural historian. She records occurrences that are new or unusual, taking care to identify the details demanding an explanation. She is careful to record the common wisdom regarding these natural phenomena, and the common wisdom more often than not appeals to superstition or mere dogmatic assertion.

Throughout these letters Elisabeth not only shows herself to be keeping abreast of the latest scientific literature but also demonstrates a real scientific curiosity. While she is an astute observer of natural phenomena, she wants a proper mechanistic causal explanation for what she observes and experiences. The standard Scholastic explanations do not satisfy her, for they either appeal to superstition or are so particular to the circumstance that they do not allow for any generalization from that experience. Elisabeth is seeking an explanation of a particular phenomenon that can shed light on other phenomena as well. The generality of mechanism, and of Cartesian physics in particular, satisfies this demand. It provides a theoretical framework through which the whole of nature can be explained.

Metaphysics

This overriding concern that one theoretical framework be able to explain the whole of nature can be seen as driving Elisabeth's metaphysical position as well.[90] As discussed above, Elisabeth was the first to pose the mind-body problem in questioning whether Descartes' dualism afforded an explanation of the ability of mind and body to causally interact with one another. Although Elisabeth poses the problem in its interactionist form, her interests extend beyond a simple concern about how two distinct substances can causally interact. At the heart of her objection is a commitment to mechanism. This commitment leads her to try to develop an account of mind — of human capacity for reason and reflection — that is materialist, thereby allowing for an efficient causal explanation of the way our thoughts and bodily states move one another, and that also respects the intuition that we have autonomy of thought.

Her commitment to mechanism emerges in her very first letter to Descartes, for, as noted earlier, there she is concerned that mechanism does not have the theoretical apparatus to account for the way an immaterial thing may move a material thing. Mechanists might not have settled on an account of causation, but they are in agreement that causal efficacy, no matter

---

90. Much of the discussion of this section derives from my "Princess Elisabeth and Descartes: The Union of Soul and Body and the Practice of Philosophy," *British Journal for the History of Philosophy* 7, no. 3 (1999): 503–20.

how it is explained, requires the properties only a material thing possesses: either being extended or having a surface. As the discussion continues, the commitment becomes clearer. Whereas Descartes is willing to entertain a species of formal causation to explain the interaction of mind and body, Elisabeth squarely rejects the idea that the Scholastic notion of a real quality demonstrates the kind of causation in play in the case of the human being. It is important to her that any causal explanation be a mechanistic one, and on the mechanist models of efficient causation both cause and effect are material.

Given her commitment to mechanist causal explanation, Elisabeth would have it that mind is just as material as body. While she does not initially state this position strongly, she does begin to intimate that perhaps mind and body are not such distinct substances as Descartes makes them out to be in his *Meditations*. She writes in her letter of 6 May 1643: "This is why I ask you for a more precise definition of the soul than the one you give in your *Metaphysics*, that is to say, of its substance separate from its action, that is, from thought." It is clear that she wants to revisit the question of how mind and body are supposed to be two really distinct things, and in particular that of what constitutes the mind as substance, in order to arrive at an account of the interaction of mind and body consistent with mechanism. In the letters that follow, Elisabeth articulates her inclinations toward a materialist account of mind more clearly. In her letter of 10 June 1643, responding to Descartes' invocation of the Scholastic account of heaviness, she admits, "it would be easier for me to concede matter and extension to the soul than to concede the capacity to move a body and to be moved by it to an immaterial thing," and she also invokes real cases to help motivate this materialist position, independently of the issue about causation. In these cases, people who would otherwise have full use of their faculty of reason fall physically ill and thereby lose the ability to think clearly. Perhaps they become delusional, or are muddle-headed, or in some other way lose the capacity to see things as they are or to draw inferences properly. Elisabeth does not see how a substance dualist like Descartes could accommodate these sorts of phenomena. For it would appear, on a strong dualist line, that even if we do have a physical illness, we should still in principle be able to think clearly: the soul, after all, on that line, is able to subsist completely independently of the body, and so it should be able to exercise its power of thought no matter what the condition of the body in which it finds itself. Elisabeth's thought is that this principle of independent subsistence is belied by the phenomena.

Nonetheless, though Elisabeth does want to defend a materialist notion of mind, she is still sympathetic to the intuition behind Descartes' substance dualism—that thought is not a mere matter of bodily motions and cannot be reduced to them. A remark in her 1 July 1643 letter suggests something like this: "Though extension is not necessary to thought, neither is it at all repugnant to it, and so it could be suited to some other function of the soul which is no less essential to it." I take her here to be suggesting that the capacity of thought might be perfectly consistent with extension, even though we can still distinguish thinking from the other actions of extended things. This suggestion goes undeveloped in the 1643 correspondence, but later in the correspondence, in the early summer of 1645, in an exchange regarding the regulation of the passions, she develops it a bit more.

There, recall, Descartes and Elisabeth discuss her persistent illness, which Descartes diagnoses as a disorder of the passions. He prescribes for Elisabeth a typically neo-Stoic remedy—simply to attend to her thoughts and to focus on those that bring her happiness, while ignoring those that prove upsetting. Elisabeth's response here is not clearly philosophical but is rather quite personal, expressing her frustration at her illness, her situation, and Descartes' own oversimplification of her situation with his pop-psychological advice. She appeals to the "weaknesses of my sex" to explain her own inability to turn her attention away from what troubles her. On its face, it seems that either she has internalized a kind of sexism or that she sounds a note of irony to bring out a certain sexism on Descartes' part. A further examination of her remarks, however, reveals a philosophical commitment related to the earlier discussion of the nature of the mind.

On the reading that takes her to have internalized a kind of sexism, Elisabeth seems to maintain that women are so closely tied to their bodies that they are subject to them, and thereby incapable, in virtue of their sex alone, of becoming fully rational. Thus, Elisabeth seems to be admitting that in principle we can regulate our bodily disposition just by using our faculty of reason, by thinking thoughts other than those we find ourselves having. She just denies that she, as a woman, is able to do so. But in making this admission, she is also implicitly accepting an aspect of Descartes' philosophical position. For she is admitting that the soul has a sort of autonomy from the body: it can engage in a certain kind of activity that allows it to maintain control over its own thoughts. She simply wants to deny that *her* mind is fully autonomous, that she has that kind of control: she suggests that her bodily condition—simply being female—deprives it of that freedom.

On the reading that takes her as sounding a note of irony, we must also take Elisabeth to be assuming the same autonomy of mind. Here, Elisabeth's invocation of the weakness of her sex is meant to bring Descartes' own assumptions to the surface—his diagnosis is colored by the fact that she is a woman and that his remedy seems to require that she deny she is a woman and be more like a man—for she is pointing out that she cannot help but be female. Her assertion in her letter of 24 May 1645 that

> if my life were entirely known to you, I think the fact that a sensitive mind, such as my own, has conserved itself for so long amidst so many difficulties in a body so weak, with no counsel but that of her own reason and with no consolation but that of her own conscience, would seem more strange to you than the causes of this present malady

would certainly seem pointedly to deflate Descartes' pop psychology while demonstrating her own strength. But here too she is both accepting the principle of the autonomy of the mind—the view that one has control over one's thoughts—and insisting that this power of thought is in some way contingent on our bodily state. While on this reading Elisabeth is maintaining that she does have her full faculty of thought, she still notes that this very fact is surprising. Her poor health and weak condition might well have obscured or otherwise impeded her ability to reason.

Within this personal response, then, and no matter which interpretation we favor, Elisabeth is seen as subscribing to a certain position on the nature of mind. On this position, the mind is autonomous: it has its own proper activity—thought—that allows us power over what we think. If we find ourselves with troubling thoughts, we need not dwell on them: we can think of other things. But Elisabeth also wants to maintain that this autonomy of mind is in a very important way dependent on the condition of the body.

This position is further articulated a little later in this part of the correspondence. In her letter of 16 August 1645, Elisabeth finally asserts her view. She writes, in raising an objection to Descartes' account of virtue as simply a matter of willing well:

> I do not yet know how to rid myself of the doubt that one can arrive at the true happiness of which you speak without the assistance of that which does not depend absolutely on the will. For there are diseases that destroy altogether the power of reasoning and by consequence that of enjoying a satisfaction of reason. There are others that diminish the force of reason and prevent one from following the maxims that good sense would have forged and that make the most moderate man subject to being carried away by his passions and less capable of disentangling himself from the accidents of fortune requiring a prompt resolution.

Here she claims both that our faculty of reason essentially involves a kind of control over our thoughts and that our physical condition can affect that faculty.

The perspective of the later letters helps to bring out the view underlying her original questions to Descartes in her letters of 1643. In this correspondence of the summer of 1645, Elisabeth points out that reason is intimately tied to our bodily condition: in order to think properly, we need to be in a state of good health. That is, while thought itself is an activity through which the mind demonstrates its essential autonomy from the body—through the mind alone we determine our thoughts—still our capacity to engage in this activity, our rational faculty, depends on our being in a certain state physiologically. In making this sort of claim about the relation between mind and body, Elisabeth need not take up a reductionist materialist position; she need not claim that all our thoughts are just bodily states and so maintain that our thoughts are essentially beyond our control, determined by the laws of nature. That our being in a certain sort of bodily state enables us to achieve rationality in this way need not compromise the *autonomy* of thought—the activity of thought—from the body. But in insisting that *we* determine our thoughts, neither need Elisabeth be committed to the kind of substance dualism that Descartes appears to espouse. For maintaining that thought is an autonomous activity does not require us to claim that it is an independent *substance;* we need not think of thought as an *entity capable of subsisting in itself,* suspended separate from body. Elisabeth's metaphysical insight, I take it, is to draw this distinction between autonomy and the sort of independence that makes something a substance.

Ethics and Political Philosophy

In the letters of 1645 and following, Elisabeth and Descartes move from considerations of the regulation of the passions to discussions of the sovereign good and even dabble in political philosophy. As noted above, in these letters we find most of Descartes' developed thought on ethics. My focus now, however, is not Cartesian ethics. Rather, I want to look closely at Elisabeth's objections (for here too she persistently raises objections) to Descartes' position in order to gain insight into her moral philosophy. We can discern three distinct points in what Elisabeth writes. The first two demonstrate that, theoretically, Elisabeth has sympathies with a virtue ethical framework for thinking about the good. However, given that our knowledge is incomplete, she is pessimistic that a virtue ethics can actually work to resolve differences. In light of this skepticism, we can read her alternatively as her searching for an ethics that might well foreshadow Thomas Hobbes's, as well as contemporary Hobbesian, contractarian accounts. To draw out Elisabeth's view, I shall focus on the letters from 21 July to 20 October 1645, though I shall draw insight from her other letters as well. After clarifying Elisabeth's objections I shall consider whether she is best read as simply raising objections in the spirit of furthering philosophical discussion or as endorsing a substantive philosophical position.

As this part of their exchange begins, Elisabeth, though she agrees with Descartes' tepid assessment of Seneca, is immediately skeptical about the view Descartes himself puts forward. In her letter of 16 August 1645 she writes, with her typical understatement, "I do not yet know how to rid myself of the doubt that one can arrive at the true happiness of which you speak without the assistance of that which does not depend absolutely on the will." Her objection cuts at two points, though she does not distinguish them explicitly. Most clearly, unlike Descartes, she takes our contentment to depend on something more than what is in our power. In her view, if we turn out to have been mistaken in the reasoning that led us to undertake the actions we did, we will regret both our error and our action, and so fail to be content. Thus, she objects that while Descartes is right to think virtue is necessary for contentment, he is wrong to think it is sufficient. In order to be virtuous, we need good fortune.

Elisabeth here seems to be aligning herself with the standard Aristotelian account of virtue. On the Aristotelian line, an agent is virtuous insofar as her actions reflect that she has character traits, or virtues, that dispose her to feel things appropriately and to act in accordance with reason or the pursuit of the human good. In addition, however, Aristotelian virtue requires an element of moral luck. In order to be virtuous, on this account, not only must we have the good intentions that come with good character, we also need to have the world accord with our intentions and our conceptions of the good. While waging a war might involve courage, it is not courageous to defend a cause grounded in falsehoods. Elisabeth here seems to grant Descartes a virtue ethical framework, but she raises what must be a standard Aristotelian objection to his view that virtue is simply being resolved to do what we judge to be best.

However, Elisabeth also wants to make a further point. For her, not only does our contentment depend on things outside our power, but also, she suggests, the very possibility of virtue, the capacity to judge well and to be resolved to act in accordance with those judgments, depends on things external to us. Our being in ill health can "destroy altogether the power of reasoning and by consequence that of enjoying a satisfaction of reason," or, to a lesser degree, affect our strength of will or simply our ability to judge things dispassionately. While she is still focused on the place of luck in achieving virtue, it is not clear that an Aristotelian would go so far as to claim that our very faculty of reason—that which defines us as human beings—is subject to fortune.

Elisabeth then focuses more and more on the limits of our knowledge of the value of things and of the outcomes of our actions, and she implies that these limits preclude our ever achieving contentment. For her, this limitation gets a grip in two ways. On the one hand, Elisabeth thinks that we cannot be properly content unless we see our good in relation to that of others; so to achieve contentment from our actions we would need to know each outcome's true value. However, since we do not have complete knowledge, we cannot properly evaluate the outcomes of our actions, and so cannot properly compare them to other goods. On the other hand, Elisabeth maintains that to act virtuously, we would need to know the consequences of our actions in advance. For acting virtuously requires that we reason or deliberate about how to act and then choose to act in the way that will yield the greatest good. However, again, we do not have the knowledge adequate to this task.

Let me suggest that Elisabeth's objection here can be resolved in this way: if we assume Descartes' account of virtue, then virtue is insufficient for contentment, insofar as we require for it, in addition to virtue, the knowledge of the just value of our actions; for virtue to be sufficient for contentment, we would need an "infinite science" to guarantee that our best judgments are correct. Whereas her first objection focused on the degree to which contentment depends on fortune, this second line of attack highlights the intrinsic limits on what does depend on us, our knowledge.

To understand this objection, it is helpful to see it in its intellectual historical context. As noted above, the seventeenth century saw a revival of Stoic writings and in particular Stoic ethics. However, there is a distinction between classical Stoic ethics, for instance that outlined in Seneca's *De vita beata*, and the neo-Stoic effort to Christianize Stoicism.[91] For one, the neo-Stoic movement selectively focused on ethics and so was not so concerned to preserve the situation of ethics within a whole system, as was classical Stoicism.[92] Nonetheless, both Stoics and neo-Stoics hold that virtue is both necessary and sufficient for true happiness or contentment, and they take this contentment to be the end of all action. Moreover, in principle at least, both Stoics and neo-Stoics take it to be possible to achieve contentment in this life. This is particularly important for the neo-Stoics, for in focusing on

91. The discussion that follows has been informed by Donald Rutherford's "Neostoicism and Early Modern Perfectionism" (MS).

92. Justus Lipsius, the instigator of the Stoic revival, did provide critical commentary on Stoic physics in his *Physiologia Stoicorum*.

this life they diverge from traditional Christian ethics. Within that tradition, virtue is not sufficient for contentment, since contentment requires divine grace and cannot be achieved in this life. However, this same focus on the pragmatics of this life would seem to motivate neo-Stoics to diverge from their classical intellectual ancestors on what virtue consists in. For the Stoics, virtue is just perfection, or the full development of a being's intrinsically good powers. In the case of a human being, our faculty of reason constitutes our perfection, and so virtue, for us, is just a fully developed or *perfected* capacity of reason, that is, complete knowledge. In achieving this perfection, we cannot but achieve true happiness. For the Stoics, then, because virtue is not a matter of degree but complete perfection, contentment is not a matter of degree but an all-or-nothing affair. The Stoic sage is one who has achieved perfect knowledge and so is virtuous and content. While the neo-Stoics agree with the Stoics that human virtue consists in the perfection of our faculty of reason, they do not want to go so far as to claim that virtue consists in *perfected* reason. Rather, virtue consists in our *perfecting* our reason, our persistent effort to keep our practical reasoning within its proper limits, limits prescribed by divine will. Thus, the virtuous person, for the neo-Stoic, disposes her will well *as far as it is in her power to do so*. For the neo-Stoic, it is our principal task to determine what is properly within our power and what is not, to firmly resolve to do what is in our power, and to resist doing what is without. In this resistance we are to remain impassive to those things that affect us. This resolution of will effectively compensates for our imperfect knowledge on the neo-Stoic view and so allows us to be virtuous simply in exercising our faculties to the best of our ability, without our yet having realized any absolute perfection of those faculties. Thus, neo-Stoic virtue, unlike Stoic virtue, comes in degrees, and so does contentment.

From this point of view, Elisabeth's second objection can be read as defending Stoic ethics against Descartes' neo-Stoic modifications. Again and again, she wants to deny that Descartes' account of virtue—simply being resolved to do what one judges to be best—is sufficient for contentment. To defend her point, she relies on another Stoic doctrine—that complete knowledge is required for contentment. For her, contentment comes only when we act on judgments that turn out to be correct. Moreover, she claims that correct judgment is required not only for contentment but also for virtue itself. She thus seems to endorse the classical Stoic point that virtue requires a faculty of reason that is fully perfected, and not merely aiming to perfect itself. Indeed, her earlier point that our possessing the faculty of reason requisite for virtue is dependent on fortune is not inconsistent with a Stoic position. Stoics maintain that individuals are constituted through the causal workings of the world and that the faculty of reason is a result of a particular distribution of rational matter (*pneuma*) in an individual. It is consistent with this view that the causal workings of the world might well have the result of compromising our faculty of reasoning. Our ability to achieve virtue would then depend on our good fortune at being properly positioned in the causal order. Though Elisabeth is no longer towing the Aristotelian line, in defending the classical Stoic position she is still advocating a virtue ethics.

Elisabeth's objections do not stop here, however. While she further develops her objection that complete knowledge is necessary for both contentment and virtuous action, the form of the objection takes another turn. If we knew the value of each thing, we would be able to measure the relative value of particular goods. However, without this complete knowledge, it is unclear what standard of evaluation we should use. Virtue and contentment might not require complete knowledge, but in its absence we still demand a measure of value. Because we do not have complete knowledge, this measure will in some way depend on personal dispositions and prejudices, but if it is to serve as a measure it must also manage to move beyond these personal perspectives.

With this attention to the measure of value, Elisabeth comes back to what motivated the discussion of the sovereign good in the first place—the passions. Our passions represent our personal perspectives in representing how things are important to us. The problem of how to regulate them is also the problem of how to measure relative value.

This move on her part suggests another reading of Elisabeth's objections, namely, motivating a contractarian ethics. Contractarian ethics takes as its starting point self-interested agents, each with his own desires. These desires may, and indeed are likely to, compete with one another. The contractarian task is for these individuals to come to an agreement about how they will value things in concert with one another, while still promoting their own interests.[93] In her early objections, Elisabeth is principally concerned with the problem of balancing self-interest against the interests of others or, more generally, with balancing competing interests. There, as we have seen, Elisabeth questions whether Descartes has the resources to reconcile competing evaluations of things and actions. Her objection presupposes that evaluations are made from a self-interested point of view. And there is no reason to think that different agents' interests, and so their evaluations, will coincide. The problem of ethics, on this view, is not to lead a good life and achieve contentment but rather to find a way of reconciling

93. Thomas Hobbes, in his *Leviathan* (1651), is usually credited with developing this account of the good.

these conflicting interests and the evaluations deriving from them. Contractarianism conceives of ethics in a similar way.

On this reading, the question of ethics, for Elisabeth, is essentially a political one. So this reading gains support from Elisabeth's request, in her letter of 25 April 1646, for Descartes' views on "the principal maxims . . . concerning civil life" and the ensuing exchange on Machiavelli's *The Prince*. Elisabeth sees that work as valuable insofar as it is concerned to promote a stable civil society; governing a state well involves balancing the competing interests of oneself as ruler and of one's subjects.

Moreover, the problem of balancing competing interests would have had some personal grip for Elisabeth. First, her family retained some hope of regaining their lost empire. At the time of this exchange with Descartes, Elisabeth was confronted by a very real case of the balancing of competing interests. Negotiations regarding the end of the Thirty Years' War were well under way, and it is certainly the case that the Palatine had interests that were not necessarily shared with other more powerful parties in these talks. In addition, although they may have been without a kingdom to rule, Elisabeth and her siblings seem to have been raised in such a way that they would be fully prepared to assume their proper places and to do so well. Their actions in their adult lives reflect as much. Charles Louis returned a war-ravaged land to economic prosperity in the small Palatinate he received at the end of the Thirty Years' War, as well as revived the university at Heidelberg; Sophie, as electress of Hanover, contributed to the success of that reign. Elisabeth's concern for the quality of life of those under her comes out in her correspondence with Descartes, both in her letter on *The Prince*, where she finds the practice of executing people "barbaric and unnatural," and in her observations on the poverty of the Berlin countryside when she is staying with her aunt at Crossen.[94] Elisabeth's tenure as abbess at Herford was also characterized by economic prosperity and a flourishing of the life of those who fell under her purview. Governing well thus seems to have been understood by the family to involve balancing the interests of individuals to promote the good of the whole.

It is not altogether clear how to understand Elisabeth's own perspective in this part of her exchange with Descartes. On the one hand, she raises objections from three different ethical frameworks—the Aristotelian, the Stoic, and the protocontractarian. She thus shows herself to be well versed in the various perspectives one can take toward one of the central questions of ethics: the nature of the good. And she is certainly availing herself of this

94. See her letters of 29 November 1646 and May 1647.

rich understanding of ethics to press Descartes to the view he is beginning to articulate here. She might thus be simply raising objections with the aim of furthering philosophical understanding. However, there is also a way of reading Elisabeth that suggests that Elisabeth herself is working to articulate an ethical theory of her own. To see this, we need to think about how her virtue ethics and skepticism work together.

As we have seen, along with a strain of Aristotelian virtue ethics, Elisabeth's second objection presupposes a Stoic account of virtue. To be truly virtuous, for her, involves having the complete knowledge that would allow us always to reason well about the right thing to do. On the other hand, she can be seen to discount the importance of virtue to focus on the practical matter of mediating differences of evaluation. Elisabeth's acceptance of the classical Stoic framework marks her as a virtue theorist. For she agrees that we are good or bad in virtue of those character traits that dispose us to act well for the right reasons. However, she also recognizes that true virtue is practically impossible in this life. Descartes, along with other neo-Stoics, recognizes the difficulty of achieving a perfect Stoic virtue in this life as well, but he responds by shifting the conditions for virtue. For the neo-Stoics one need not succeed in doing good to be virtuous; one need only be resolved to act well; virtue is a matter of good intentions and does not hinge on the outcomes of our actions. Elisabeth, however, demands more consistency between the ethical context and other areas of philosophical inquiry, and in particular epistemology.

In the *Meditations*, Descartes is unwilling to grant that we have knowledge just by judging the best we can. Rather, we have knowledge only when we follow the rule for avoiding error, that is, when we affirm only those ideas we perceive clearly and distinctly. Certainly, we are to work to arrive at those clear and distinct perceptions, but if we fall short, we are to suspend judgment; we err when we do not, and we do not yet have knowledge. We can see Elisabeth as demanding a symmetry between the epistemic and the ethical contexts. Whereas in the ethical context, Descartes is willing to maintain that we can actually be virtuous even though we err and, moreover, that we can achieve contentment in the face of this error with the assurance that we did the best we could, for her we cannot be virtuous unless we see clearly the true value of things and the outcomes of our actions.

Nonetheless, Elisabeth recognizes that ethics is concerned with how we should act, and she admits that in the practical context we cannot suspend judgment as we can in the epistemic, or theoretical, context. Moreover, given that our knowledge is incomplete, our evaluations are driven by our passions, those thoughts that represent the importance of things to us. Resolution of will, in her view, is an insufficient compensation for our ignorance. For, of course, different people will take things to be important in different ways, depending on their natural temperaments or the passions they are currently feeling. And herein lies the problem. It seems that these differences in passionate evaluations can lead only to intractable disagreement, more intractable the more resolute each individual is. For there is nothing reason can say to alter our temperament or to get us to shift our focus away from the passion that grips our perspective. It is in this context of practical ignorance that Elisabeth's rational theoretical suggestions emerge. For she wants a measure whereby we might have a standard for our evaluations, one independent of any one particular perspective. With this measure in hand we might arrive at a calculus for choosing one alternative or another, given imperfect knowledge. This measure can allow us to achieve, if not virtue, then an appropriate degree of contentment in this life.

In this correspondence, however, this idea is left simply as a demand and is not fleshed out. Still, an examination of how Elisabeth's objections progress gives us insight into how a revival of Stoic virtue ethics and skepticism in the seventeenth century may well have motivated the development of contractarian ethics. Of course, here I am making only a suggestion, and more work needs to be done to articulate how these strands of thought come together.

VOLUME EDITOR'S BIBLIOGRAPHY

PRIMARY SOURCES

Aquinas, Thomas. *Summa Theologica*. Trans. Fathers of the English Dominican Province. 3 vols. New York: Benziger Brothers, 1947–48.

Barclay, Robert. *Reliquiae Barclaianae: Correspondence of Colonel David Barclay and Robert Barclay of Urie and his son Robert, including letters from Princess Elisabeth of the Rhine, William Penn, George Fox and others, etc.* London: Winter and Bailey, 1870.

Beverwyck, Johan. *Van de Uitnementheyt des vrouwelicken Geslachts*. Dordrecht, 1639.

Burton, Robert. *Anatomy of Melancholy*. Oxford: Henry Cripps, 1628. Modern ed., ed. J. B. Bamborough and Martin Dodsworth. New York: Oxford University Press, 2001.

Calendar of State Papers, Domestic and Calendar of State Papers and Manuscripts, Relating to English Affairs, existing in the archives and collections of Venice, and in other libraries of Northern Italy. 24 vols. London: HMSO, 1864–1923.

Calendar of State Papers, Domestic Series, of the reign of Charles I. 23 vols. London: Longmans, 1856–1924.

Cavendish, Margaret. *Observations upon Experimental Philosophy*. Ed. Eileen O'Neill. Cambridge: Cambridge University Press, 2001.

———. *Philosophical Letters, or Modest Reflections on some Opinions in Natural Philosophy*. London, 1664.

Cicero. *Tusculan Disputations*. Trans. J. E. King. Cambridge: Harvard University Press, 1927, 1960.

Conway, Anne Finch, Viscountess. *Principles of the Most Ancient and Modern Philosophy* (1690). Ed. Allison P. Coudert and Taylor Corse. Cambridge: Cambridge University Press, 1996.

Descartes, René. *Correspondance avec Elisabeth*. Ed. Jean-Marie Beyssade and Michelle Beyssade. Paris: Garnier-Flammarion, 1989.

———. *The Correspondence of René Descartes 1643*. Ed. Theo Verbeek, Erik-Jan Bos, and Jeroen van de Ven. Utrecht: Zeno Institute for Philosophy, 2003.

———. *Ecrits physiologiques et médicaux*. Ed. Vincent Aucante. Paris: Presses Universitaires de France, 2000.

———. *Lettres de Monsieur Descartes*. Ed. Claude Clerselier. 3 vols. Paris: Angot, 1657–67.

———. *Lettres sur la morale*. Ed. Jacques Chevalier. Paris: Boivin, 1935.

————. *Lettres sur la morale: corréspondence avec la princesse Elisabeth, Chanut et la reine Christine.* Ed. Jacques Chevalier. Paris: Hatier-Boivin, 1955.

————. *Oeuvres de Descartes.* Ed. Charles Adam and Paul Tannery. 11 vols. Paris: Cerf, 1897–1913. New ed., Paris: Vrin, 1964–71. Rpt., Paris: Vrin, 1996. (Cited as AT.)

————. *The Philosophical Writings of Descartes.* Vols. 1–3, ed. John Cottingham, Robert Stoothoff, and Dugald Murdoch. Vol. 3, ed. Cottingham, Stoothoff, Murdoch, and Anthony Kenny. Cambridge: Cambridge University Press, 1984–1991. (Cited as CSM or CSMK.)

Digby, Kenelm. *Two Treatises, in the one of which the Nature of Bodies, in the other the Nature of Man's soul is looked into, in way of discovery of the immortality of reasonable souls.* London: John Williams, 1645. Rpt., New York: Garland, 1978.

Du Châtelet, Emilie. *Institutions de la physique.* Paris: Prault fils, 1740.

Du Vair, Guillaume. *De la sainte philosophie* and *La philosophie morale des Stoiques.* In *Oeuvres.* Lyon: B. Nugo, 1641. Rpt., Geneva: Slatkine, 1970.

Eustachius a Sancto Paulo. *Summa philosophiae quadripartite* (1609).Cologne, 1629

————. *Summa Theologica tripartite.* Paris, 1613–16.

Fonte, Moderata (Modesta Pozzo). *The Worth of Women.* Ed. and trans. Virginia Cox. Chicago: University of Chicago Press, 1997.

Foucher de Careil, Alexandre. *Descartes, la Princesse Elisabeth et la Reine Christine.* Paris and Amsterdam: Germer-Ballière/Muller, 1879. New ed., Paris: Felix Alcan, 1909.

Grotius, Hugo. *De jure belli ac pacis. libri tres* (1625). Trans. Francis W. Kelsey et al. Introd. James Brown Scott. New York: Oceania, 1964.

Harriot, Thomas. *Artes analyticae praxis.* London: Robert Barker, 1631.

Hobbes, Thomas. *Leviathan.* London: Andrew Crooke, 1651. Modern eds., ed. C. B. Macpherson. Baltimore: Penguin, 1968. Ed. Edwin Curley. Indianapolis: Hackett, 1994.

Hogelande, M. de. *Cogitationes, quibus Dei existential, item animae spiritalitas, et possibilis cum corpore unio demonstratur, nec non brevis historia oeconomiae corporis animalis preponitur atque mechanice explicatur.* Amsterdam: Ludovicus Elzevirium, 1646.

Huygens, Constantijn. *De Briefwisseling van Constantijn Huygens, 1608–1687.* Ed. J. A. Worp. 6 vols. The Hague: Martinus Nijhoff, 1911–17.

La Framboisière, Abraham Nicholas de. *Oeuvres.* Lyon: Jean Antoine Huguetan, 1644

Lipsius, Justus. *De Constantia.* Antwerp: Christoph Plantin,1584.

————. *Manductio ad Stoicam Philosophiam.* Antwerp: Christoph Plantin, 1604.

————. *Physiologia Stoicorum.* Antwerp: Christoph Plantin, 1604.

Machiavelli, Niccolò. *The Discourses.* Ed. and introd. Bernard Crick. Trans. Leslie J. Walker, S.J. Rev. Brian Richardson. New York: Penguin Books, 1970, 1983.

————. *The Prince.* Ed. Quentin Skinner and Russell Price. Cambridge: Cambridge University Press, 1988.

Malebranche, Nicholas. *Oeuvres complètes.* Ed. André Robinet. Paris: Vrin, 1958–84.

Montaigne, Michel de. *The Complete Essays.* Trans. M. A. Screech. New York: Penguin Books, 1987.

Norris, John. *Letters concerning the Love of God.* London: Samuel Manship and Richard Wilkin, 1695.

Pell, John. Letter book of John Pell, 1655–58. British Library Additional MSS 4364
     f.150, 4365.f.196 and 198.

Penn, William. *An Account of W. Penn's Travails in Holland and Germany, Anno MDCLXXVII.*
     2nd corrected ed. London: T. Sowle, 1695.

Plato. *Complete Works.* Ed. John Cooper. Assoc. ed. D. S. Hutchinson. Indianapolis:
     Hackett, 1997.

Regius [le Roy], Henri. *Fundamenta Physica.* Utrecht: Roman, 1646.

————. *Physiologia sive cognitio sanitatis.* Utrecht: Roman, 1641.

————. *Utrajectini Fundamenta Medica.* Amsterdam: Theodorum Ackersdycium, 1647.

Reynolds, Edward. *Treatise of the Passions and Faculties of the Soule of Man.* London: Robert
     Bostock, 1640. Facsimile reproduction, ed. Margaret Lee Wiley. Gainesville, FL:
     Scholars' Facsimiles and Reprints, 1971.

Seneca. *De vita beata.* In *Seneca: Moral Essays II,* trans. J. W. Basore. Cambridge: Harvard
     University Press, 1932, 1965.

Sorbière, Samuel. *Lettres et discours de M. de Sorbière.* Paris: F. Clousier, 1660.

————. *Sorbierana, ou bons mots, rencontres agreables, pensées judicieuses, et observations curieuses
     de M. Sorbiére.* Amsterdam: George Gallet, 1694.

Stampioen, Johan. *Algebra ofte Nieuwe Stel-Regel.* The Hague: by the author, 1639.

Van Schurman, Anna Maria. *Whether a Christian Woman Should Be Educated.* Ed. and
     trans. Joyce L. Irwin. Chicago: University of Chicago Press, 1998.

White, Thomas. *De mundo dialogi tres, quibus materia, forma, caussae.* Paris: Dionysium
     Moreaum, 1642.

————. *Institutionum Peripateticarum ad mentem summi viri, clarissimique Philosophi Kenelmi
     Euitis Digboeii.* 2nd corrected ed. London, 1647.

SECONDARY SOURCES

Biographies of Elisabeth

Blaze de Bury, Marie Pauline Rose Stewart. *Memoirs of the Princess Palatine, Princess of
     Bohemia including her correspondence with the great men of her day.* London: Richard Bent-
     ley, 1853.

Creese, Anna. "The Letters of Elisabeth, Princess Palatine: A Seventeenth Century
     Correspondence." Ph.D. diss., Princeton University, 1993.

Godfrey, Elizabeth. *A Sister of Prince Rupert: Elizabeth Princess Palatine and Abbess of Herford.*
     London: John Lane, 1909.

Zendler, Beatrice. "The Three Princesses." *Hypatia* 4, no.1 (1989): 28–63.

Works about the Family Palatine

Benger, Elizabeth. *Memoirs of Elizabeth Stuart, Queen of Bohemia, Daughter of James I.* Vols. 1
     and 2. London: Longman, Hurst, Rees, Orme, Brown and Green, 1825.

Marshall, Rosalind K. *The Winter Queen: The Life of Elizabeth of Bohemia, 1596–1662.* Ed-
     inburgh: Scottish National Portrait Gallery, 1998.

Morrah, Patrick. *Prince Rupert of the Rhine.* London: Constable, 1976.

Oman, Carola. *Elizabeth of Bohemia.* London: Hodder and Stoughton, 1938, 1964.

Biographies of Descartes

Baillet, Adrien. *Vie de Descartes*. Paris, 1691. Rpt., Paris: La Table Ronde, 1946.

Gaukroger, Stephen. *Descartes: An Intellectual Biography*. New York: Oxford University Press, 1995.

Rodis-Lewis, Genevieve. *Descartes: His Life and Thought*. Trans. Jane Marie Todd. Ithaca: Cornell University Press, 1998.

The Intellectual-Historical Context

Ackrill, J. L. *Aristotle the Philosopher*. Oxford: Oxford University Press, 1980.

Adam, Charles. *Descartes et ses amitiés féminines*. Paris: Boivin, 1917.

Ariew, Roger. *Descartes and the Last Scholastics*. Ithaca: Cornell University Press, 1999.

Des Chene, Dennis. *Physiologia: Natural Philosophy in Late Aristotelian and Cartesian Thought*. Ithaca: Cornell University Press, 1996.

————. *Spirits and Clocks: Mechanism and Organism in Descartes*. Ithaca: Cornell University Press, 2001.

Dijksterhuis, E. J., et al. *Descartes et le cartésianisme hollandaise*. Paris and Amsterdam: PUF and Editions Françaises d'Amsterdam, 1950.

Foucher de Careil, Alexandre. *Descartes et la Princesse Palatine, ou de l'influence du cartésianisme sur les femmes au XVIIe siécle*. Paris: Auguste Durand, 1862.

Harth, Erica. *Cartesian Women: Versions and Subversions of Rational Discourse in the Old Regime*. Ithaca: Cornell University Press, 1992.

Levi, Anthony. *French Moralists: The Theory of the Passions, 1585–1649*. Oxford: Clarendon Press, 1964.

O'Neill, Eileen. "Disappearing Ink: Early Modern Women Philosophers and Their Fate in History." In *Philosophy in a Feminist Voice*, ed. Janet A. Kourany. Princeton: Princeton University Press, 1998. 17–62.

————. "Women Cartesians, 'Feminine Philosophy' and Historical Exclusion." In *Feminist Interpretations of René Descartes*, ed. Susan Bordo. University Park: Pennsylvania State University Press, 1999. 232–57.

Schiebinger, Londa. *The Mind Has No Sex? Women in the Origins of Modern Science*. Cambridge: Harvard University Press, 1989.

Verbeek, Theo. *Descartes and the Dutch: Early Reactions to Cartesianism (1637–1650)*. Carbondale: Southern Illinois University Press, 1992.

Verbeek, Theo, and Jean-Luc Marion, eds. *La querelle d'Utrecht: René Descartes et Martin Schoock*. Paris: Les Impressions Nouvelles, 1988.

Waterlow, Sarah. *Nature, Change and Agency in Aristotle's "Physics."* Oxford: Oxford University Press, 1982.

Seventeenth-Century Accounts of Causation and Conceptions of the Physical World

Clatterbaugh, Kenneth. *The Causation Debate in Modern Philosophy, 1637–1739*. New York: Routledge, 1999.

Cottingham, John, ed. *The Cambridge Companion to Descartes*. Cambridge: Cambridge University Press, 1992.

Gabbey, Alan. "The Case of Mechanics: One Revolution or Many?" In *Reappraisals of the Scientific Revolution*, ed. David C. Lindberg and Robert S. Westman. Cambridge: Cambridge University Press, 1990. 493–528.

Garber, Daniel. *Descartes' Metaphysical Physics.* Chicago: University of Chicago Press, 1992.

———. "Descartes' Physics." In *The Cambridge Companion to Descartes,* ed. John Cottingham. Cambridge: Cambridge University Press, 1992. 286–334.

Garber, Daniel, John Henry, Lynn Joy, and Alan Gabbey. "New Doctrines of Body and Its Powers, Place and Space." In *The Cambridge History of Seventeenth Century Philosophy,* ed. Daniel Garber and Michael Ayers. Cambridge: Cambridge University Press, 1998. 553–623.

Hatfield, Gary. "Descartes' Physiology and Its Relation to His Psychology." In *The Cambridge Companion to Descartes,* ed. John Cottingham. Cambridge: Cambridge University Press, 1992. 335–70.

Lindeboom, G. A. *Descartes and Medicine.* Amsterdam: Rodopi, 1979.

Maguire, J. E. "Boyle's Conception of Nature." *Journal of the History of Ideas* 33, no. 4 (1972): 523–42.

Nadler, Steven, ed. *Causation in Early Modern Philosophy.* University Park: Pennsylvania State University Press, 1993.

———. "Doctrines of Explanation in Late Scholasticism and in the Mechanical Philosophy." In *The Cambridge History of Seventeenth Century Philosophy,* ed. Daniel Garber and Michael Ayers. Cambridge: Cambridge University Press, 1998. 513–52.

The Descartes-Elisabeth Correspondence

Blom, John. *Descartes: His Moral Philosophy and Psychology.* New York: New York University Press, 1978.

Broad, Jacqueline. *Women Philosophers of the Seventeenth Century.* Cambridge: Cambridge University Press, 2002.

Néel, Marguerite. *Descartes et la princess Elisabeth.* Paris: Editions Elzévier, 1946.

Nye, Andrea. *The Princess and the Philosopher: Letters of Elisabeth of the Palatine to René Descartes.* Lanham, MD: Rowman and Littlefield, 1999.

Petit, Léon. *Descartes et la Princesse Elisabeth: roman d'amour vécu.* Paris: A-G Nizet, 1969.

Rodis-Lewis, Genevieve. "Descartes et les femmes: l'exceptionnel apport de la princesse Elisabeth." In *Donna Filosofia e cultura nel seicento,* ed. Pina Totaro. Rome: Consiglio Nazionale delle richerche, 1999. 155–72.

Wartenburg, Thomas. "Descartes's Mood: The Question of Feminism in the Correspondence with Elisabeth." In *Feminist Interpretations of René Descartes,* ed. Susan Bordo. University Park: Pennsylvania State University Press, 1999. 190–212.

The Real Distinction, Mind-Body Interaction, and the Union of Mind and Body

Alanen, Lilli. *Descartes's Concept of Mind.* Cambridge: Harvard University Press, 2003.

Broughton, Janet, and Ruth Mattern. "Reinterpreting Descartes on the Notion of the Union of Mind and Body." *Journal of the History of Philosophy* 16, no. 1 (1978): 23–32.

Garber, Daniel. "Understanding Interaction: What Descartes Should Have Told Elisabeth." *Southern Journal of Philosophy,* supp. 21 (1983): 15–37.

Garber, Daniel, and Margaret Wilson. "Mind-Body Problems." In *The Cambridge History of Seventeenth Century Philosophy,* ed. Daniel Garber and Michael Ayers. Cambridge: Cambridge University Press, 1998. 833–67.

Mattern, Ruth. "Descartes's Correspondence with Elizabeth: Concerning Both the Union and Distinction of Mind and Body. " In *Descartes: Critical and Interpretative Essays*, ed. Michael Hooker. Baltimore: Johns Hopkins University Press, 1978. 212–22.

O'Neill, Eileen. "Mind-Body Interaction and Metaphysical Consistency: A Defense of Descartes." *Journal of the History of Philosophy* 25, no. 2 (1987): 227–45.

Radner, Daisie. "Descartes' Notion of the Union of Mind and Body." *Journal of the History of Philosophy* 9 (1971): 159–71.

Richardson, R. C. "The 'Scandal' of Cartesian Interactionism." *Mind* 92 (1982): 20–37.

Rozemond, Marleen. *Descartes's Dualism*. Cambridge: Harvard University Press, 1998.

Shapiro, Lisa. "Princess Elizabeth and Descartes: The Union of Soul and Body and the Practice of Philosophy." *British Journal for the History of Philosophy* 7, no. 3 (1999): 503–20.

Tollefson, Deborah. "Princess Elisabeth and the Problem of Mind-Body Interaction." *Hypatia* 14, no. 3 (1999): 59–77.

Wilson, Margaret. *Descartes*. New York: Routledge, 1978.

Yandell, David. "What Descartes Really Told Elisabeth: Mind-Body Union as a Primitive Notion." *British Journal for the History of Philosophy* 5, no. 2 (1997): 249–73.

Descartes' and Elisabeth's Moral Philosophy

Marshall, John. *Descartes's Moral Theory*. Ithaca: Cornell University Press, 1998.

Mesnard, Pierre. *Essai sur la morale de Descartes*. Paris: Boivin, 1936.

Nye, Andrea. "Polity and Prudence: The Ethics of Elisabeth, Princess Palatine." In *Hypatia's Daughters*, ed. Linda Lopez McAlister. Bloomington: Indiana University Press, 1996. 68–91.

Rodis-Lewis, Genevieve. *La morale de Descartes*. Paris: PUF, 1957.

Other Cited Works

Muller, Frederick. "27 onuitgegeven brieven aan Descartes." *De Nederlandsche Spectator* (1876): 336–39.

Von Staden, Heinrich. "In a Pure and Holy Way: Personal and Professional Conduct in the Hippocratic Oath." *Journal of the History of Medicine and Allied Sciences* 51 (1996): 406–8.

NOTE ON TEXTS AND TRANSLATION

In the preparation of this translation, I have relied largely on the Adam and Tannery edition of Descartes' *Oeuvres*, though I have also consulted Foucher de Careil's original publication of Elisabeth's letters, as well as the editions of Jacques Chevalier and of Jean-Marie and Michelle Beyssade (who rely on Chevalier). I also consulted the original manuscript, now in the care of the Geldersch Landschap and Geldersche Kasteelen in Arnhem, Netherlands, as part of the Rosendael collection. This manuscript is not in Elisabeth's own hand but consists of copies, written all at once. Jeroen van de Ven, a member of Professor Theo Verbeek's team, thinks the copies were made in the early eighteenth century. The letters were copied out of chronological sequence and in no particular order. They are bracketed by copies of two letters from Queen Christina of Sweden to Descartes. The first, of 2 December 1648, is familiar (see AT 5:251–52, there dated 12 December 1648): the second concerns Christina's abdication but was written a good four years after Descartes' death. This second letter seems to be a form letter with a wide circulation.

The dating of several of Elisabeth's letters is problematic, in a way similar to that of the 1648 letter from Christina. In redating Christina's letter to 12 December, Adam and Tannery (following Foucher de Careil) assume that the date follows the Julian rather than the Gregorian calendar. They make a similar assumption with a number of Elisabeth's letters, though they are not consistent in diverging from the manuscript date. When their dating does differ from that of the manuscript they do not always offer adequate reasons. In this edition, I have chosen to follow the manuscript uniformly, simply because there is no good basis for choosing one calendar over another. Here I follow the choice of Theo Verbeek, Erik-Jan Bos, and Jeroen van de Ven in their edition of Descartes' correspondence of 1643. The letters where my date diverges from Adam and Tannery are: 6 May 1643 (AT date: 6/16 May); 10 June 1643 (AT date: 10/20 June); 30 September 1646 (AT date: 10 October).

In another matter, the signature of Elisabeth's letter of 4 December 1649 refers to a previous letter of 10/20 November, but this letter is not part of the manuscript and appears to be no longer extant.

It is very difficult to determine the provenance of these copies. Whoever arranged for Elisabeth's letters to be copied must have also had access to Christina's letters—and been given notice of Christina's abdication. Verbeek speculates that they are a copy of a copy made surreptitiously by Chanut at the time of Descartes' death, even though Chanut assured Elisabeth he would do no such thing. But there is no known connection between Chanut and Rosendael. The letters may also have been copied by someone associated with Elisabeth. Here there is scant evidence. In 1722, one Petronella Wilhelmina van Hoorn married the owner of Rosendael, and she may have been related to Elisabeth's close companion at the convent at Herford, Countess Anna Maria van Hoorn. Van Hoorn is referred to in the correspondence with Barclay and Penn included in this volume, but little information is known about her. However, even if Anna Maria van Hoorn did possess Elisabeth's letters, and copies were in the possession of Petronella Wilhelmina, there is still the problem of explaining how Christina's letters come into the mix. Perhaps Elisabeth had these in her possession as well.

As regards the translation itself, I have benefited from the excellent translation of Descartes' letters published in volume 3 of *The Philosophical Writings of Descartes*, edited and translated by John Cottingham, Richard Stoothoff, Dugald Murdoch, and Anthony Kenny, and I have consulted the translations of John Blom and Andrea Nye. These translations derive from the Adam and Tannery *Oeuvres*. Outside of the dating question, the Adam and Tannery transcription of the manuscripts is accurate.

Edward Reynolds's dedication of his *Treatise on the Passions and Faculties of the Soule of Man* to Elisabeth has been transcribed from the 1640 edition of that work.

The correspondence with Robert Barclay is a transcription from *Reliquiae Barclaianae: Correspondence of Colonel David Barclay and Robert Barclay of Urie* (London: Winter & Bailey, Lithograph, 1870). I thank the library at Haverford College for access to this work. The original material is a lithograph of handwritten copies of Barclay's letters and contains very little punctuation. I have added contemporary punctuation as seemed appropriate.

The correspondence with William Penn is a transcription from Penn's *An Account of W. Penn's Travails in Holland and Germany, Anno MDCLXXVII* (London: T. Sowle, 1695). This account was published after being found among Anne Conway's papers.

THE CORRESPONDENCE

AT 3:660[1]

ELISABETH TO DESCARTES

[The Hague] 6 May 1643

M. Descartes,

I learned, with much joy and regret, of the plan you had to see me a few days ago; I was touched equally by your charity in willing to share yourself with an ignorant and intractable person and by the bad luck that robbed me of such a profitable conversation. M. Palotti[2] greatly augmented this latter passion in going over with me the solutions you gave him to the obscurities contained in the physics of M. Regius.[3] I would have been better instructed

1. I provide the reader with the volume and page references from the Adam and Tannery edition of Descartes' *Oeuvres.* The page number indicates the beginning of the page.

2. Alphonse Pollot (1602–68), whom Elisabeth refers to as Palotti, was a gentleman-in-waiting to the prince of Orange. In his letter to Pollot of 6 October 1642, Descartes notes his happiness that Elisabeth has read and seems to approve of his *Meditations,* as well as his intention to visit The Hague to meet her (see *Oeuvres de Descartes,* ed. Charles Adam and Paul Tannery, 11 vols. [Paris: Cerf, 1897–1913; new ed., Paris: Vrin, 1964–7; reprint, Paris: Vrin, 1996; cited hereafter as AT] 3:577–78) This letter would seem to mark Descartes' attempt at this meeting. Pollot's relation to Descartes began in 1638 with an exchange, through Henricus Reneri, about Descartes' *Discourse on the Method.* Pollot, as suggested here, effected the introduction between Descartes and Elisabeth. He appears to have tutored Elisabeth in geometry (see Descartes to Elisabeth, November 1645) and often served as the courier of their correspondence (see Elisabeth's letter of 24 May 1645, below). Reneri (1593–1639), a French philosopher, was a professor of philosophy at the University of Utrecht.

3. Henri le Roy or Regius (1598–1679) was a Dutch physician who took up Descartes' physics and physiology and taught them as chair of medicine at the University of Utrecht, beginning in 1638. Elisabeth's remarks here suggest that she was tutored by Regius or at least read his *Physiologia sive cognitio sanitatis* (Utrecht: Roman, 1641). While at Utrecht, beginning in 1642, Regius was attacked as promulgator of Cartesian philosophy by Professor of Theology Voetius. He was supported by Descartes in these battles until 1646. At that time there was a public falling out between Descartes and Regius upon publication of Regius's *Fundamenta Physica.* Descartes' side of this dispute can be seen in the French preface to the *Principles* and the *Comments on a Certain Broadsheet.* One can see trouble ahead in their earlier 1641 correspondence: see

661   on these from your mouth, as I would have been on a question I proposed to that professor while he was in this town, and regarding which he redirected me to you so that I might receive a satisfactory answer. The shame of showing you so disordered a style prevented me, up until now, from asking you for this favor by letter.

But today M. Palotti has given me such assurance of your goodwill toward everyone, and in particular toward me, that I chased from my mind all considerations other than that of availing myself of it. So I ask you please to tell me how the soul of a human being (it being only a thinking substance) can determine the bodily spirits, in order to bring about voluntary actions. For it seems that all determination of movement happens through the impulsion of the thing moved, by the manner in which it is pushed by that which moves it, or else by the particular qualities and shape of the surface of the latter. Physical contact is required for the first two conditions, extension for the third. You entirely exclude the one [extension] from the notion you have of the soul, and the other [physical contact] appears to me incompatible with an immaterial thing.[4] This is why I ask you for a more precise definition of the soul than the one you give in your *Metaphysics*, that is to say, of its substance separate from its action, that is, from thought.[5] For even if we were to suppose them inseparable (which is however difficult to prove in the mother's womb and in great fainting spells) as are the attributes of God, we could, in considering them apart, acquire a more perfect idea of them.

662   Knowing that you are the best doctor for my soul, I expose to you quite freely the weaknesses of its speculations, and hope that in observing the Hippocratic oath,[6] you will supply me with remedies without making them public; such I beg of you to do, as well as to suffer the badgerings of

Your affectionate friend at your service,

Elisabeth.

Descartes to Regius, May 1641 (AT 3:371–72, *The Philosophical Writings of Descartes*, ed. John Cottingham, Robert Stoothoff, and Dugald Murdoch, and for vol. 3, Anthony Kenny, 3 vols. [Cambridge: Cambridge University Press, 1984–1991, cited hereafter as CSM or CSMK, respectively] 181–82), December 1641 (AT 3:454–55, CSMK 199), December 1641 (AT 3:460, CSMK 200–201), January 1642 (AT 3:491, CSMK 491–92).

4. For a clear statement of this claim, see the Sixth Meditation argument for the real distinction of mind and body (AT 7:78, CSM 2:54).

5. Elisabeth here seems to be referencing the discussion in the paragraph subsequent to that containing the real distinction argument (AT 7:78–80, CSM 2:54–55), wherein Descartes details the "faculties" of extended and intellectual substances.

6. While Foucher de Careil, following Clerselier's rendering of Descartes' response, has "serment de Harpocrates" here, AT change it to Hippocrates. AT's reasoning seems sound. Not only do they follow the manuscripts, but the Hippocratic oath would have been well known to both Descartes and Elisabeth. Fabricius alludes to it, and by 1643 his work had seen more than thirty editions, one even published in Leiden in 1643 with a commentary by Meibomius.

DESCARTES TO ELISABETH

Egmond du Hoef, 21 May 1643

Madame,

The favor with which your Highness has honored me, in allowing me to receive her orders in writing, is greater than I would ever have dared to hope; and it is more consoling to my failings than what I had hoped for with passion, which was to receive them by mouth, had I been able to be admitted the honor of paying you reverence, and of offering you my very humble services when I was last in The Hague. For in that case I would have had too many marvels to admire at the same time, and seeing superhuman discourse emerging from a body so similar to those painters give to angels, I would have been delighted in the same manner as it seems to me must be those who, coming from the earth, enter newly into heaven. This would have made me less capable of responding to your Highness, who without doubt has already noticed in me this failing, when I had the honor of speaking with her before; and your clemency wanted to assuage it, in leaving me the traces of your thoughts on a paper, where, in rereading them several times and accustoming myself to consider them, I would be truly less dazzled, but I instead feel more wonder, in noticing that these thoughts not only seem ingenious at the outset, but also even more judicious and solid the more one examines them.

I can say with truth that the question your Highness proposes seems to me that which, in view of my published writings, one can most rightly ask me.[7] For there are two things about the human soul on which all the knowledge we can have of its nature depends: one of which is that it thinks, and the other is that, being united to the body, it can act on and be acted

664

Elisabeth's later letters show her familiarity with the medical establishment, and Descartes too had interests in medicine. Moreover, while Harpocrates, or Horus, the child, is the Egyptian god of silence, and was taken up as the god of secrecy by the Greeks and Romans, there is no oath associated with him. While Harpocrates is associated with a secret medical profession in certain monuments, this same secret is contained in the Hippocratic oath: "About whatever I may see or hear in treatment, or even without treatment, in the life of human beings—things that should not ever be blurted out outside—I will remain silent, holding such things to be unutterable [sacred, not to be divulged]. " Translation by Heinrich Von Staden, "In a Pure and Holy Way: Personal and Professional Conduct in the Hippocratic Oath, " *Journal of the History of Medicine and Allied Sciences* 51 (1996): 406–8.

7. At this point, Descartes had published the *Discourse on the Method,* with accompanying essays (1637), and the *Meditations,* along with Objections and Replies (1641, 1642). He says little in those works about the philosophical basis of mind-body interaction. Gassendi, in the Fifth Objections, had raised a similar question, though he met with a much less hospitable reply. See AT 7:343–44, 7:389–90, 9:213, CSM 2:238–39, 266, 275–76.

Crispyn Van den Queborne. *Elisabeth, Princess Palatine* (mid-seventeenth century). Engraving, 3 3/8 × 5 1/4 in. (NPG D18201). Courtesy National Portrait Gallery, London.

upon by it.[8] I have said almost nothing about the latter, and have concentrated solely on making the first better understood, as my principal aim was 665 to prove the distinction between the soul and the body. Only the first was able to serve this aim, and the other would have been harmful to it. But, as your Highness sees so clearly that one cannot conceal anything from her, I will try here to explain the manner in which I conceive of the union of the soul with the body and how the soul has the power [*force*] to move it.

First, I consider that there are in us certain primitive notions that are like originals on the pattern of which we form all our other knowledge. There are only very few of these notions; for, after the most general—those of being, number, and duration, etc. —which apply to all that we can conceive, we have, for the body in particular, only the notion of extension, from which follow the notions of shape and movement; and for the soul alone, we have only that of thought, in which are included the perceptions of the understanding and the inclinations of the will; and finally, for the soul and the body together, we have only that of their union, on which depends that of the power the soul has to move the body and the body to act on the soul, in causing its sensations and passions.

I consider also that all human knowledge [*science*] consists only in distinguishing well these notions, and in attributing each of them only to those things to which it pertains. For, when we want to explain some difficulty 666 by means of a notion which does not pertain to it, we cannot fail to be mistaken; just as we are mistaken when we want to explain one of these notions by another; for being primitive, each of them can be understood only through itself. Although the use of the senses has given us notions of extension, of shapes, and of movements that are much more familiar than the others, the principal cause of our errors lies in our ordinarily wanting to use these notions to explain those things to which they do not pertain. For instance, when we want to use the imagination to conceive the nature of the soul, or better, when one wants to conceive the way in which the soul moves the body, by appealing to the way one body is moved by another body.

That is why, since, in the *Meditations* which your Highness deigned to read, I was trying to make conceivable the notions which pertain to the soul alone, distinguishing them from those which pertain to the body alone, the first thing that I ought to explain subsequently is the manner of conceiving

---

8. *Agir et patir avec lui:* In English, it is difficult to bring out the parallel between active and passive, which preserves the tie to the passions of the soul that will figure prominently in the later correspondence.

those which pertain to the union of the soul with the body, without those which pertain to the body alone, or to the soul alone. To which it seems to me that what I wrote at the end of my response to the sixth objections can be useful;[9] for we cannot look for these simple notions elsewhere than in our soul, which has them all in itself by its nature, but which does not always

667   distinguish one from the others well enough, or even attribute them to the objects to which it ought to attribute them.

Thus, I believe that we have heretofore confused the notion of the power with which the soul acts on the body with the power with which one body acts on another; and that we have attributed the one and the other not to the soul, for we did not yet know it, but to diverse qualities of bodies, such as heaviness, heat, and others, which we have imagined to be real, that is to say, to have an existence distinct from that of body, and by consequence, to be substances, even though we have named them qualities. In order to understand them, sometimes we have used those notions that are in us for knowing body, and sometimes those which are there for knowing the soul, depending on whether what we were attributing to them was material or immaterial. For example, in supposing that heaviness is a real quality, of which we have no other knowledge but that it has the power to move a body in which it is toward the center of the earth, we have no difficulty in conceiving how it moves the body, nor how it is joined to it; and we do not think that this happens through a real contact of one surface against another, for we experience in ourselves that we have a specific notion for conceiving

668   that; and I think that we use this notion badly, in applying it to heaviness, which, as I hope to demonstrate in my Physics, is nothing really distinct from body.[10] But I do think that it was given to us for conceiving the way in which the soul moves the body.

If I were to employ more words to explain myself, I would show that I did not sufficiently recognize the incomparable mind of your Highness, and I would be too presumptuous if I dared to think that my response should be entirely satisfactory to her; but I will try to avoid both the one and the other in adding here nothing more, except that if I am capable of writing or saying something that could be agreeable to her, I would always take it as a great honor to take up a pen or to go to The Hague for this end, and that there is nothing in the world which is so dear to me as the power to obey her commandments. But I cannot find a reason to observe the Hippocratic oath that she enjoined me to, since she communicated nothing to me that does not

9. AT 7:444–45, CSM 2:299–300.
10. *Principles* 4.20–27 (AT 7A:212–16, CSM 1:268–70).

merit being seen and admired by all men. I can only say, on this matter, that esteeming infinitely your letter to me, I will treat it as the misers do their treasures: the more they value them the more they hide them away, and begrudging the rest of the world a view of them, they make it their sovereign good to look at them. Thus, it will be easy for me alone to enjoy the good of seeing it, and my greatest ambition is to be able to say and to be truly, Madame,

Your Highness's very humble and obedient servant,

Descartes.

ELISABETH TO DESCARTES

[*The Hague*] 10 *June 1643*

AT 3:683

M. Descartes,

Your goodwill appears not only in your showing me the faults in my reasoning and correcting them, as I expected, but also in your attempt to console me about them in order to make the knowledge of them less annoying for me. But, in detriment to your judgment, you attempt to console me about those faults with false praise. Such false praise would have been necessary to encourage me to work to remedy them had my upbringing, in a place where the ordinary way of conversing has accustomed me to understand that people are incapable of giving one true praise, not made me presume that I could not err in believing the contrary of what people speak, and had it not rendered the consideration of my imperfections so familiar that they no longer upset me more than is necessary to promote the desire to rid myself of them.

This makes me confess, without shame, that I have found in myself all 684 the causes of error which you noticed in your letter, and that as yet I have not been able to banish them entirely, for the life which I am constrained to lead does not leave enough time at my disposal to acquire a habit of meditation in accordance with your rules.[11] Now the interests of my house, which I must not neglect, now some conversations and social obligations which I cannot avoid, beat down so heavily on this weak mind with an-

---

11. Elisabeth here seems to be referring to what Descartes writes in the preface to reader of the *Meditations*, and in the postulates of the geometrical exposition of his philosophy in the Second Replies, where he requires that his readers "meditate seriously with me, and withdraw their minds from the senses and from all preconceived opinions" (AT 7:9, CSM 2:8; see also AT 7:162ff., CSM 2:114ff.). Doing so, however, requires that one be able to "expressly rid [one's] . . . mind of all worries and arrange for [oneself] . . . a clear stretch of free time," as the meditator does in the First Meditation (AT 7:18, CSM 2:17). It is this luxury Elisabeth cannot afford.

noyance or boredom, that it is rendered useless for anything else at all for a long time afterward: this will serve, I hope, as an excuse for my stupidity in being unable to comprehend, by appeal to the idea you once had of heaviness, the idea through which we must judge how the soul (nonextended and immaterial) can move the body; nor why this power [*puissance*] to carry the body toward the center of the earth, which you earlier falsely attributed to a body as a quality, should sooner persuade us that a body can be pushed by some immaterial thing, than the demonstration of a contrary truth (which you promise in your physics) should confirm us in the opinion of its impossibility. In particular, since this idea (unable to pretend to the same perfection and objective reality as that of God) can be feigned due to the ignorance of that which truly moves these bodies toward the center, and since no material cause presents itself to the senses, one would then attribute this power to its contrary, an immaterial cause. But I nevertheless have never been able to conceive of such an immaterial thing as anything other than a negation of matter which cannot have any communication with it.

685

I admit that it would be easier for me to concede matter and extension to the soul than to concede the capacity to move a body and to be moved by it to an immaterial thing. For, if the first is achieved through *information*, it would be necessary that the spirits, which cause the movements, were intelligent, a capacity you accord to nothing corporeal.[12] And even though, in your *Metaphysical Meditations*, you show the possibility of the second, it is altogether very difficult to understand that a soul, as you have described it, after having had the faculty and the custom of reasoning well, can lose all of this by some vapors, and that, being able to subsist without the body, and having nothing in common with it, the soul is still so governed by it.

But after all, since you have undertaken to instruct me, I entertain these sentiments only as friends which I do not intend to keep, assuring myself that you will explicate the nature of an immaterial substance and the manner of its actions and passions in the body, just as well as you have all the other things that you have wanted to teach. I beg of you also to believe that you

---

12. I have here retained the French *information*. It is hard to determine what theoretical model Elisabeth is adverting to. On the one hand, it is tempting to think that she is invoking the Aristotelian doctrine that the soul is the form of the body and so informs the body. On the other hand, her concern with the intelligence of corporeal spirits suggests that she is referring to a Stoic account of cognitive faculties and intentional action. The Stoics explained the cohesion of bodies and their motions toward some end, as well as the rational faculties Descartes accords to the soul (and so, one might say, the information of substances), by appeal to that part of matter termed *pneuma*.

could not perform this charity to anyone who felt more the obligation she has to you as?

    Your very affectionate friend,

        Elisabeth.

DESCARTES TO ELISABETH

AT 3:690

28 June 1643, Egmond du Hoef

Madame,

    I have a very great obligation to your Highness in that she, after having borne my explaining myself badly in my previous letter, concerning the question which it pleased her to propose to me, deigns again to have the patience to listen to me on the same matter, and to give me occasion to note the things which I omitted. Of which the principal ones seem to me to be that, after having distinguished three sorts of ideas or primitive notions which are each known in a particular way and not by a comparison of the one with the other—that is, the notion that we have of the soul, that of the body, and the union which is between the soul and the body—I ought to have explained the difference between these three sorts of notions and between the operations of the soul through which we have them, and to have stated how we render each of them familiar and easy to us. Then, after that, having said why I availed myself of the comparison with heaviness, I ought to have made clear that, even though one might want to conceive of the soul as material (which, strictly speaking, is what it is to conceive its union with the body), one would not cease to know, after that, that the soul is separable from it. That is, I think, all of what your Highness has prescribed me to do here.

    First, then, I notice a great difference between these three sorts of notions. The soul is conceived only by the pure understanding [*l'entendement*]; the body, that is to say, extension, shapes, and motions, can also be known by the understanding alone, but is much better known by the understanding aided by the imagination; and finally, those things which pertain to the union of the soul and the body are known only obscurely by the understanding alone, or even by the understanding aided by the imagination; but they are known very clearly by the senses. From which it follows that those who never philosophize and who use only their senses do not doubt in the least that the soul moves the body and that the body acts on the soul. But they consider the one and the other as one single thing, that is to say, they conceive of their union. For to conceive of the union between two things is

691

692

to conceive of them as one single thing. Metaphysical thoughts which exercise the pure understanding serve to render the notion of the soul familiar. The study of mathematics, which exercises principally the imagination in its consideration of shapes and movements, accustoms us to form very distinct notions of body. And lastly, it is in using only life and ordinary conversations and in abstaining from meditating and studying those things which exercise the imagination that we learn to conceive the union of the soul and the body.

I almost fear that your Highness will think that I do not speak seriously here. But this would be contrary to the respect I owe her and that I would never neglect to pay her. And I can say with truth that the principal rule I have always observed in my studies, and that which I believe has served me the most in acquiring some bit of knowledge, is that I never spend more than a few hours each day in thoughts which occupy the imagination, and very few hours a year in those which occupy the understanding alone, and that I give all the rest of my time to relaxing the senses and resting the mind; I even count, among the exercises of the imagination, all serious conversations and everything for which it is necessary to devote attention. It is this that has made me retire to the country. For even though in the most populated city in the world I could have as many hours to myself as I now employ in study, I would nevertheless not be able to use them so usefully, since my mind would be distracted by the attention the bothers of life require. I take the liberty to write of this here to your Highness in order to show that I truly admire that, amid the affairs and the cares which persons who are of a great mind and of great birth never lack, she has been able to attend to the meditations which are required in order to know well the distinction between the soul and the body.

But I judged that it was these meditations, rather than these other thoughts which require less attention, that have made her find obscurity in the notion we have of their union; as it does not seem to me that the human mind is capable of conceiving very distinctly, and at the same time, the distinction between the soul and the body and their union, since to do so it is necessary to conceive them as one single thing and at the same time to conceive them as two, which is contradictory. On this matter (supposing your Highness still had the reasons which prove the distinction of the soul and body at the forefront of her mind and not wanting to ask her to remove them from there in order to represent to herself the notion of the union that each always experiences within himself without philosophizing, in knowing that he is a single person who has together a body and a thought, which are of such a nature that this thought can move the body and sense what happens to it), I availed myself in my previous letter of a comparison between heaviness and those other qualities which we commonly imagine to be united to some bodies just as thought is united to our own, and I was not worried that this comparison hangs on qualities that are not real, even though we imagine them so, since I believed that your Highness was already entirely persuaded that the soul is a substance distinct from body.

But since your Highness notices that it is easier to attribute matter and extension to the soul than to attribute to it the capacity to move a body and to be moved by one without having matter, I beg her to feel free to attribute this matter and this extension to the soul, for to do so is to do nothing but conceive it as united with the body. After having well conceived this and having experienced it within herself, it will be easy for her to consider that the matter that she has attributed to this thought is not the thought itself, and that the extension of this matter is of another nature than the extension of this thought, in that the first is determined to a certain place, from which it excludes all other extended bodies, and this is not the case with the second. In this way your Highness will not neglect to return easily to the knowledge of the distinction between the soul and the body, even though she has conceived their union.

695

Finally, though I believe it is very necessary to have understood well once in one's life the principles of metaphysics, since it is these that give us knowledge of God and of our soul, I also believe that it would be very harmful to occupy one's understanding often in meditating on them. For in doing so, it could not attend so well to the functions of the imagination and the senses. The best is to content oneself in retaining in one's memory and in one's belief the conclusions that one has at one time drawn from such meditation, and then to employ the rest of the time one has for study in those thoughts where the understanding acts with imagination or the senses.

The extreme devotion which I have to serve your Highness makes me hope that my frankness will not be disagreeable to her. She would have here received a longer discourse in which I would have tried to clarify all at once the difficulties of the question asked, but for a new annoyance which I have just learned about from Utrecht, that the magistrate summons me in order to verify what I wrote about one of their ministers—no matter that this is a man who has slandered me very indignantly and that what I wrote about him in my just defense was only too well known to the world—and so I am constrained to finish here, in order that I may go find the means to extricate myself as soon as I can from this chicanery.[13] I am, &c.

---

13. See the Letter to Voetius, AT 8B:3–194. Parts of this very long letter are translated in CSMK 220–24. This letter, which was published in Latin and simultaneously in Flemish translation in May 1643, was written as a reply to the pointed published attacks on Cartesianism by Voetius. Voetius, as rector of the University of Utrecht, had earlier arranged for the formal condemnation of Cartesian philosophy at the university. For further reading on this dispute, see Verbeek and Marion, *La querelle d'Utrecht*); and Verbeek, *Descartes and the Dutch*. See also Descartes to Father Dinet, esp. AT 7:582ff., CSM 2:393ff., and the postscript of Elisabeth's letter of 22 June 1645 below.

ELISABETH TO DESCARTES

[The Hague] 1 July 1643

M. Descartes,

I see that you have not received as much inconvenience from my esteem for your instruction and the desire to avail myself of it, as from the ingratitude of those who deprive themselves of it and would like to deprive the human species of it. I would not have sent you new evidence of my ignorance until I knew you were done with those of that mindset, if Sieur Van Bergen [14] had not obliged me to it earlier, through his kindness in agreeing to stay in town, just until I gave him a response to your letter of 28 June. What you write there makes me see clearly the three sorts of notions that we have, their objects, and how we ought to make use of them.

I also find that the senses show me that the soul moves the body, but they teach me nothing (no more than do the understanding and the imagination) of the way in which it does so. For this reason, I think that there are some properties of the soul, which are unknown to us, which could perhaps overturn what your *Metaphysical Meditations* persuaded me of by such good reasoning: the nonextendedness of the soul. This doubt seems to be founded on the rule that you give there, in speaking of the true and the false, that all error comes to us in forming judgments about that which we do not perceive well enough. [15] Though extension is not necessary to thought, neither is it at all repugnant to it, and so it could be suited to some other function of the soul which is no less essential to it. At the very least, it makes one abandon the contradiction of the Scholastics, that it [the soul] is both as a whole in the whole body and as a whole in each of its parts. [16] I do not excuse myself at all for confusing the notion of the soul with that of the body for the same reason as the vulgar; but this doesn't rid me of the first doubt, and I will lose hope of finding certitude in anything in the world if you, who alone have kept me from being a skeptic, do not answer that to which my first reasoning carried me.

---

14. Anthonie Studler Van Surck, sieur de Bergen (1606–66), was Descartes' banker in Holland and sometimes acted as intermediary for Descartes' letters. In particular he often served as intermediary in Descartes' correspondence with Huygens. Elisabeth might well have known him through this connection with Huygens, since she too corresponded with Constantijn Huygens (1596–1687), a noted humanist scholar and father of the mathematician and physicist Christian Huygens (1629–95)). In addition, the sieur de Bergen was charged with the distribution of the *Principles* in Holland, while Descartes was in France in 1644.

15. See the rule arrived at and articulated in the Fourth Meditation: "If, however, I simply refrain from making a judgment in cases where I do not perceive the truth with sufficient clarity and distinctness, then it is clear that I am behaving correctly and avoiding error" (AT 7:59, CSM 2:41).

16. See for example, Aquinas, *Summa Theologica*, I, q.76 a.8.

Even though I owe you this confession and thanks, I would think it strongly imprudent if I did not already know your kindness and generosity, equal to the rest of your merits, as much by the experience that I have already had as by reputation. You could not have attested to it in a manner more obliging than by the clarifications and counsel you have imparted to me, which I hold above all as one of the greatest treasures that could be possessed by

> Your very affectionate friend at your service,
>
> Elisabeth.

DESCARTES TO ELISABETH

Egmond, 17 November 1643 [17]

AT 4:37

Madame,

Having learned from M. de Pollot that your Highness has taken the [38] trouble to consider the problem of three circles, [18] and that she has found the way to solve it by supposing but one unknown quantity, I thought that my duty obliged me to set out here the reason why I had proposed using several unknown quantities and in what way I solve for them.

In considering a problem in geometry, I always make it so that the lines which I use to find the solution to the problem are parallel or intersect at right angles as much as is possible; and I do not consider any other theorems but that the sides of similar triangles have a similar proportion between them, and that in right triangles, the square of the base is equal to the sum of the squares of the sides. I do not fear supposing more unknown quantities to reduce the problem to such terms so that it depends only on these two theorems. On the contrary, I prefer to suppose more of them than fewer. For, by this means, I see more clearly all that I do, and in solving for them I do better at finding the shortest paths and avoid superfluous multiplications. On the other hand, if one draws other lines and makes use of other theorems, even though it could

---

17. Verbeek et al., *Correspondence,* were able to date this letter more precisely from the covering note to Pollot. They also note that the British Library contains two manuscript copies of this and the subsequent letter in the papers collected by Thomas Birch (Add. 4278 [Birch], fols. 150r–151v and Add. 4278 [Birch], fols. 159r–160v. These contain the papers and correspondence of John Pell, and so indicate that Pell had copies made. In between the two copies is Pell's translation.

18. The problem here is to find the radius of a fourth circle whose circumference touches those of three given ones, or what is usually called Apollonius's problem. Elisabeth seems to have learned her geometry from a textbook (*Algebra ofte Nieuwe Stel-Regel*) written by Johan Stampioen, which Descartes had criticized. See Stephen Gaukroger, *Descartes: An Intellectual Biography* (New York: Oxford University Press, 1995), 334–35, 387. After setting this problem, Descartes was concerned that he had set the bar too high. See his letter to Pollot, 21 October 1643, AT 4:26.

still happen that by chance the path one finds is shorter than mine, all the same, it almost always turns out the other way. One does not see what one does as well, except if one has the demonstration of the theorem which one is using fully present to the mind. In this case one finds, almost always, that it depends on the consideration of some triangles that are either right triangles or similar to one another and thus one falls back on the path I take.[19]

For example, in considering this problem of the three circles, we need only suppose one unknown quantity, with the help of a theorem that shows us how to find the area of a triangle by its three sides. For if A, B, and C are the centers of three given circles, and D is the center of the one we are looking for, the three sides of triangle ABC are given, and the three lines AD, BD, and CD are composed of three radii of the given circles, joined to a radius of the circle we are looking for, so that, supposing x for this radius, we have all the sides of the triangles ABD, ACD, and BCD. [See fig. 1.][20] By consequence we can have their areas which, added together, are equal to the area of the triangle given by ABC. And we can by this equation come to know the radius x, which alone is required for the solution of this question. But this route seems to me to lead to so many superfluous multiplications that I would not want to undertake to solve them in three months. This is why, instead of the two oblique lines, AB and BC, I take the three perpendiculars BE, DG, and DF, and setting three unknown quantities, one for DF, one for DG, and the other for the radius of the circle I am looking for, I have all the sides of the three right triangles ADF, BDG, and CDF, which gives me three equations, for in each of these the square of the base is equal to the sum of the squares of the sides. [See figs. 2 and 3.]

After having made as many equations as I supposed unknown quantities, I consider whether, from each equation, I can find one in simple enough terms. If I cannot do so, I try to arrive at one by joining two or more equations by addition or subtraction. Finally, only if this does not suffice, I examine whether it would be any better to change the terms in some way. For, in making this examination skillfully, one easily comes upon the shortest paths and one can try an infinity of things in very little time.

Thus, in this example, I suppose that the three bases of the right triangles are:

$$AD = a + x,$$
$$BD = b + x,$$
$$CD = c + x.$$

19. Descartes is here reiterating the method he elaborates and demonstrates in the *Géometrie*, published as an essay accompanying his *Discourse on the Method*, in 1637.

20. These figures were inserted by Clerselier.

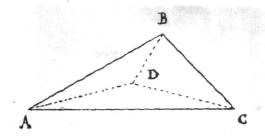

Figure 1

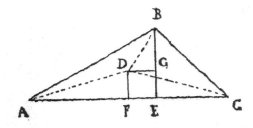

Figure 2

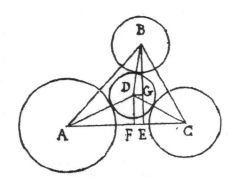

Figure 3

And making AE = d, BE = e, and CE = f,

$$\text{DF or GE} = y, \text{DG or FE} = z,$$

I have for the sides of the same triangles:

$$AF = d - z \ \& \ FD = y,$$
$$BG = e - y \ \& \ DG = z,$$
$$CF = f + z \ \& \ FD = y.$$

41

Then, making the square of each of the bases equal to the sum of the squares of the two sides, I have the three following equations:

$$aa + 2ax + xx = dd - 2dz + zz + yy,$$
$$bb + 2bx + xx = ee - 2ey + yy + zz,$$
$$cc + 2cx + xx = ff + 2fz + zz + yy,$$

and I see that by one of these alone I cannot find any of the unknown quantities, without drawing the square root, which would complicate the question too much. This is why I come to the second way, which is to join two equations together, and I cannot but perceive that the terms *xx*, *yy*, and *zz* being similarly in all three equations, if I take away the one from the other, as I would like, they cancel one another, and so I would have no unknown terms other than *x*, *y*, and *z* on their own. I see also that if I take away the second from the first or from the third, I would have all these three terms, *x*, *y*, and *z*; but that, if I take away the first from the third, I would have only *x* and *z*. Thus, I choose this last path and I find:

$$cc + 2cx - aa - 2ax = ff + 2fz - dd + 2dz$$

or better

$$z = \frac{cc - aa + dd - ff + 2cx - 2ax}{2d + 2f}$$

or better

$$1/2\,d - 1/2\,f + \frac{cc - aa + 2cx - 2ax}{2d + 2f}$$

42   Then, taking the second equation from the first or from the third (since the one reduces to the other) and replacing z with the terms I just found, I have from the first and the second:

$$aa + 2ax - bb - 2bx = dd - 2dz - ee + 2ey$$

or better

$$2ey = ee + aa + 2ax - bb - 2bx - dd + dd - df + \frac{ccd - aad + 2cdx - 2adx}{d + f}$$

or better

$$y = \frac{1}{2}e - \frac{bb}{2e} - \frac{bx}{e} - \frac{df}{2e} + \frac{ccd + aaf + 2cdx + 2afx}{2ed + 2ef}$$

Finally, returning to one of the first three equations, and in place of *y* or of *z* putting the quantities that are their equals, and the squares of these quanti-

ties for *yy* and *zz*, we find an equation where only *x* and *xx* are unknown. In
this way, then, the problem is planar or of the second degree, and it is no
longer necessary to go on. For the rest does not serve to cultivate or entertain the mind, but only to exercise one's patience for laborious calculations.
Even so I fear that I have made myself boring to your Highness, because I
stopped to write those things that she no doubt knew better than I and that
are easy, but which are nevertheless the keys to my algebra. I ask her quite
humbly to believe that it is the devotion with which I honor her which has
carried me away, and that I am, Madame,
Your Highness's very humble and very obedient servant,
Descartes.

ELISABETH TO DESCARTES

[The Hague] 21 *November* 1643

M. Descartes,

 If I were as adept in following your advice as I have desire to be, you
would already find the effects of your kindness in the progress I would have
made in reasoning and in algebra, whereas at this time I can show you only
faults. But I am so accustomed to showing them to you that like old sinners
I have lost all shame. For this reason I had planned to send you the solution
to the question you had given me, arrived at by the method they had taught
me earlier, as much to oblige you to tell me what is missing as because I am
not as well versed in your own method.[21] For I well noticed that there were
things missing in my solution, as I did not see it clearly enough to arrive at
a theorem. But I would never have found the reason without your last letter,
which gives me all the satisfaction that I demanded, and teaches me more
than I would have learned in six months with my master. I am very much in
your debt for it, and would never have pardoned M. de Palotti[22] if he had
used your solution in accordance with your order. All the same, he did not
want to give it to me, except under the condition that I send you what I have
done. Thus do not mind that I give you an unneeded inconvenience, since
there are few things that I would not do to obtain the effects of your good
will, which is infinitely esteemed by
 Your very affectionate friend at your service,
Elisabeth.

21. See above, note 18.
22. See Descartes to Pollot, November 1643, AT 4:43–44.

DESCARTES TO ELISABETH

Egmond du Hoef, 29 November 1643[23]

Madame,

46   The solution which it pleased your Highness to do me the honor of sending[24] is so just that it is not possible to desire anything more, and not only was I surprised from astonishment at seeing it, but I cannot stop myself from adding that I was also filled with joy, and I was taken with a bit of vanity in seeing that the calculation which your Highness used is entirely similar to that which I proposed in my *Geometry.* Experience has taught me that most minds who have the facility to understand the reasoning of metaphysics are not able to understand that of algebra, and reciprocally that those who easily understand the latter are ordinarily incapable of other sorts of reasoning.[25] I see no one but your Highness for whom all things are equally easy. It is true that I have had proof enough of this already, so that I could not have any doubts about it, but I feared only that the patience that is necessary to overcome the difficulties at the beginning of the calculation was lacking in her. For this is a quality extremely rare in excellent minds and in persons of great station.

Now that this difficulty has been overcome, she will have much more pleasure in the rest, and in substituting but one letter in place of many, just as she has done here quite often, the calculation will not be tedious to her. One can almost always do this when one only wants to see the nature of a problem, that is, to see if it can be solved with a ruler and compass, or if it is necessary to employ some other curved lines of the first or the second kind, etc., and which is the path for finding the solution. I ordinarily con-
47   tent myself with doing just this with particular problems. For it seems to me

23. Verbeek, et al., *Correspondence,* 60, were able to date this letter more precisely from copies in the British Library.

24. We do not have a record of the letter in which Elisabeth relays her solution.

25. Descartes reiterates this view publicly in the dedicatory letter to his *Principles of Philosophy:* "I have even greater evidence of your powers—and this is special to myself—in the fact that you are the only person I have so far found who has completely understood all my previously published works. Many other people, even those of the utmost acumen and learning, find them very obscure; and it generally happens with almost everyone else that if they are accomplished in Metaphysics they hate Geometry, while if they have mastered Geometry they do not grasp what I have written on First Philosophy. Your intellect is, to my knowledge, unique in finding everything equally clear; and this is why my use of the term 'incomparable' is quite deserved" (AT 8A:4, CSM 1:192).

that what remains—seeking the construction and the demonstration by the propositions of Euclid, and couching the process in algebra—is nothing but an amusement for little geometers, who do not require much intelligence or much knowledge. But when one has some problem which one wants to solve, in order to arrive at a theorem which can serve as a general rule for solving other similar ones, it is necessary to retain all the same letters that one set out at the beginning just up until the end. Or better, if one changes some of them in order to facilitate the calculation, it is necessary to replace them at the end, because, ordinarily, most cancel one another out, which one cannot see when one has changed them.

It is also good to make sure that the quantities one denotes by letters have similar relations to each other, as much as is possible. This renders the theorem more elegant and shorter; for what is evoked by one of these quantities, is evoked in the same manner by the others, and this helps to prevent mistakes in calculations. For those letters signifying quantities that have the same relations, must distribute themselves in the same manner, and when this is missing, one notices one's error.

Thus, in order to find a theorem which shows what is the radius of the circle that touches three given by position, it is not necessary, in this example, to suppose the three letters a, b, c for the lines AD, DC, DB but for the lines AB, AC, and BC, for these last have the same relation to one another that the three AH, BH, and CH do, and the first set of three do not. In following the calculation with these six letters, without changing them or adding any others to them, along the path which your Highness has taken (for it is better for this than that which I had proposed), one should come to quite a regular equation and one which will furnish a short enough theorem. For the three letters a, b, c are there disposed in the same manner, as the three d, e, f. [See fig. 4.]

Because the calculation of this is tedious, if your Highness has the desire to try it, it will be easier for her to suppose that the three given circles touch one another, and so to employ through the whole calculation only the letters d, e, f, x which, being the radii of the four circles, have a similar relation to one another. In the first place, she will find

$$AK = \frac{dd + df + dx - fx}{d + f}, \text{ \& } AD = \frac{dd + df + de - fe}{d + f}$$

where she can already notice that x is in the line AK as e is in the line AD, since it is found by the triangle AHC, as the other is by the triangle ABC. Then finally, she will have this equation:

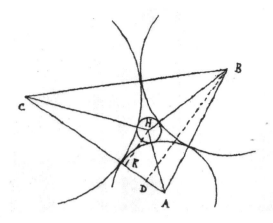

Figure 4

$$ddeeff + ddeexx + ddffxx + eeffxx = 2deffxx + 2deeffx + 2deefxx + 2ddeffx$$
$$+ 2ddefxx + 2ddeefx.$$

From this one draws, as a theorem, that the four sums which are produced by multiplying together the squares of three of these radii are equal to double the six sums which are produced by multiplying two of the radii by one another, and by the squares of the two others. All of which suffices to serve as a rule for finding the radius of the largest circle that can be drawn between three given circles that touch one another. For if the radii of these three given circles are, for example, $d/2$, $e/3$, $f/4$, I will have 576 for $ddeeff$, 36xx for $ddeexx$, and so on for the others. From which I will have

$$x = \frac{-156}{47} + \sqrt{\frac{31104}{2209}}$$

if I am not mistaken in the calculation I just did.

Your Highness can see here two very different procedures for solving one problem, according to the different aims one has. For wanting to know the nature of the problem, and by what device one can solve it, I take as given perpendicular or parallel lines, and suppose more unknown quantities, with the aim of making no superfluous multiplications and seeing more clearly the shortest paths. On the other hand, in wanting to find the solution, I take as given the sides of the triangle and suppose but one unknown letter. But there are a number of problems where the same path leads to the satisfaction of both aims, and I do not doubt that your Highness will soon see just how far the human mind can reach with this science. I would count myself happy if I could contribute something to it, since I have a great zeal to be, Madame,

> Your Highness's very humble and very obedient servant,
> Descartes.

DESCARTES TO ELISABETH

Paris, 8 July 1644[26]

Madame,

My voyage could not be accompanied with any misfortune since I was so happy as to make it with the good wishes of your Highness.[27] The very favorable letter, which gives me some indication of being so remembered,[28] is the most precious thing I could have received in this country. It would have made me happy if it had not informed me that the malady your Highness had before I left The Hague has left her with still some remains of this indisposition in her stomach. The remedies she has chosen—that is, those of diet and exercise—in my opinion are the best of all, after, however, those of the soul, which has, without a doubt, a great power over the body, as is shown by the great changes that anger, fear, and the other passions excite in it. But it is not by its will directly that the soul conducts the animal spirits to the places where they can be useful or harmful; it is only in willing or thinking of some other thing.[29] For the construction of our body is such that certain movements follow in it naturally from certain thoughts, as one sees that a redness of the face follows from shame, tears from compassion, and laughter from joy.[30]

65

---

26. Originally, Adam and Tannery, following Clerselier, dated this letter July 1647. Upon reflection on the whole body of the Descartes-Elisabeth correspondence, however, they redated it to July 1644. See AT 5:553. I follow AT's redating here, as have both Cottingham and Beyssade. The argument is convincing, as the letter does fit with Elisabeth's reply of 1 August 1644. Moreover, Elisabeth was in Holland in 1644, but she was at Crossen in 1647. My one concern here is that Descartes' thinking about the passions in this letter seems quite developed, and he does not seem to start thinking about the passions seriously until their later correspondence in 1645. Still, Descartes does make mention of the expressions of the passions (what he focuses on here) in animals as early as 1637, in the *Discourse*, so the redating is still quite plausible.

27. Descartes was undertaking a trip to France to settle family matters in Brittany and Poitou, including his father's estate, but he also stopped in Paris, where he reinforced his ties to the intellectual community. See Geneviève Rodis-Lewis, *Descartes: His Life and Thought*, trans. Jane Marie Todd (Ithaca: Cornell University Press, 1998), 152ff.

28. To my knowledge no copy of this letter is extant.

29. Descartes maintains this position in the *Passions of the Soul*. See a. 41 (AT 9:359–60).

30. Descartes discusses the expressions of the passions extensively in the *Passions*. See aa.112–35 (AT 11:411–28).

I know of no other thought more proper to the conservation of health than a strong conviction and firm belief that the architecture of our body is so good that, once one is healthy, one cannot easily fall ill, unless one does something remarkably excessive, or else the air or other external causes harm us. When one has an illness, one can restore one's health solely by the power of nature, especially when one is still young. This conviction is without doubt much more true and more reasonable than that of certain men, who, under the influence of an astrologer or a doctor, make themselves believe that they must die in a certain amount of time, and by this alone become sick and even die often enough, as I have seen happen to different people.[31] But I would not fail to be extremely sad if I thought that your Highness still suffered this indisposition. I prefer to hope that she is all through it, and at the same time a desire to be certain this is so makes me feel extremely eager to return to Holland.

I propose to leave here in four or five days in order to pass through Poitou and Brittany, where the business that brought me here is. But as soon as I can put those matters in a little bit of order, I wish nothing so much as to return to the place where I was fortunate to have the honor of speaking with your Highness sometimes. For, even though there are many people here whom I honor and esteem, I have all the same not yet seen any who can make me stay. I am more than any thing I can say, &c.

AT 4:131   ELISABETH TO DESCARTES

[The Hague] 1 August 1644

Mr. Descartes,

I am obliged to thank you for the present M. Van Bergen gave me on your behalf, though my conscience tells me that I will not be able to do so adequately.[32] If I had received from it only the benefit brought to our century[33]—this one here owing you all that the preceding ones have paid to innovators in the sciences, since you alone have demonstrated that there is such innovation—to what degree will my debt to you amount, I, whom you

---

31. See AT 3:15. There, in a letter to Mersenne of 29 January 1640, Descartes details the deadly effect on Hortensius of having his horoscope done.

32. Van Surck, sieur de Bergen, presented Elisabeth with a copy of Descartes' *Principles of Philosophy*, which Descartes had dedicated to Elisabeth, with effusive praise of her intellectual acumen. See AT 8A:1–4, CSM 1:190–92.

33. Adam and Tannery insert *siècle* into the gap in the MS. This suggestion does seem to fit with Elisabeth's sense here.

have given, with instruction, a part of your glory in the public testimony which you give me of your friendship and your approval? The pedants will say that you are forced to build a new morality in order to render me worthy of it.[34] But I take this morality as a rule of my life, feeling myself to be only at the first stage which you approve there, the will to inform my understanding and to follow the good it knows. It is to this will that I owe an understanding of your works, which are obscure only to those who examine them by the principles of Aristotle, or with very little care. Indeed, the most reasonable of our doctors in this country have confessed to me that they have not studied them at all, because they are too old to start a new method, having exhausted the power of the body and of the mind in the old method.

132

But I fear that you will, with justice, retract your assessment of my ability to grasp things, when you find out that I do not understand how quicksilver is constituted, such that it is both as agitated as it is and as heavy at the same time, for that is contrary to the definition you have given of heaviness;[35] and even though the body E, in the figure on page 225,[36] presses upon it when it is underneath, why should it still feel this constraint when it is above, any more than air feels constrained in leaving a vessel in which it has been contained?

The second difficulty I found is that of getting those particles that are twisted into the shape of shells[37] to pass through the center of the earth without being bent or disfigured by the fire found there, as they were in the beginning in forming the body M. Only their speed can save them from it, and you say on pages 133 and 134[38] that, since speed is not at all necessary in order for them to travel in a straight line, these are the least agitated parts of the first element which flow in this way through the globules of the

---

34. Elisabeth is here referring to the distinction between apparent and true virtues that Descartes makes in his dedication of the *Principles*.

35. Descartes' account of heaviness appears in *Principles* 4.20–27. In article 22, he claims that lightness results from an excess of agitation of the particles of heavenly matter. Descartes discusses the nature of quicksilver in 4.58. It poses a problem for him because it is a heavy, nontransparent liquid, and he tries to explain these properties by claiming that quicksilver is both heavy and easily agitated. Elisabeth here is suggesting that his account of heaviness does not afford him this explanation, since, insofar as it is agitated it should be light rather than heavy.

36. See fig. 18 at AT 8:240.

37. Elisabeth is here discussing Descartes' account of a magnet in *Principles* 4.133ff. She here appeals to particles "twisted like the shell of snail," as Descartes describes them in *Principles* 3.90. Descartes also refers to them as "grooved particles," and it is this locution he employs in his discussion of the magnet.

38. *Principles* 3.88–90.

second. I am equally surprised that they take such a long route in leaving the poles of body M and pass along the surface of the earth in order to return to the other pole, because they could have found a shorter route through body C.[39]

I represent to you here only the reasons for my doubts about matters in your book; the reasons for my wonder are innumerable, as are also those for my obligation, among which I count again the kindness you demonstrated in telling me of your news and in giving me the precepts for the conservation of my health. The former have brought me much joy, through the great success of your voyage and the continuation of the plan you have to return, and the latter much profit, since I have already felt the benefit of them. You have not displayed to M. Voetius[40] the danger he has in being your enemy, as you have to me the advantage of your goodwill; otherwise, he would as much shun the title, as I seek to deserve that of

Your very affectionate friend at your service,

Elisabeth.

AT 4:135

DESCARTES TO ELISABETH

Le Crevis, August 1644

Madame,

The honor that your Highness does me in not being displeased that I dared to express in public how much I esteem and honor her is greater, and obliges me more, than any other honor I could receive from elsewhere. I do not fear being accused of having changed anything in moral philosophy in order to make my feelings on this subject understood. For what I have written on it is so true and so clear that I am sure that there is no reasonable man who does not subscribe to it. But I do fear that what I have put in the rest of the book is more dubious and more obscure since your Highness finds difficulties there.

That regarding the heaviness of quicksilver is very considerable, and I would have tried to clarify it if I did not fear saying something contrary to what I might be able to learn later, not having examined the nature of this metal enough. All I can say about it now is that I am convinced that the little particles of air, of water, and of all the other terrestrial bodies have several pores through which the very subtle matter can pass, and this follows well

39. Elisabeth here seems to be referring to Descartes' discussion in *Principles* 4.146–51.

40. Elisabeth adverts here to the controversy at the University of Utrecht. See above, note 13.

enough from the way in which I have said these particles are formed. Thus, it suffices to say that the particles of quicksilver and of other metals have fewer such pores in order to understand how these metals are heavy. For, for example, even if we were to admit that particles of water and those of quicksilver were of the same size and shape and that their movements were similar, to explain how quicksilver ought to be much heavier than water, it suffices to suppose only that each particle of water is like a little cord which is very soft and very loose and that those of quicksilver, having fewer pores, are like other little cords which are much harder and tighter.

As for the little particles turned into the shape of shells, it is not a marvel that they are not destroyed by the fire at the center of the earth. For this fire, being composed only of very subtle matter, can very well carry them very fast but cannot make them crash up against other hard bodies, which would be required to break or to divide them.

As for the rest, these shell-like particles do not take too long a route at all to return from one pole to the other. For I suppose that most of them pass through the center of the earth. In this way, only those that do not find any passage lower down return through our air. This is the reason that I give for why the magnetic strength of the entire mass of the earth does not appear to us to be as strong as that of little magnetic stones.

But I ask your Highness very humbly to pardon me if I have written nothing here but what is very confusing. I do not yet have the book in which she has deigned to mark the pages and I continue to be in the midst of traveling, but I hope to have the honor of making my bows to her in The Hague in two or three months.

I am, &c.

137

138

DESCARTES TO ELISABETH

Egmond, 18 May 1645

AT 4:200

Madame,

I was extremely surprised to learn from the letters of M. de Pollot[41] that your Highness has been ill for a long time, and I rue my solitude, for it is the reason I did not know anything of this sooner. It is true that I am so removed from the world that I do not learn anything at all about what happens. But all the same the zeal I have for serving your Highness would not have let me

---

41. Pollot's letters to Descartes are not available. Descartes' reply indicates they were dated on or about 1 May 1645. For Descartes' reply see AT 4:204ff.

go so long without knowing the state of her health, even if I had to go to The Hague expressly to inquire about it, had not M. de Pollot, who wrote me very hastily about two months ago, promised to write me again by the next regular mail. Because he never neglects to send me news of how your Highness is doing, when I did not receive any letters from him, I supposed

201   that you were still in the same state. But I learned from his last letters that your Highness has had a low-grade fever, accompanied by a dry cough, which lasted three or four weeks, and that after you had recovered from this for five or six days, the illness returned. However, at the time that he sent me his letter (which was almost fifteen days en route), your Highness was beginning to get better once again. In regard to all this, I note the signs of a quite considerable illness, but nevertheless one from which it seems that your Highness can so certainly recover that I cannot abstain from writing her my feelings on the matter. Thus, even though I am not a doctor, the honor that your Highness gave me last summer of wanting to know my opinion regarding another indisposition that she then had, makes me hope that the liberty I take will not be disagreeable to her.[42]

The most common cause of a low-grade fever is sadness, and the stubbornness of fortune in persecuting your house continually gives you matters for annoyance which are so public and so terrible that it is necessary neither to conjecture very much nor to be particularly experienced in social matters to judge that the principal cause of your indisposition consists in these.[43]

---

42. See Descartes to Elisabeth, 8 July 1644. Though Descartes claims he is not a doctor, there is a bit of dissimulation here. He is deeply interested in medical matters. Throughout his works he insists that he is concerned with the conduct of life, and in part 6 of the *Discourse*, he makes it clear that "the maintenance of health, which is undoubtedly the chief good and the foundation of all the other goods in this life, " is a large part of this concern (AT 6:62, CSM 1:143).

Descartes was, however, committed to a mechanist account of the workings of the human body, still being worked out in the mid-seventeenth century, not only by Descartes himself, in his posthumously published *Treatise of Man,* but also by the likes of William Harvey in *De Motu Cordis.* As becomes clear in what follows, the competing medical theories were derived from Galenic medicine and sought to cure disease by rebalancing the humors. For discussion of Descartes' medical writings see G. A. Lindeboom, *Descartes and Medicine* (Amsterdam: Rodopi, 1979); and a recent annotated edition of Descartes' medical writings: *Ecrits physiologiques et médicaux,* ed. Vincent Aucante (Paris: Presses Universitaires de France, 2000). For an interesting comparison with Descartes' prescription below, see the cures for melancholy in the Second Parturition of Robert Burton, *Anatomy of Melancholy,* ed. J. B. Bamborough and Martin Dodsworth. (New York: Oxford University Press, 2001). Burton's work was originally published in 1621 and revised through 1651.

43. Descartes is here referring to a cluster of events. Elisabeth's uncle, Charles I of England, was facing the English Civil War. The English and Dutch governments had helped to support Elisabeth's family since the death of her father in 1632. The Civil War thus exacerbated an already precarious financial situation as well as caused personal pain.

One would fear that you would not be able to recover from it at all, if it were not that by the force of your virtue you were making your soul content, despite the disfavor of fortune. I know well that it would be imprudent to want to cheer up a person to whom fortune sends new occasions for displeasure each day, and I am not one of those cruel philosophers who want their sage to be insensible.[44] I know also that your Highness is nowhere near as affected by that which regards her personally as by that which regards the interest of her house and the persons whom she cares about. I take this as the most lovable virtue of all. But it seems to me that the difference between the greatest souls and the base and vulgar souls consists principally in that the vulgar souls give themselves over to their passions and are happy or sad only according to whether those things that happen to them are agreeable or unpleasant; whereas the others [i.e., the great souls] have reasoning so strong and so powerful that, even though they too have passions, and often even more violent ones than most do, their reason nevertheless remains mistress and makes it such that even afflictions serve them and contribute to the perfect felicity which they can enjoy already in this life. Thus, on the one hand, considering themselves to be immortal and capable of receiving very great contentment, and, on the other hand, considering that they are joined to mortal and fragile bodies which are subject to many infirmities and which cannot fail to perish in a few years, they do nearly everything that is in their power to render fortune favorable in this life, but nevertheless they esteem this life so little with respect to eternity that they give events no more consideration than we do events in comedies. Just as those sad and lamentable stories which we see represented on a stage often entertain us as much as the happy ones, even though they bring tears to our eyes, in this way the greatest souls of which I speak draw a satisfaction in themselves from all the things that happen to them, even the most annoying and insupportable.[45] In this way, when they feel pain in their bodies they make an effort to support it patiently, and this show of their strength is agreeable to them; in this way, seeing their friends under some great affliction, they feel compassion at the friend's ill fortune and do everything possible to deliver the friend from it, and they do not fear even exposing themselves to death to this end if it is necessary. But, in the meantime, their conscience tells them

202

203

44. Descartes seems here to be trying to distance himself from neo-Stoic moralists such as Guillaume Du Vair. See Du Vair's *De la sainte philosophie* and *La philosophie morale des Stoïques* (1641), in *Oeuvres*.

45. Descartes continues to draw on this example, and even on this analogy with the theater. See also his letters to Elisabeth of May or June 1645 and 6 October 1646 below, as well as *Passions of the Soul* aa. 94, 147, 187.

that they fulfill their duty and that this is what makes an action praiseworthy and virtuous. This testimony makes them more happy, so that all the sadness their compassion affords them does not afflict them. Finally, just as the greatest prosperity of fortune never intoxicates them or makes them insolent, so too the greatest adversities are unable to defeat them or render them so sad that the body, to which they are joined, becomes sick.

I would fear that this style would be ridiculous if I were using it in writing someone else; but as I consider your Highness to be the most noble and the most upstanding soul I know, I believe that she should also be the most happy and that she will be so truly, if only it would please her to cast her eyes on that which is right under her and to compare the value of those goods she possesses, and which can never be taken away from her, with that of those goods which fortune has plucked from her and the losses with which fortune persecutes her in the person of those near to her. Then she will see all the many reasons she has to be content with her own goods. The extreme zeal that I have for her is the cause of my having let myself go on in this discourse, and I beg her very humbly to excuse it, as it comes from a person who is, &c.

204

AT 4:207

ELISABETH TO DESCARTES

[The Hague] 24 May [1645]

M. Descartes,

I see that the charms of solitary life have not destroyed in you in the least the virtues requisite for society. Such generous kindness as you have for your friends, and as you express to me with the concern you have for my health. But I would be annoyed if it had made you undertake a voyage here, since M. de Palotti has told me that you judge rest necessary to your good health. I assure you that the doctors, who saw me every day and examined all the symptoms of my illness, did not in so doing find its cause, or order such helpful remedies, as you have done from afar. Even if they had been smart enough to suspect the part that my mind plays in the disorder of the body, I would not have had the frankness to admit it to them at all. But to you, Monsieur, I do it without scruple, assuring myself that such a naive recounting of my faults would not in the least destroy the place I have in your friendship, but would confirm it all the more, because you will see from it that the friendship is necessary to me.

Know thus that I have a body imbued with a large part of the weaknesses of my sex, so that it is affected very easily by the afflictions of the soul and has none of the strength to bring itself back into line, as it is of a temperament subject to obstructions and resting in an air which contributes

208

strongly to this. In people who cannot exercise much, it does not take a long oppression of the heart by sadness to obstruct the spleen and infect the rest of the body by its vapors. I myself imagine that the low fever and dry throat—which have not yet left me, even with the warmth of the season, and though the walks I take bring back my strength a little—come from this. This is what made me consent to follow the doctors' advice to drink the waters of Spa here for a month,[46] as I have found by experience that they get rid of obstructions (the waters are brought all the way here without going bad). But I will not take them at all before I know your view, since you have the kindness to want to cure my body with my soul.

I will continue by confessing to you also that, although I do not rest my felicity on things which depend on fortune or on the will of men at all, and although I do not judge myself to be absolutely wretched knowing I will never see my house in order or those near to me away from misery, I still do not know how to consider the injurious accidents that befall them under any other notion than that of evil, nor how to consider the useless efforts I make in their service without some sort of anxiety. This anxiety is no sooner calmed by reasoning than a new disaster produces another anxiety.[47] If my life were entirely known to you, I think the fact that a sensitive mind, such as my own, has conserved itself for so long amidst so many difficulties, in a body so weak, with no counsel but that of her own reason and with no consolation but that of her own conscience, would seem more strange to you than the causes of this present malady.

I spent all of last winter performing the most annoying tasks, which prevented me from taking advantage of the opportunity you gave me of presenting you with the difficulties I find in my studies. These tasks in turn give me other difficulties that I would need to be even more stupid than I am to rid myself of. I only found time just before my indisposition to read the philosophy of the chevalier Digby,[48] which he has written in English, from which

209

46. Spa is a town in Belgium, famed for the healing powers of its mineral hot springs. From as early as the sixteenth century its waters were being exported. Currently, they are commercially available under the "Spa" label.

47. With this remark Elisabeth begins her critique of Descartes' Stoic-informed ethics. She develops this critique, just as Descartes develops his ethics, in the letters which follow.

48. Sir Kenelm Digby (1603–65) published his *Two Treatises, in the one of which the Nature of Bodies, in the other the Nature of Man's soul is looked into, in way of discovery of the immortality of reasonable souls* in English in 1644 with Gilles Blaizot while in exile in Paris. It was published in London in 1645 and has been reprinted (New York: Garland, 1978). Elisabeth is referring to the first *Treatise*, on the nature of bodies, here. Descartes and Digby seem to have met in person, when Digby took a trip to Holland in 1641 especially to meet Descartes. In fall of 1642 Digby was arrested, and Descartes was apprised of this, as well as of his release, by Mersenne (see Descartes to Mersenne, 12 October 1642, AT 3:582, and 20 October 1642, AT 3:590).

I was hoping to draw arguments with which to refute your own, since the chapter summaries showed me two places where he claimed to do so. But when I got there, I was completely surprised to see that he had understood nothing as little as what he approves in your account of reflection. With respect to that which he denies in your account of refraction, he draws no distinction between the movement of a ball and its determination, and does not consider why a soft body that gives way slows down the former, and that a hard body can only resist the latter.[49] He is more excusable for part of what he says about the movement of the heart, as he has not read what you have written about it to the doctor from Louvain.[50] Doctor Jonson[51] told me that he will translate these two chapters for you; and I think that you will not be curious about the rest of the book, because it is of the caliber and follows the method of that English priest who goes by the name Albanus[52] (although the book does have in it some very nice meditations), and because one can hardly expect more from a man who has passed most of the time of his life following designs of love or ambition. I will never have stronger or more constant designs than that of being all my life, Your very affectionate friend, at your service,

Elisabeth.

49. Elisabeth is no doubt referring to chapter 13, *Of three sorts of Violent Motion: Reflexion, Undulation and Refraction,* of Digby's *Treatise on the Nature of Bodies.* The table of contents refers directly to Descartes' account and Digby's effort to refute it. Digby's attack is on Descartes' *Dioptrics.*

50. Digby discusses the movement of the heart in chapter 26 of the first *Treatise.* Adam and Tannery claim that the "doctor from Louvain" is Johan Beverwyck. For Descartes' exchange with Beverwyck, which he apparently shared with Elisabeth, see Beverwyck to Descartes, 10 June 1643, AT 3:682, and Descartes to Beverwyck, 5 July 1643, AT 4:3–6. Johan Beverwyck (1594–1647) was a Dutch physician who published a number of medical works in Dutch. Interestingly, he also wrote a catalogue of learned women, *Van de Uitnementheyt des vrouwelicken Geslachts* (Dordrecht, 1639), which included Anna Maria van Schurman, author of *On Whether a Christian Woman Should Be Educated,* of whom he was a great admirer.

51. Samson Jonsson (1603–61) was the chaplain to the court of Queen Elisabeth of Bohemia, Elisabeth's mother. He seems to have had some interest in physics and metaphysics as well, as Elisabeth, in her letter of 11 April 1647, suggests that Regius has availed himself of Jonsson's assistance in his *Fundamenta Physica.*

52. Thomas White, author of *Institutionum Peripateticarum ad mentem summi viri, clarissimique Philosophi Kenelmi Euitis Digboeii* (the second corrected edition was published in London in 1647, though Elisabeth must here be referring to the first edition). An earlier work of his, *De mundo dialogi tres; quibus materia, forma, caussae* (Paris: Dionysium Moreaum, 1642), was sent to Descartes through Constantijn Huygens in late 1642. See AT 3:485 and a letter from Descartes to Huygens of 13 October 1642 (AT 3:578). Constantijn Huygens served as a tutor to Elisabeth and her siblings as well as consultant to the queen of Bohemia, Elisabeth's mother. Correspondence between Huygens and Elisabeth and members of her family can be found in *De Briefwisseling van Constantijn Huygens,* ed. J. A. Worp, 6 vols. (The Hague: Martinus Nijhoff, 1911–17), vols. 3–6.

24 May

M. Descartes,

I realize now that in what I send you, I am forgetting one of your max-   211
ims, which is never to put anything in writing which can by interpreted
badly by less charitable readers. But I have enough faith in the care of M. de
Palotti that I know that my letter will truly be delivered to you, and in your
discretion that you will destroy it by fire, because of the danger that it will
fall into evil hands.

DESCARTES TO ELISABETH   *AT* 4:218

Egmond, May or June 1645

Madame,

I could not read the letter your Highness did me the honor of writing without being extremely affected at seeing that a virtue so rare and so
accomplished was not accompanied by good health or the prosperity she
merits. I easily conceive the many unpleasant things which are continually
presented to her, and are all the more difficult to overcome, in that often
they are of such a nature that true reason does not demand that one oppose them directly or that one try to chase them away. These are domestic
enemies with which we are constrained to interact, and so we are obliged to
stand on guard incessantly in order to prevent them from doing harm. I find
for this but one remedy, which is to divert one's imagination and one's senses
as much as possible and to employ only the understanding alone to consider
them when one is obliged to by prudence.

One can, it seems to me, here easily notice the difference between un-   219
derstanding, on the one hand, and imagination or sensation on the other.
Consider for instance a person who otherwise has all sorts of reasons to be
content, but who sees continually represented before her tragedies full of
dreadful events, and who occupies herself only in considering these objects
of sadness and pity. Even though these events are feigned and fabulous, so
that they only draw tears from her eyes and move her imagination without
touching her understanding, I believe, I say, that this alone would suffice to
accustom her heart to close itself up and to emit sighs. Following this, the circulation of the blood would be blocked and slowed, and the largest particles
of the blood, attaching one to the other, could easily grind up the spleen by
getting caught and stopping in its pores, and the more subtle particles, retaining their agitation, could alter her lungs and cause a cough, which in the long
term would give good cause for fear. Now, on the contrary, consider a person

who has an infinite number of true sources of displeasure, but takes great care to turn her imagination from them so that she thinks of them only when practical matters oblige her to, and so that she considers only those objects which are capable of bringing her contentment and joy. Not only would this be of great use to her in enabling her to judge more soundly those things which matter to her, since she would regard them without passion, but also I do not doubt that this alone would be capable of bringing her back to health, even though her spleen and lungs were already ill disposed by the bad temperament of the blood caused by her sadness. This would be especially the case if she also uses the medical remedies of the doctors to cure the part of the blood which causes the obstructions. In this regard, I judge the waters of Spa very appropriate, especially if your Highness in taking them observes what the doctors usually recommend, and clears her mind entirely of all sorts of unhappy thoughts, and even also of all sorts of serious meditations concerning the sciences. She should occupy herself by imitating those who convince themselves they think of nothing in looking at the greenery of a wood, the colors of a flower, the flight of a bird, and such things that require no attention. This is not to waste time but to employ it well. For one can, in doing this, satisfy oneself by the hope that by this means one will recover perfect health, which is the foundation of all the other goods that one can have in this life.

I know well that I write nothing here that your Highness does not know better than I, and that it is not so much the theory but the practice which is difficult in this matter. But the extreme honor that she does me in expressing that she is not averse to hearing my opinions leads me to take the liberty of writing them as they are. And I do so again here in adding that I have experienced in myself an illness nearly similar and even more dangerous, which was cured by the remedy I just outlined. For being born of a mother who died just a few days after my birth[53] of a disease of the lungs caused by some unhappiness, I inherited from her a dry cough and a pale color which stayed with me until I was more than twenty years old and which led all the doctors who saw me up to that point to condemn me to an early death. But I believe I have always had the inclination to regard things which present themselves to me from the most favorable perspective and to make my principal contentment depend on myself alone, and I believe that this inclination caused this indisposition, which was almost natural to me, to pass away little by little.

I have a great obligation to your Highness for giving me her opinion of the book of Chevalier D'Igby,[54] which I will not be able to read until

53. Descartes' mother actually died on 13 May 1597, fourteen months after his birth.
54. That is, Kenelm Digby, mentioned in Elisabeth's previous letter.

it is translated into Latin, which M. Jonson, who was here yesterday, said some people want to do. He also said that I could send my letters for your Highness through ordinary messengers, which I would not have dared to do without his having said so, and I have put off writing this one, as I was waiting for one of my friends to go to The Hague so that I might give it to him. I regret infinitely the absence of M. de Pollot, since I could have learned from him the state of your health, but the letters which are sent to me through the Alkmaar postman never fail to reach me. As there is no one in the world whom I desire to be able to serve with as much passion as your Highness, there is also nothing which could make me more happy than to have the honor of receiving her orders. I am, &c.

222

ELISABETH TO DESCARTES

AT 4:233

[The Hague] 22 June 1645

M. Descartes,

Your letters, when they do not teach me, always serve me as the antidote to melancholy, turning my mind from the disagreeable objects that come to it every day to the happiness that I possess in the friendship of a person of your merit, to whose counsel I can commit the conduct of my life. If I could yet make my mind conform to your last precepts, there is no doubt that I would cure myself promptly of maladies of the body and weaknesses of the mind. But I confess that I find it difficult to separate from the senses and the imagination those things that are continuously represented to them in conversation and in letters, so that I do not know how to avoid them without sinning against my duty. I know well that in removing everything upsetting to me (which I believe to be represented only by imagination) from the idea of an affair, I would judge it healthily and would find in it the remedies as well as the affection which I bring to it. But I have never known how to put this into practice until the passion has already played its role. There is something surprising in misfortunes, even those that have been foreseen, of which I am mistress only after a certain time; my body becomes so strongly disordered that several months are necessary for me to restore it, and those months hardly pass without some new subject of trouble. Besides this, I must govern my mind with care, giving it agreeable objects, for the least laziness makes it fall back onto those subjects, all too readily available, which afflict it. I fear that if I do not use my mind at all while I am taking waters of Spa, it will only become more melancholy. If I were able to profit, as you do, from everything that presents itself to my senses, I would divert myself without difficulty. It is at this moment that I feel the inconvenience of being but a

234

little rational. For if I were not so at all, I would find pleasures in common with those among whom I must live and so be able to take this medicine and have it do something. And if I were as rational as you, I would cure myself as you have done. In addition, the curse of my sex keeps me from the contentment a voyage to Egmond, where I might learn of the truths you draw from your garden, would have brought me. All the same I console myself with the liberty you give me to ask from time to time for news of it as

Your very affectionate friend at your service,
Elisabeth.

235   M. Descartes, I learned with great joy that the Academy of Groningen did you justice.[55]

AT 4:236

DESCARTES TO ELISABETH

Egmond, June 1645

Madame,

I ask your Highness very humbly to pardon me, for I cannot feel sorry for her indisposition when I have the honor of receiving her letters. I always note in them thoughts so distinct and reasoning so firm that it is not possible for me to convince myself that a mind capable of conceiving them is lodged in a weak and sickly body. Whatever the case might be, the knowledge that your Highness demonstrates of the illness and of the remedies that can overcome it assures me that she will not fail to have the skill required to employ them.

I know well that it is nearly impossible to resist the first troubles that new misfortunes excite in us, and even that it is ordinarily the best minds in whom the passions are the most violent and act more strongly on their bodies. But it

237   seems to me that the following day, when sleep has calmed emotions in the blood that occur in such circumstances, one can begin to get one's mind in order and make it tranquil. This is done by making an effort to consider all the benefits one can take from that thing which one had taken the preceding day for a great mishap, and by turning one's attention away from the evils one had imagined there. For there are no events so disastrous, or so absolutely

---

55. Elisabeth is here referring to the decision in favor of Descartes and against Martin Schoock in the matter concerning Voetius at Utrecht. Most at issue was a question of whether Descartes had ever been suspected of atheism. Descartes was most concerned to vindicate himself of this charge. For further details see AT 4:196ff.; Verbeek, *Descartes and the Dutch;* Gaukroger, *Descartes,* 360–61; and Rodis-Lewis, *Descartes,* 163–72.

bad in the judgment of people, that a reasonable person could not look at them from an angle which will make them appear favorable. Your Highness can draw this general consolation from the ill favors of fortune: that they have perhaps contributed a lot toward enabling her to cultivate her mind to the point that she has. This is a good that she should value more than an empire. Great prosperity often dazzles and intoxicates in such a way that it sooner possesses those that have it than is possessed by them. Even though this does not happen to those with minds of a temperament like your own, it would all the same furnish her with fewer occasions to exercise her mind than does adversity. I believe that as there is no good in the world except good sense which we can call absolutely good, there is also no evil from which we cannot draw some benefit, having good sense.

I have tried before to recommend carefreeness to your Highness, thinking that too serious occupations would weaken the body in tiring the mind, but I would not want this to dissuade her from those measures necessary for turning her thought from objects which can sadden her. And I do not doubt that the diversions of study, which would be very difficult for others, could serve her as a release. I would count myself happy if I could contribute to making these diversions easier for her. And I have even more desire to go to The Hague to learn about the virtues of the Spa waters, than to know here those of the plants of my garden, and much more than I care what is happening at Groningen or at Utrecht,[56] whether to my benefit or harm. This will oblige me in four or five days to follow this letter, and I will be all the days of my life, &c.

238

DESCARTES TO ELISABETH

AT 4:251

Egmond, 21 July 1645

Madame,

Since I had the honor of seeing your Highness, the air has been so inconstant, and some days have been so unseasonably cold that I have often been worried and afraid that the waters of Spa would not be as healthy or useful as they would have been in more serene weather. Since you have done me the honor of telling me that my letters could serve as a kind of diversion for you, though the doctors recommend that you not occupy your mind with anything that might tax it, I would be a bad caretaker of the favor it has

---

56. See above, note 13. Descartes appealed the decision at Utrecht to the State of Groningen, which referred the matter to the University of Groningen.

pleased you to do me in permitting me to write you if I were remiss in taking the first occasion to do so.

252   I imagine that most of the letters you receive from others give you some distress and that before you even read them you dread finding in them some news that will upset you, since bad fortune has long accustomed you to receiving such bad news. Whereas for my letters, you can at least be assured that, even if they give you no cause for joy, they will also give you no reason for sadness. You can open them at any time without fearing that they will interfere with the digestion of the waters you take. As I learn nothing of what is going on in the rest of the world in this desert, and have no thoughts more frequently than those which, representing to me the virtues of your Highness, make me wish to see her as happy and as content as she deserves to be, the only subject I have with which to engage you is how philosophy teaches us to acquire this sovereign felicity which vulgar minds vainly expect from fortune, but which we can obtain only from ourselves.

One of the ways that seems most useful to me to acquire this felicity is to examine what the ancients wrote about it and to try to go beyond what they said by adding something to their precepts. For in this way one can make these precepts perfectly one's own and dispose oneself to put them into practice. So, in order to supplement the defect in my mind, which on its own can produce nothing I deem worthwhile for your Highness to read, and so that my letters are not entirely empty and useless, I propose to fill them henceforth with considerations which I will draw from the reading of

253   a particular book, namely, Seneca's *De vita beata*,[57] unless you would rather choose another, or unless this plan is disagreeable to you. But if you approve of it (as I hope you will), and especially if it pleases you to share with me your remarks about the same book, then, besides the fact that they will serve to instruct me, they will give me occasion to make my own thoughts more exact. And I will develop my thoughts with more care the more I judge that this exchange is agreeable to you. For there is nothing in the world that I desire with more zeal than to demonstrate, in everything which is in my power, that I am, Madame,

Your Highness's very humble and very obedient servant,

Descartes.

---

57. Lucius Annaeus Seneca (5–65 CE) was a Roman philosopher with strong Stoic leanings, though he was also influence by Epicurean doctrine. He also served as the tutor to Nero. When he came under suspicion of trying to overthrow Nero, he was sentenced to death by a method of his own choosing. He chose to open his veins.

DESCARTES TO ELISABETH

Egmond, 4 August 1645

Madame,

When I chose Seneca's *De vita beata* as the book to propose to your Highness as an agreeable topic of discussion, I did so only on the basis of the reputation of the author and the dignity of the subject matter, without thinking of the manner in which he treats it. Having since considered this manner, I do not find it sufficiently exact to merit following it through. But in order that your Highness can judge of it more easily, I will here try to explain in what way it seems to me that this subject ought to have been treated by a philosopher like him who, not having been enlightened by faith, had only natural reason as a guide.

He says very well at the beginning that *Vivere omnes beate volunt, sed ad pervidendum quid sit quod beatam vitam efficiat, caligant.*[58] But it is necessary to know what *vivere beate*[59] means; I would say in French, to live happily [*vivre heureusement*], if there wasn't a difference between good fortune [*l'heur*] and true happiness [*beatitude*].[60] This good fortune depends only on those things that are external to us; so those to whom some good comes without their having done anything to try to attain it are deemed more fortunate [*plus heureux*] than sages. On the other hand, true happiness consists, it seems to me, in a perfect contentment of the mind and an internal satisfaction that those who are the most favored by fortune ordinarily do not have and that the sages acquire without fortune's favor. Thus, to live *beate*, to live happily, is nothing but to have a mind that is perfectly content and satisfied.

264

Considering, after this, what *quod beatam vitam efficiat* means, that is to say, what those things are which can give us this sovereign contentment, I note that they are of two sorts: those which depend on us, such as virtue and wisdom, and those which do not depend on us at all, such as honors, riches, and health. For it is certain that a wellborn man who is never ill, who lacks noth-

58. "All men want to live happily, but as to seeing clearly what brings about a happy life, they are in a fog." This sentence is the first of Seneca's dialogue.

59. Since Descartes is here attempting to interpret the Latin, I shall leave *beate* untranslated.

60. *L'heur* here adverts to good fortune, and so *heureux* is best rendered in this letter as "fortunate" in keeping with this. *La béatitude* is the sovereign felicity Descartes adverts to in his previous letter, or "sovereign contentment" below. I translate it here as "true happiness." In keeping with this I will translate its adverbial form *en béatitude* as "happily." In later letters, however, Descartes uses *heureux* to mean "happy" in concert with achieving the sovereign good. Other uses of the term are ambiguous, and many certainly include both being happy and fortunate.

ing, and who with all this is as wise and virtuous as another who is poor, un-
healthy, and deformed can enjoy a greater contentment than the latter can.
All the same, as a small vessel can be just as full as a larger one even though
it contains less fluid, so too, taking the contentment of each for the fullness
and fulfillment of desires regulated according to reason, I do not doubt that
those poorer and more disfavored by fortune or nature can be fully content
and satisfied just as well as others, even though they do not enjoy as many
goods.⁶¹ It is only this sort of contentment that is here in question. For since
the other sort is not at all in our power, seeking it would be superfluous.

So it seems to me that each person can make himself content by himself and without waiting on something from elsewhere just so long as he
observes three things, which are related to the three rules of conduct that I
set out in the *Discourse on the Method*.⁶²

The first is that he always try to make use of his mind as well as he can,
in order to know what must be done, or not done, in all the events of life.

The second is that he have a firm and constant resolution to execute all
that reason advises him to do, without having the passions or appetites turn
him away from it. It is the firmness of this resolution that I believe ought to be
taken to be virtue, even though I know of no one who has ever explained it in
this way. Instead it has been divided into many types, to which diverse names
have been given in accordance with the diverse objects to which it extends.

The third is that, while he so conducts himself as much as he can in
accordance with reason, he keep in mind that all the goods he does not
possess are, each and every one of them, entirely outside of his power. By
this means, he will accustom himself not to desire them at all. For there is
nothing but desire and regret or repentance that can prevent us from being
content. But if we always do all that our reason tells us, we will never have
any grounds to repent, even though events afterward make us see that we
were mistaken. For our being mistaken is not our fault at all. What makes it
the case that, for example, we do not desire to have more arms, or better, to
have more tongues than we have, but that we do desire to be in better health
or to have more riches, is only that we imagine that these latter things can
be acquired by our conduct, or even that they are due to our nature, and that
the same is not true of the others. We can strip ourselves of this opinion in

---

61. Interestingly, Moderata Fonte, in her *Worth of Women*, 85, uses a similar metaphor to argue
that women are just as capable as men of achieving virtue.

62. See the "provisional moral code consisting of just three or four maxims" Descartes outlines
in part 3 of the *Discourse* (AT 6:22ff., CSM 1:122ff.).

considering that, since we have always followed the advice of our reason, we have omitted nothing that was in our power, and that maladies and bad fortune are no less natural to man than prosperity and health.

For the rest, all sorts of desires are not incompatible with true happiness; only those that are accompanied by impatience and sadness are. It is also not necessary that our reason never be mistaken. It suffices that our conscience testifies that we have never lacked resolution and virtue to execute all the things that we have judged to be the best. Thus, virtue alone is sufficient to render us content in this life. Nevertheless, when virtue is not made clear by the intellect, it can be false. That is to say, our will and resolution to do well can carry us toward bad things, even though we think them good. The contentment that comes from such virtue is not solid, and, since we ordinarily oppose this virtue to pleasures, appetites, and passions, it is very difficult to put into practice. On the other hand, the right use of reason, giving us a true knowledge of the good, prevents virtue from being false. In making virtue accord with licit pleasures, reason makes practicing virtue quite easy; and in giving us knowledge of the condition of our nature, it restrains our desires in such a way that one must admit that the greatest felicity of man depends on this right usage of reason and, by consequence, that the study that serves in acquiring it is the most useful occupation that one can have, as it is also without doubt the most agreeable and the most sweet.

267

From all this it seems to me that Seneca ought to have taught us all the principal truths we are required to know to facilitate the practice of virtue and to regulate our desires and passions, and thus to enjoy a natural and true happiness. This would have made his book the best and the most useful that a pagan philosopher could have written. All the same, this is only my opinion, which I submit to the judgment of your Highness, and if she does me such a favor as to alert me to what I am missing, I would owe her a great obligation and will show in correcting myself that I am, Madame,

268

Your Highness's very humble and very obedient servant,
Descartes.

ELISABETH TO DESCARTES

The Hague, 16 August 1645

M. Descartes,

In examining the book that you recommended to me, I found quite a few nice parts and sentences well conceived to give me a subject for an

269   agreeable meditation, but not for instructing me in what it treats. For they are written without method, and the author does something other than he set out to do. Instead of demonstrating the shortest path toward true happiness, he contents himself with revealing that his riches and his luxury do not preclude his reaching it. This I am obliged to write to you, so that you will not think that I am of your opinion by prejudice or by laziness. I demand nothing other than that you continue to correct Seneca. I do so, not because your manner of reasoning is most extraordinary, but because it is the most natural that I have encountered and seems to teach me nothing new, but instead allows me to draw from my mind pieces of knowledge I have not yet apprehended.[63]

It is for this reason that I do not yet know how to rid myself of the doubt that one can arrive at the true happiness of which you speak without the assistance of that which does not depend absolutely on the will. For there are diseases that destroy altogether the power of reasoning and by consequence that of enjoying a satisfaction of reason. There are others that diminish the force of reason and prevent one from following the maxims that good sense would have forged and that make the most moderate man subject to being carried away by his passions and less capable of disentangling himself from the accidents of fortune requiring a prompt resolution. When Epicurus was struggling to convince his friends that he felt no pain from his kidney stones, instead of crying like the vulgar, he was leading the life of the philosopher and not that of a prince or a captain or a courtier. For he knew that nothing could come to him from outside that would make him forget his role and cause him to fail to rise above his circumstances according to

270   his philosophy.[64] On these occasions regret seems to me inevitable, and the knowledge that to err is as natural to man as it is to be sick cannot protect us. For we also are not unaware that we were able to exempt ourselves of each particular fault.

But I assure myself that you will elucidate these points of difficulty for me, as well as many others, of which I am not aware at this moment, when you teach me the truths which must be known to facilitate the exercise of virtue. Do not forget, I pray you, your plan to honor me with your precepts and believe that I esteem them as much as they deserve it.

---

63. Elisabeth here seems to be referring to the Platonic model of knowledge as recollection as presented in his dialogue *Meno*.

64. Elisabeth is here no doubt referring to the death of Epicurus: he died of kidney failure after trying for two weeks to pass kidney stones. It is unclear where Elisabeth would have read of this story. Montaigne alludes to it in his essay *On the Resemblance of Children to Their Fathers*. See *The Complete Essays*, trans. M. A. Screech (New York: Penguin Books, 1987), 858–87.

It has been eight days since the bad humor of a sick brother prevented me from making this request of you, since I have had to stay near him every day, either to make him, through the fondness he has for me, abide by the rules set by the doctors, or to show him my fondness by diverting him, because he is persuaded that I am capable of diverting him. I hope to divert you also in assuring you that I will be all my life, M. Descartes,

Your very affectionate friend at your service,

Elisabeth.

DESCARTES TO ELISABETH

AT 4:271

Egmond, 18 August 1645

Madame,

Even though I do not know if my last letters were delivered to your Highness, or if I can write anything on the subject on which I have the honor of engaging you that I don't have to think you understand better than myself, I will all the same not fail to continue, in the belief that my letters will not be any more tiresome to you than the books in your library. For although they contain no news that you have an interest in knowing promptly, nothing forces you to read them when you have some business to attend to. I will take the time I put into writing them as very well spent if you give them only the time you want to waste.

I said in my previous letter what it seemed to me Seneca ought to have treated in his book. I will now examine what he does treat there. I note in general only three things: the first is that he tries to explain what the sovereign good is and that he gives different definitions; the second, that he argues against the opinion of Epicurus;[65] and the third, that he responds to those who object that philosophers do not live in accordance with the rules they prescribe. But in order to see the particular way in which he treats these things, I will spend a little time on each chapter.

272

In the first, he takes to task those who follow custom and example more than reason. *In the matter of how to live,* he says, *people always rely on belief, never*

---

65. Epicurus (c. 341–271 BCE) was a major Hellenistic philosopher whose work enjoyed a substantial revival in the seventeenth century. His philosophy is characterized by a thoroughgoing materialist metaphysics, which maintains that the world is composed of indestructible atoms which move through empty space, as well as an apparently hedonistic ethics, for he maintains that happiness consists quite simply in pleasure. However, both Descartes below and Elisabeth in what follows interpret Epicurus as meaning by "pleasure" something more than sensual pleasure and akin to contentment.

on judgment.[66] He approves nonetheless of our taking the advice of those he believes to be the wisest. But he wants us also to use our own judgment to examine their opinions. In this I am strongly of his opinion. For even though most people are not capable of finding the right path for themselves, there are few who cannot recognize it well enough when someone else points it out to them clearly. No matter what happens, one has grounds to be satisfied in one's conscience, and to be assured that the opinions one has concerning morality are the best that one could have, when, instead of letting oneself be led blindly by example, one has taken the care to find the most able advice, and when one has employed all the force of one's mind to examine what path one ought to follow. But while Seneca strives to hone his eloquence here, he is not always exact enough in the expression of his thought. For instance, when he says, *We will become wise insofar as we separate ourselves from the crowd,*[67] he seems to teach that it is sufficient to act extravagantly to be wise, but this is not his intention.

273

In the second chapter he does almost nothing but repeat, in other terms, what he said in the first. He adds only that what is commonly judged to be good is not so.

Then, in the third, after having again employed many superfluous words, he finally states his opinion concerning the sovereign good, which is that *it accords with the nature of things,*[68] and that *wisdom is conforming to its law and example*[69] [i.e., of nature], and that *the truly happy life is one in accordance with one's own nature.*[70] All these explications seem very obscure to me. For it is without doubt that by "nature" he does not understand our natural inclinations, seeing as they ordinarily carry us to pursue pleasure, and he argues against doing that. But what follows in his discourse makes me think that by "the nature of things" he means the order established by God in all things that there are in the world. Considering this order as infallible and independent of our will, he says that *wisdom is being in accord with the nature of things and conforming to its law and example,*[71] that is to say that it is wisdom to acquiesce to

66. The Latin Descartes quotes reads "Nunquam de vita iudicatur . . . semper creditur." Seneca, *De vita beata*, 1.4; *Seneca: Moral Essays II*, trans. J. W. Basore (Cambridge: Harvard University Press, 1932, 1965), 100–101.

67. The Latin Descartes quotes reads "Sanabimur, si modo separemur a coetu" (ibid., 1.5, 100–103).

68. The Latin reads: "rerum naturae assentitur" (ibid., 3.3, 106–7).

69. The Latin reads: "ad illius legem exemplumque formari sapientia est" (ibid., 3.3, 106–7).

70. The Latin reads: "beata vita est conveniens naturae suae" (ibid., 3.3, 106–7).

71. The Latin reads: "rerum naturae assentiri & ad illius legem exemplumque formari, sapientia est" (ibid., 3.3, 106–7).

the order of things, and to do what we believe ourselves to be born to do, or better, to speak as a Christian, that it is wisdom to submit to the will of God and to follow it in all one's actions. And *the good life is one in accordance* 274 *with one's own nature* is to say that true happiness consists in following in this way the order of the world and accepting the good part of everything that happens to us. This explains practically nothing, and it is not clear enough what the connection is with what he adds immediately after—that this true happiness cannot be achieved *unless the mind is healthy* [72]—unless he means also that *to live according to nature* [73] is to live following true reason.

In the fourth and fifth chapters, he gives some other definitions of the sovereign good, all of which have some relation to the sense of the first, but none of which explains it sufficiently. Through their diversity, they make it appear that Seneca has not understood clearly what he wanted to say. For the better one conceives of something, the more determined one is to express it in only one way. That formulation where he seems to me to have hit upon it best is in the fifth chapter, where he says that *a truly happy person is one who, by benefit of reason, neither desires nor fears* [74] and that *the good life is one grounded in right and certain judgment.* [75] But so long as he does not teach any of the reasons why we ought to neither fear nor desire anything, all this helps us very little.

In these same chapters he begins to argue against those who locate true happiness in pleasure, and he continues to do so in the following chapters. This is why, before examining them, I will state my view on this question.

I note, first, that there is a difference between true happiness, the sov- 275 ereign good, and the final end or goal to which our actions ought to tend. True happiness is not the sovereign good; but it presupposes it, and it is the contentment or satisfaction of the mind that comes from possessing it. But, by the end of our actions, we can understand either the one or the other. For the sovereign good is without doubt the thing which we ought to put forward to ourselves as the goal of all our actions, and the contentment of mind that comes from it is also rightly called our end, as it is what attracts us and so makes us seek the sovereign good.

Other than this, I note that Epicurus understood the word "pleasure" in a different sense than did those who argued against him. For all his adversaries restricted the signification of this word to the pleasures of the senses. He,

---

72. The Latin Descartes quotes reads: "nisi sana mens est" (ibid., 6.1, 114–15).

73. The Latin Descartes quotes reads: "secundum naturam vivere" (ibid., 7.2, 116–19).

74. The Latin reads: "beatus est qui nec cupit nec timet beneficio rationis" (ibid., 5.1, 110–11).

75. The Latin reads: "beata vita est in recto certoque iudicio stabilita" (ibid., 5.3, 112–13).

on the other hand, extended it to every contentment of the mind, as one can easily judge from what Seneca and some others have written about him.

So, there were three opinions on the sovereign good and the end of our actions among the pagan philosophers: Epicurus claimed that it was pleasure; Zeno[76] wanted it to be virtue; and Aristotle made it consist of all the perfections, as much those of the body as those of the mind. These three opinions can, it seems to me, be received as true and in accord with one another, provided they are interpreted favorably.

For Aristotle considered the sovereign good of the whole of human nature in general, that is, that which the most accomplished of all men can have, and so he was right to have it consist of all the perfections of which human nature is capable. But that meaning is not useful to us.

Zeno, on the contrary, considered that which each man could possess on his own. This is why he too was quite right to say that the sovereign good consists only in virtue, for it is only virtue, among the goods we can have, which depends entirely on our free will. But he represented this virtue as so severe and so opposed to pleasure, in making all the vices equal, that it seems to me that only melancholic people or minds entirely detached from bodies were able to be among his followers.

Finally, Epicurus was not wrong, in considering what true happiness consists in and the motive or the end to which our actions tend, to say that it is pleasure in general. For even though the mere knowledge of our duty could oblige us to do good actions, this would not, all the same, make us enjoy any true happiness if we did not receive any pleasure from it. But because the name "pleasure" is often given to false pleasures that are accompanied or followed by anxiety, trouble, and repentance, many have thought that this view of Epicurus teaches vice. And, in fact, it does not teach virtue. When there is a prize for hitting a bull's-eye, one makes people want to hit the bull's-eye by showing them this prize. Still they cannot win the prize if they do not see the bull's-eye. And those who see the bull's-eye cannot be induced to aim for it if they do not know that there is a prize to win. Similarly, virtue, which is the bull's-eye, does not come to be strongly desired when it is seen on its own; contentment, which is the prize, cannot be acquired unless it is pursued.

This is why I think I can conclude here that true happiness consists only in the contentment of the mind, that is, in contentment in general. For even though there are kinds of contentment that depend on the body, and others which do not depend on it all, there is, all the same, no contentment but that of the mind. However, to have a contentment that is solid, it is necessary

---

76. Zeno of Citium (c. 344–262 BCE) was the founder of the Stoic school of philosophy.

to follow virtue, that is, to have a firm and constant will to execute all that we judge to be the best and to employ all the force of our understanding to judge well. I reserve for another time a consideration of what Seneca wrote on this, because my letter is already too long, and I have only sufficient space   278
to write that I am, Madame,

      Your Highness's very humble and very obedient servant,
           Descartes.

ELISABETH TO DESCARTES   *AT* 4:278

The Hague, August 1645

M. Descartes,

    I believe that you will have already seen in my last letter of the sixteenth that your letter of the fourth was given to me. I have no need to add that that letter shed more light on the subject it treats than anything else I have   279
been able to read or meditate on about it. You understand too well what you do, what I can do, and have examined what others have done so well for me to be able to doubt it, even though through an excess of generosity you pretend to be unaware of the extreme obligation I have to you for having given me an occupation so useful and so agreeable as that of reading and considering your letters. Without the last one, I would not have understood so well as I think I do now what Seneca judges true happiness to be. I attributed the obscurity I found in the said book, as I do that in the books of most ancients, to the manner of explication and the scanty connection and order they observe. Their style is altogether different from our own. The things which are problematic to us pass for hypotheses to them, and they write with the idea of accumulating admirers by surprising the imagination, rather than disciples by shaping the faculty of judgment. In this way, Seneca makes use of nice words to attract the young to follow his views, as others do by means of poetry and fables. The way he refutes the view of Epicurus seems to confirm this impression. He attributes this to that philosopher: that which we say is a law for virtue, he says he does for pleasure.[77] A little before that he says that these followers claim: I hold in effect that one does not know how to live pleasantly without living also, at the same time, honorably.[78]

---

77. Elisabeth quotes the following passage: "nos virtuti legem dicimus, eam ille dicit voluptati" (*De vita beata*, 13.1, 130–31).

78. Elisabeth quotes this passage: "ego enim nego quemquam posse iucunde vivere, nisi simul et honeste vivat" (ibid., 10.1, 122–23).

From which it seems clear that what they call "pleasure" is the joy and satisfaction of the mind which Seneca counts as the consequences of the supreme
280 good. Nevertheless, throughout the book he speaks of this Epicurean pleasure more as a satirist than as a philosopher, as if it were purely sensual. But
I want to be charitable to him, and this is caused by your having taken the
care to explicate their opinions and reconcile their differences better than
they themselves knew how to do. Thereby you refute a powerful objection
against the search for this sovereign good that not one of these great thinkers was able to define, and also against the authority of human reason, for
it has not enlightened these excellent personages at all with the knowledge
of what is most necessary to them and is closest to their hearts. I hope that
you will continue, with what Seneca said, or with what he should have said,
in teaching me the means of strengthening the understanding, so as to judge
the best in all the actions of life. For this seems to be the only difficulty, since
it is impossible not to follow the good path when it is known. Have again, I
pray you, the frankness to tell me if I abuse your kindness in demanding too
much of your time in the satisfaction of

Your very affectionate friend, at your service,

Elisabeth.

AT 4:281

DESCARTES TO ELISABETH

Egmond, 1 September 1645

Madame,

As I was uncertain whether your Highness was in The Hague or in
Rhenen, I addressed my letter through Leiden, and that letter you have done
the honor of writing me was delivered to me only after the postman who
carried it to Alkmaar had left. This has kept me from expressing earlier how
full of glory I am that my own judgment of the book that you have taken the
trouble to read is no different from your own, and that my way of reasoning
appears natural enough to you. I assure myself that if you had had the leisure
to think about the things of which he treats as much as I have, I could not have
written anything that you could not have noted better than I. But because the
age, birth, and occupations of your Highness have not been able to permit
this, perhaps then what I write will be able to serve to save you a little time,
and my mistakes themselves can furnish you with occasions to note the truth.

When I spoke of a true happiness which depends entirely on our free will
and which all men can acquire without any assistance from elsewhere, you
282 note quite rightly that there are illnesses which, taking away the power of

reasoning, also take away that of enjoying the satisfaction of a rational mind. This shows me that what I have said generally about all men should be extended only to those who have free use of their reason and with that know the path necessary to take to reach this true happiness. For there is no one who does not desire to make himself happy [*heureux*], but many do not know the means to do so, and often a bodily indisposition prevents the will from being free. Something similar also happens when we sleep, for the most philosophical person in the world does not know how to prevent himself from having bad dreams when his temperament disposes him to them. All the same, experience shows that if one has often had some thought while one has had a free mind, one returns to it often afterward, no matter what indisposition the body has. Thus, I can say that my dreams never represent to me anything upsetting. And without doubt, one has a great benefit from being accustomed for a long time to having no sad thoughts. But we are able to be absolutely responsible for ourselves only so long as we are in our own power, and it is less upsetting to lose one's life than to lose the use of reason. For even without the teachings of faith, natural philosophy alone makes us hope for our soul to have a happier state after death than that it has at present. No fear is more upsetting to it than that of being joined to a body that entirely takes away its freedom.

For the other indispositions, which do not altogether trouble the senses but simply alter the humors and make one find oneself extraordinarily inclined to sadness, anger, or some other passions, they no doubt give trouble, but they can be overcome and even give the soul occasion for a satisfaction all the greater insofar as those passions are difficult to vanquish. I also believe something similar of all external obstacles, such as the brilliance of high birth, the flatteries of the court, the adversities of fortune, and also great prosperity, which ordinarily gets more in the way of our being able to play the role of philosopher than do misfortunes. For when one has everything one wishes, one forgets to think of oneself, and, afterward, when fortune changes, one finds oneself the more surprised the more one put one's trust in it. Finally, one can say generally that nothing can entirely take away the means of making ourselves happy so long as it does not trouble our reason, and it is not always those things that appear the most upsetting that are the most harmful. 283

But in order to know exactly how much each thing can contribute to our contentment, it is necessary to consider what the causes that produce it are, and this is also one of the principal pieces of knowledge that can serve to facilitate virtue. For all the actions of our mind which bring us some perfection are virtuous, and all our contentment consists only in our inner testimony of having some perfection. Thus, we know of no exercise of virtue (that is to say, what our reason convinces us we ought to do) from which we do not receive 284 satisfaction and pleasure. But there are two sorts of pleasures: those which pertain to the mind alone and others which pertain to the human being, that is, to the mind insofar as it is united to a body. These latter ones, presenting themselves confusedly to the imagination, often appear to be much greater than they are, especially before we possess them; and this is the source of all the evils and errors of life. For, according to the rule of reason, each pleasure ought to be measured by the greatness of the perfection it produces, and this is how we measure those whose causes are clearly known to us. But often passion makes us believe that certain things are much better and more desirable than they are. Then, when we have taken great pain to acquire them and lost, in the meantime, the occasion to possess other truer goods, the enjoyment makes us know their defects and from this arises disdain, regret, and repentance. That is why the true duty of reason is to examine the just value of all the goods whose acquisition seems to depend in some way on our conduct, in order that we will never fail to employ all our care in trying to procure those which are, in fact, the most desirable. In regard to which, if fortune is opposed to our plans and prevents them from succeeding, we will have at least the satisfaction of having lost nothing by our fault, and will not fail to enjoy the natural true happiness which will have been in our power to acquire.

285

Thus, for example, anger can sometimes excite in us desires for vengeance so violent that it makes us imagine more pleasure in punishing our enemy than in protecting our honor or our life, and we will expose ourselves imprudently to losing both the one and the other for this end. On the other hand, if reason examines what is the good or the perfection on which this pleasure drawn from vengeance is founded, it will find none other there (at least when this vengeance does not serve to prevent the recurrence of what we take offense at) but that it makes us imagine that we have some sort of superiority and some advantage over those on whom we seek vengeance. This is often only a vain imagination, which does not merit being valued in comparison with honor or life, or even in comparison with the satisfaction one would have in seeing oneself master of one's anger in abstaining from seeking vengeance.

And something similar occurs with all other passions. For there are none which do not represent to us the good to which they tend more vividly than is merited and which do not make us imagine pleasures much greater before we possess them than we find them afterward, once we have them. Because of this we commonly blame pleasure, since we use this word only to signify

286

pleasures that often trick us by their appearance, and make us neglect other much more solid ones, which we do not so much look forward to and which are ordinarily those of the mind alone. I say "ordinarily," for all of the pleasures of the mind are not praiseworthy, since they can be founded on a false opinion, as is the pleasure we take in slander, which is founded only on the fact that we think we will be valued more, the less others are valued. They can also trick us by their appearance, when some strong passion accompanies them, as we see in the pleasure of ambition.

But the principal difference between the pleasures of the body and those of the mind consists in this: the body is subject to perpetual change, and even its conservation and its well-being depend on this change; so all the pleasures proper to it hardly last. For these proceed only from the acquisition of something that is useful to the body at the moment it receives them, and as soon as this something ceases to be useful to it, the pleasures also cease. On the other hand, the pleasures of the soul can be as immortal as can it, so long as they have a foundation so solid that neither knowledge of the truth nor any false belief can destroy it.

For the rest, the true use of our reason in the conduct of life consists only in examining and considering without passion the value of all perfections, those of the body as much as those of the mind, that can be acquired by our conduct, in order that, being ordinarily obliged to deprive ourselves of some of them in order to have others, we will always choose the best. And since those of the body are the lesser, one can say generally that there is a way to make oneself happy without them. All the same, I am not of the opinion that we need to despise them entirely, nor even that we ought to free ourselves from having the passions. It suffices that we render them subject to reason, and when we have thus tamed them they are sometimes the more useful the more they tend to excess. I would have none more excessive than that which leads me to the respect and veneration I owe you and makes me be, Madame,

Your Highness's very humble and very obedient servant,

Descartes.

ELISABETH TO DESCARTES

[The Hague] 13 September 1645

M. Descartes,

If my conscience were to rest satisfied with the pretexts you offer for my ignorance, as if they were remedies for it, I would be greatly indebted to it, and would be exempted from repenting having so poorly employed the time I have enjoyed the use of reason, which I have had longer than others of my age, since my birth and fortune have forced me to exercise my judgment earlier than most, in order to lead a life that is very trying and free of the prosperity that could prevent me from thinking of myself and also free of the subjection that would have obliged me to rely on the prudence of a governess.

All the same, neither this prosperity nor the flatteries which accompany it are, I believe, absolutely capable of removing the strength of mind of well-born minds and of preventing them from receiving any change of fortune as a philosopher. But I am persuaded that the multitude of accidents which surprise persons governing the public, without giving them the time to examine the most useful expedient, often lead them (no matter how virtuous they are) to perform actions which afterward cause them to repent. And, as you say, repenting is one of the principal obstacles to true happiness. It is true that a habit of esteeming good things according to how they can contribute

289   to contentment, measuring this contentment according to the perfections which give birth to the pleasures, and judging these perfections and these pleasures without passion will protect them from a number of faults. But in order to esteem these goods in this way, one must know them perfectly. And in order to know all those goods among which one must choose in an active life, one would need to possess an infinite science. You say that one cannot fail to be satisfied when one's conscience testifies that one has availed oneself of all the possible precautions. But this circumstance never arrives when one misses one's mark. For one always changes one's mind about the things that remained to be considered. In order to measure contentment in accordance with the perfection causing it, it would be necessary to see clearly the value of each thing, so as to determine whether those that are useful only to us or those that render us still more useful to others are preferable. The latter seem to be esteemed by those with an excess of a humor that torments itself for others, and the former by those who live only for themselves. Nevertheless each of these sorts of persons supports their inclinations with reasons strong enough to make them each continue all their lives in the same way. It is similar with other perfections of the body and of the mind, which a tacit sentiment makes reason endorse. This sentiment ought not to be called a passion because we are born with it. So tell me, if you please, just up to what point one must follow this sentiment (it being a gift of nature) and how to correct it.

I would also like to see you define the passions, in order to know them better.[79] For those who call the passions perturbations of the mind would persuade me that the force of the passions consists only in overwhelming

290   and subjecting reason to them, if experience did not show me that there are

---

79. This demand on Elisabeth's part can reasonably be seen as leading Descartes to write *The Passions of the Soul*. As subsequent letters reveal, Descartes responds by beginning to draft what will become that work. It was first published, in French, in 1649.

passions that do carry us to reasonable actions. But I assure myself that you will shed more light on this subject, when you explicate how the force of the passions renders them even more useful when they are subject to reason.

I will receive this favor in Riswyck in the house of the prince of Orange,[80] where we are moving, since this house is to be cleaned; but for this reason you have no need to change the address of your letters to

Your very affectionate friend at your service,

Elisabeth.

DESCARTES TO ELISABETH

AT 4:290

Egmond , 15 September 1645

Madame,

Your Highness has noted so exactly all the causes which have prevented Seneca from presenting his opinion regarding the sovereign good to us clearly, and your having taken the pain to read his book with such care makes me fear making myself tiresome if I continue here to examine all his chapters in order. Your care in reading makes me defer responding to the difficulty it pleased you to propose to me concerning the means to strengthen the understanding in order to discern the best course in all actions of life. This is why, without ceasing now to continue with Seneca, I will try only to explain my opinion concerning this matter.

291

It seems to me that only two things are required in order to be always disposed to judge well: one is the knowledge of the truth, and the other is the habit of remembering and acquiescing to this knowledge every time the occasion requires. But since only God knows all things perfectly, it is necessary that we content ourselves in knowing those things that are most useful to us.

Among these, the first and the principal one is that there is a God on whom all things depend, whose perfections are infinite, whose power is immense, and whose decrees are infallible. For this teaches us to appreciate all the things that come to us, as they are sent to us expressly by God. Since the true object of love is perfection, when we elevate our mind to considering God as He is, we will find ourselves naturally so inclined to love him that we will draw joy even from our afflictions, in thinking that His will is carried out as we receive them.

292

80. The prince of Orange and Stadholder of the Netherlands at this time was Frederick Henry. Frederick Henry was, incidentally, the brother of Elisabeth's grandmother Juliana. His son William II married Mary Henrietta Stuart, the daughter of Charles I of England.

The second thing it is necessary to know is the nature of our mind, insofar as it subsists without the body and is much more noble than it and capable of enjoying an infinite number of contentments which are not found in this life. For this prevents us from fearing death and detaches our affection from the things of the world so much that we regard all that is in the power of fortune only with contempt.

In this regard, what can also serve greatly is to judge in a dignified way the works of God, and to have an idea of the vast extent of the universe, as I have tried to present it in the third book of my *Principles*. For when we imagine that beyond the heavens there is nothing but imaginary spaces, and that all the heavens are made only for the service of the earth and the earth only for man, this makes us inclined to think that this earth is our principal home and this life our best. Instead of knowing the perfections that are truly in us, we attribute to other creatures imperfections they do not have in order to elevate ourselves above them. And entering into an impertinent presumption, we want to be counsel to God and to take charge with him of conducting the world; and this causes an infinity of anxieties and annoyances.

293   After having thus recalled the goodness of God, the immortality of our souls and the greatness of the universe, there is also one more truth the knowledge of which seems to me quite useful. This is that, even though each of us is a person separate from others and, by consequence, with interests that are in some manner distinct from those of the rest of the world, one must, all the same, think that one does not know how to subsist alone and that one is, in effect, one part of the universe and, more particularly even, one part of this earth, one part of this state, and this society, and this family, to which one is joined by his home, by his oath, by his birth. It is always necessary to prefer the interests of the whole, of which one is a part, to those of one's person in particular, though with measure and discretion. For one would be wrong to expose oneself to a great evil in order to procure only a small good for one's parents or one's country. If a man is worth more on his own than all the rest of his city, he would not be right to sacrifice himself to save it. But if one related everything to oneself, one would not fear harming other men greatly when one wanted to take something small for oneself. One would have no true friends, no faithfulness, and in general no virtue. On the other hand, in considering oneself as a part of the public, one takes pleasure in acting well toward everyone, and one does not fear even exposing one's life for the service of others when the occasion occurs. That is, one would lose one's soul, if one could, in order to save others. And

294   so this consideration is the source and origin of all the most heroic actions men do. As for those who expose themselves to death for reasons of vanity, because they hope to be praised, or of stupidity, because they do not appre-

hend the danger, I believe that they are more to be pitied than to be prized. But when someone does expose himself to death because he thinks it is his duty, or better, when he suffers some other evil in order to bring about good to others—even if he perhaps does not think upon reflection that he did it because he owes more to the public of which he is a part than to himself in particular—he does it all the same in virtue of this consideration, which is confused in his mind. One is naturally drawn to have it, when one knows and loves God as one should. For then, abandoning oneself completely to His will, one divests oneself of one's proper interests, and one has no other passion than that of doing what one believes would be agreeable to Him. In consequence of which one has satisfactions of the mind and contentments that are incomparably more valuable than all the little passing joys that depend on the senses.

Outside of these truths, which concern all our actions in general, it is necessary also to know several others, which relate more particularly to each one of them. The principal ones seem to me to be those that I noted in my last letter. That is, that all our passions represent to us the goods they incite   295
us to seek as much greater than they actually are, and that the pleasures of the body are never as lasting as those of the mind, or as large when we possess them as they appear when we hope for them. This we must note carefully, so that when we sense ourselves moved by some passion, we suspend our judgment until the passion abates, and so that we do not allow ourselves to be easily deceived by the false appearance of the goods of this world.

To this I cannot add anything else except that it is also necessary to examine in particular all the mores of the places where one lives in order to know just how far they must be followed. Even if we cannot have certain demonstrations of everything, we ought nevertheless to take a side and embrace the opinions which seem to us the most true, concerning all those things which come into play, in order that, when there is a question of action, we will never be irresolute. For it is irresolution alone that causes regret and repentance.

For the rest, I have said before that besides the knowledge of the truth, habituation is also required for being always disposed to judge well. For since we cannot always be attentive to the same thing—even though we have been convinced of some truth by reason of some clear and evident perceptions—we will be able to be turned, afterward, to believing false appearances, if we do not, through a long and frequent meditation, imprint it   296
sufficiently in our mind so that it turns into habit. In this sense, the Schools are right to say that the virtues are habits, for one rarely makes a mistake because one doesn't have theoretical knowledge of what to do, but only because one doesn't have practical knowledge, that is to say, because one doesn't have a firm habit of believing it. And so, while I here examine these

truths, I also augment my habit of believing them, I am particularly obligated to your Highness for permitting me this exchange, and there is no way that I could better employ my leisure than in expressing that I am, Madame,

Your Highness's very humble and very obedient servant,

Descartes.

When I ended this letter, I received that from your Highness of the thirteenth, but I found so many things to consider there that I dare not undertake to respond off the cuff, and I assure your Highness that I will much prefer to take a little time to think on it.

AT 4:301

ELISABETH TO DESCARTES

[Riswyck] 30 September [1645]

M.Descartes

302   Even though your observations on Seneca's attitude toward the sovereign good have made me profit from reading that work more than I would have known how to on my own, I am not the least bit sorry to exchange them for truths as necessary as those which include the means of strengthening the understanding in order to discern which is the best of all the actions one can take in life, on the condition that you still add the explication my stupidity is in need of, that concerning the usefulness of those pieces of knowledge you set out.

The knowledge of the existence of God and his attributes can console us from the mishaps which come to us from the ordinary course of nature and from the order He has established there, such as losing one's well-being [*le bien*] in a storm, or health by an infection of the air, or friends through death. But it cannot console us from those mishaps that are brought upon us by other men. For it seems to us that the will of these men is entirely free, as we have nothing but faith alone to persuade us that God cares to rule these wills and that He has determined the fate of each person before the creation of the world.

The knowledge of the immortality of the soul, along with the knowledge that it is much more noble than the body, is as capable of making us seek death as of making us despise it, since we cannot doubt that we will live more happily exempt from the maladies and passions of the body. And I am surprised that those who claimed to be persuaded by this truth and lived without the revealed law preferred a painful life to an advantageous death.

The knowledge of the great extent of the universe, which you have 303   shown in the third book of your *Principles*, serves to detach our affections from that which we see in it; but it also separates the particular providence, which is the foundation of theology, from the idea we have of God.

The consideration that we are part of a whole of which we must seek the advantage is, surely enough, the source of all generous actions; but I find many difficulties in the conditions which you prescribe for them. How is one to measure the evils that one brings upon oneself for the sake of the public against the good which will accrue to the public, without the evils' seeming greater to us inasmuch as our idea of them is more distinct? And which measure will we have for comparing those things that are not known to us equally well, such as our own merit and that of those with whom we live? A naturally arrogant person will always tip the balance in his favor, and a modest one will esteem himself less than he is worth.

In order to profit from the particular truths of which you speak, it is necessary to know exactly all the passions we feel and the prejudices we have, most of which are imperceptible. In observing the customs of the countries where we are, we sometimes find some very unreasonable ones that it is necessary to follow in order to avoid even greater inconveniences. Since I have been here, I have experienced a very trying illustration of this truth. For I was hoping to profit from this stay in the country by having more time to employ in study, and I have found here, without comparison, less leisure than I ever had at The Hague, because of the distractions of those who don't know what to do with themselves. And even though it is very unjust of them to deprive me of real goods so that I might give them imaginary ones, I am constrained to abide by the impertinent established laws of civility so that I do not acquire any enemies. Since I began writing this letter I have been interrupted more than seven times by these annoying visits. It is an excess of goodness [on your part] which guarantees that my letters will not suffer a parallel predicament on your end and which obliges you to want to solidify my habit of receiving your thoughts by relaying them to such an unruly person as

Your very affectionate friend at your service,
Elisabeth.

DESCARTES TO ELISABETH

Egmond, 6 October 1645

Madame,

I have sometimes asked myself a question: whether it is better to be gay and content, in imagining the goods one possesses to be greater and more valuable than they are and not knowing or stopping to consider those one lacks, or to have more consideration and knowledge in order to know the just value of the one and the other, and to become sadder. If I were to think that the sovereign good consisted of joy, I would not doubt at all that one should try to make oneself joyful, no matter at what price it comes, and I would approve of the brutality of those who drown their sorrows in wine or dull them with tobacco. But I distinguish between the sovereign good, which consists in the exercise of virtue, or what is the same thing, in the possession of all the goods whose acquisition depends on our free will, and the satisfaction of mind which follows this acquisition. This is why, seeing that it is a greater perfection to know the truth, even though it is to our disadvantage, than not to know it, I admit that it would be better to be less gay and to have more knowledge. It is not common that when one is more gay, one has a more satisfied mind. On the contrary, great joys are ordinarily somber and serious, and it is only the mediocre and passing ones that are accompanied by laughter. Thus, I do not approve of trying to deceive oneself in going over false imaginings. For all the pleasure arising in that way can only touch the surface of the soul, which, at the same time, feels an inner bitterness in perceiving that they are false. Even if it could happen that the soul is so continually diverted elsewhere that it never perceives they are false, it would not because of this diversion enjoy the true happiness which is in question, for this must depend on our conduct and could not come from fortune.

But as one can have different but equally true considerations, some of which some lead us to be content, and others on the contrary prevent us from being so, it seems to me that prudence demands that we dwell principally on those which give us satisfaction. Almost all the things in the world are such that we can regard them from a side which makes them appear good and from another which makes us notice defects. And I believe that if one must make use of one's skill in something, it is principally to know how to look at them from the angle which makes them appear most to our advantage, as long as this does not involve our deceiving ourselves.

So, when your Highness notes the causes which have allowed her more leisure to cultivate her reason than many others of her age, if it pleases her also to consider how much she has profited from this compared with others, I am assured she will have reason to be content. I do not see why she likes better to compare herself to those who give her cause to complain, than to those who can give her some satisfaction. The constitution of our nature is such that our mind needs a lot of rest so that it can usefully devote a few moments to seeking the truth, and it will be numbed instead of polished if it is applied too much in study, and so we ought not to measure the time we were able to use in instructing ourselves by the number of hours we have to ourselves. Rather, it seems to me, we should measure it by the example of what we see commonly occurring with others, as being a mark of the ordinary comportment of the human mind.

It seems to me as well that one has no reason to repent when one has done what one judges to be the best at the time that one had to be resolved to act, even if afterward, in rethinking the matter with more leisure, one judges that one was wrong. But one would sooner repent if one had done something against one's conscience, even if one discovered afterward that one did better than one would have thought. For we are responsible only for our thoughts, and human nature is such that we do not know everything or always judge so well off the cuff as when we have a lot of time to deliberate.

For the rest, even if the vanity, which makes one have a better opinion of oneself than one should, is a vice which belongs only to weak and base souls, this is not to say that stronger and more generous ones should despise themselves. But one must do justice to oneself in discovering one's perfections as much as one's faults. Even if decency prevents one from making them public, it does not prevent us from being conscious of them. 308

Finally, even if we do not have an infinite science so that we can know perfectly all the goods we must choose among in the diverse occasions of life, one must, it seems to me, content oneself in having a mediocre knowledge of those things most necessary, such as those which I enumerated in my last letter.

In it I already declared my opinion concerning the difficulty your Highness proposes, that is, whether those who relate everything to themselves are more reasonable than those who torment themselves for others. For if we think only of ourselves alone, we can enjoy only the goods that are particular to us. On the other hand, if we consider ourselves as a part of some other body, we participate as well in those goods held in common, without being deprived of any of those that are proper to ourselves. It is not the same with the evils. For according to philosophy, evil is nothing real but only a privation. When we become sad because of some evil that has befallen our friends, in doing so we do not participate in the defect in which this evil consists. And no matter what sadness or what pain we have on such an occasion, it cannot be so great as the interior satisfaction which always accompanies good actions and principally those which proceed from a pure affection for others and which we do not relate to ourselves, that is, to the Christian virtue which we call charity. Thus, one can, even in crying and taking a great deal of trouble, have more pleasure than when one laughs or rests. 309

It is easy to prove that the pleasure of the soul in which true happiness consists is not inseparable from the gaiety and ease of the body, as much from the example of tragedies,[81] which please us more the more they excite sadness in us, as from those of the exercises of the body, such as hunting, tennis, and other similar exercises, which do not cease to be agreeable even if they are very difficult. We even find that often fatigue and difficulty augment pleasure. The cause of the contentment the soul receives from these exercises consists in that they make it notice the strength, or the skill, or some other perfection of the body to which it is joined. But the contentment that it has from crying upon seeing some pitiable and disastrous action represented in the theater comes principally from its seeming to it that it is doing something virtuous in having compassion for the afflicted. And generally, the soul is pleased in feeling itself moved by passions, no matter what nature they are, so long as it remains in control.

310   But it is necessary that I examine these passions more particularly to be able to define them, which will be easier for me here than were I to write to someone else. For your Highness, having taken the trouble to read the treatise I sketched out before concerning the nature of animals,[82] knows already how I conceive diverse impressions to be formed in their brain. Some are formed by exterior objects which move their senses, others by the interior dispositions of the body, or by the vestiges of the preceding impressions which remain in the memory, or by the agitation of the spirits which come from the heart, or in a human, by the action of the soul, which has some force for changing the impressions in the brain, as, reciprocally, these impressions have the force to excite thoughts in the soul that do not depend on its will. From all this it follows that one can generally call passions all the thoughts that are excited in the soul in this way without the concurrence of its will, and by consequence, without any action coming from it, but only from the impressions in the brain. For everything that is not an action is a passion. But one ordinarily reserves this word for the thoughts that are caused by some particular agitation of the spirits. Those that come from exterior objects or even the interior dispositions of the body, such as the perceptions of colors, sounds, odors, light, thirst, pain, and similar ones, are
311   called sensations, some external, some internal. Those which depend only on what the preceding impressions left in the memory and the ordinary

81. See above, note 45, for Descartes' other appeals to the theater.

82. It is unclear what work Descartes is referring to here. The *Principles* projects a treatise on animal physiology, but it is unlikely he would have something new to present to Elisabeth so soon after the publication of that work. In letters to Père Guillaume Gibieuf (19 January 1642, AT 3:479, CSMK 203–4) and to Mersenne (November or December 1632, AT 1:263, CSMK 40, and 20 February 1639, AT 2:525, CSMK 134) he refers to work he has done on animal physiology.

agitation of the spirits are dreams, whether they come while asleep or when one is awake, and the soul, determining itself to nothing on its own, follows nonchalantly the impressions found in the brain. But when the soul uses its will to determine itself to some thought which is not only intelligible but also imaginable, this thought makes a new impression in the brain, and this thought is not a passion in it, but an action which is properly called imagination. Finally, when the ordinary course of the spirits is such that it regularly excites thoughts that are sad or gay, or other similar ones, we do not attribute this to passion but to the nature or humor of those in which they are excited. This makes us say that this man is of a sad nature, this other of a gay humor, etc. There remain only those thoughts which come from some particular agitation of the spirits, and of which we sense the effects in the soul itself, which are properly called passions.[83]

It is true that we hardly ever have any thoughts that do not depend on several of the causes that I just distinguished. But we denominate them in accordance with their principal cause or their principal aspect, and this makes many confuse the sensation of pain with the passion of sadness, and the sensation of tickling [*chatouillement*] with the passion of joy, which they also call voluptuousness or pleasure, and sensations of thirst or hunger with the desires to drink and to eat, which are passions. For ordinarily the causes of pain also agitate the spirits in the manner that is required for exciting sadness, and those that make us feel some tickling agitate them in the manner required for exciting joy, and so on for the others.[84]

312

We also sometimes confuse the inclinations or the habits that dispose us to some passion with the passion itself, though these are nevertheless easy to distinguish. For example, let's say that, in a town to which the enemies have just laid siege, the first judgment the inhabitants make of the evil that might come to them is an action of their soul, not a passion. Even if similar such judgments are made by several townspeople, they will not, all the same, be equally moved, but rather some will be more so, others less, according to whether they have more or less of a habit or inclination toward fear. Before their soul receives the emotion in which alone the passion consists, it is nec-

83. The discussion in *Passions of the Soul* aa.17–26 parallels Descartes' discussion here.

84. As Descartes notes in *Passions of the Soul* a.51, bodily motions are insufficient to distinguish passions from one another. In a.52 he rejects a taxonomy of the passions by their objects per se in favor of a system which distinguishes them by "the different ways they can harm or benefit us or, generally, be important to us" (AT 11:372). He then goes on, following on his point in the next paragraph here, to stipulate that the use of the passions, kept separate from the principle of their enumeration, is to "dispose the soul to will the things nature tells us are useful and to persist in this volition" (ibid.)

essary that it make this judgment, or better, without judging, that it conceive at least the danger and imprint the image of it in the brain (which is made by another action which we call imagining). It is also necessary that, by this same means, it determine the spirits which go from the brain via the nerves to the muscles, to enter into those muscles which tighten the openings of the heart. This tightening retards the circulation of the blood, from which it follows that the whole body becomes pale, cold, and trembling, and the new spirits which come from the heart to the brain are agitated in such a way that they cannot aid in forming any other images but those which excite in the soul the passion of fear. All of these things follow one another so closely that it seems that there is only one operation.[85] And so with the all the other passions there is some particular agitation in the spirits that come from the heart.

There you have what I was thinking of writing to your Highness eight days ago. My plan was to add a particular explication of all the passions, but having found it difficult to enumerate them, I was constrained to let the postman leave without my letter, and having in the meantime received that which your Highness has done me the honor of writing me, I had a new occasion to respond. I am thus obliged to leave to another time this examination of the passions, so that I might say here that all the reasons that prove the existence of God and his being the first and immutable cause of all the effects which do not depend on the free will of men, in the same way prove, it seems to me, that He is also the cause of all the effects that do depend on it. For we cannot demonstrate He exists except by considering Him as a supremely perfect being. He would not be supremely perfect if something could happen in the world that did not come entirely from Him. It is true that faith alone teaches us what grace is, by which God elevates us to a supernatural true happiness. But philosophy alone is sufficient for knowing that the slightest thought could not enter into the mind of man unless God wants and has wanted from all eternity that thought to enter there. And the distinction of the Schools between universal and particular causes has no place here. The sun, for example, is the universal cause of all the flowers, but the sun is not the reason that tulips differ from roses. The production of tulips also depends on some other particular causes that are not subordinate to the sun. But God is such a universal cause of everything that He is in the same way the total cause, and thus nothing can happen without His will.

85. In the *Passions of the Soul*, Descartes tries to separate these operations, treating separately the physiology proper to each passion (aa.96–106), the explanation for why certain physiological motions are associated with the passions they are (aa.107–11), and the expressions of the passions (aa.113–35).

It is also true that the knowledge of the immortality of the soul and of the felicities of which it will be capable outside of this life, could give reasons to exit this life to those who are weary of it, if they were assured that they would enjoy all these felicities afterward. But no reason so assures them, and there is only the false philosophy of Hegesias, whose book was prohibited by Ptolemy [86] and was the cause that many killed themselves after having read it, as it tried to argue that this life is evil. The true teaching, altogether on the contrary, is that even among the saddest accidents and the most pressing pains one can always be content, so long as one knows how to use one's reason.

As for the extent of the universe, I do not see how, in considering it, one is invited to separate particular providence from the idea that we have of God. For God is completely different from finite powers. Finite powers can be used up, and seeing that they are employed to many great effects, we are right to judge that it is not likely that they will extend just as well to the lesser ones. But the more we judge the works of God to be greater, the more we notice the infinity of his power, and the more this infinity is better known to us, the more are we assured that it extends to all the particular actions of men.

I also do not believe that by this particular providence of God, which your Highness has said is the foundation of theology, you understand some change that comes to His decrees on the occasion of the actions that depend on our free will. Theology does not admit such a change. When it demands that we pray to God, this is not so that we may instruct him as to what we need, or so that we may try to move him so that he changes something in the order established from all eternity by His providence. Both would be blameworthy. It is only so that we might obtain what he has wanted from all eternity to be obtained from our prayers. I think that all the theologians are in agreement here, even the Arminians,[87] who seem to be those who defer the most to free will.

I confess that it is difficult to measure exactly just to what degree reason ordains that we be interested in the public good. But also this is not a matter in which it is necessary to be very exact. It suffices to satisfy one's conscience, and one can in this matter give a lot to one's inclination. For

---

86. Hegesias of Magnesia (c. 300 BCE) was a rhetorician and historian. This story is related in Cicero's *Tusculan Disputations* 1.83.

87. The Arminians, or Remonstrants, a breakaway sect from Calvinist doctrine, formed by Jacob Arminius (1560–1609), held a doctrine that put the free will of man at the center of their theological position. The position was condemned at the Calvinist Synod at Dordrecht in 1619 and branded the "Remonstrant heresy."

God has so established the order of things and conjoined men together in so tight a society that even if each person related himself wholly to himself, and had no charity for others, he would not ordinarily fail to work for them in everything that would be in his power, so long as he used prudence, and

317   principally if he lived in a time when mores were not corrupted. And aside from this, as it is a higher and more glorious thing to do good to others than to procure goods for oneself, so are the greatest souls those which have the most inclination to it and who take the least account of the goods they possess. Only the weak and base esteem themselves more than they ought and are like little vessels which three drops of water can fill. I know that your Highness is not among these. Whereas one can excite base souls to take pains for others only by making them see that they can draw a profit for themselves by doing so, it is necessary, for the interest of your Highness, to represent to her that she could not be useful to those for whom she cares for very long if she were to neglect herself, and to beg her to take care of her health. This is what does, Madame,

Your Highness's very humble and obedient servant,
Descartes.

AT 4:320

ELISABETH TO DESCARTES

The Hague, 28 October [1645]

321   M. Descartes,

Since you have given such good reasons demonstrating that it is better to know truths to our disadvantage than to be agreeably deceived, and that only in those cases which admit of different but equally true considerations ought we to rest with those which will bring us more contentment, I am surprised that you want me to compare myself to those of my age with respect to something unknown to me rather than with respect to something I can't possibly be ignorant of, even though the latter would be more to my advantage. There is nothing which could clarify for me whether I have profited more from cultivating my reason than others have in doing what they are moved to do, and I have no doubt that if I relaxed for as much time as my body requires, there would still be enough time to move me beyond what I am. If we measured the scope of the human mind by the example of the common people, it would be of very small extension, because most people use their capacity for thought only in matters regarding the senses. Even among those who apply themselves to study, there are few who use anything but their memory or who have the truth as the goal of their labor. So if there is a vice in my taking no pleasure in considering whether I have gained more than these people, I do not think that it is an excess of humility, which is just as harmful as presumption, though not as common. We are more inclined to fail to recognize our faults than our perfections. In running from repentance for the mistakes we have made as if it were an enemy of our felicity, we run the risk of losing the desire to correct ourselves. The risk is particularly great when some passion has produced the mistakes, because we naturally love to be moved by our passions and to follow their movements, and only the inconveniences proceeding from this course teach us that such mistakes can be harmful. This is, in my judgment, what makes tragedies more pleasing the more they excite sadness, because we know that the sadness will not be violent enough to carry us to extravagances or lasting enough to corrupt our health.

But this will not suffice at all to support the doctrine contained in one of your earlier letters—that the passions are the more useful the more they tend to excess, so long as they are subject to reason. It seems that the passions can never be both excessive and subject to reason. But I think you will elucidate this doubt in taking the trouble to describe how this particular agitation of the spirits serves to form all the passions we experience and in what way it corrupts reason. I would not dare to ask this of you if I did not know that you never leave a work imperfect and that in undertaking to teach a stupid person, such as myself, you are prepared for all the inconveniences that brings you.

It is this which makes me continue and say to you that the reasons which prove the existence of God and that he is the immutable cause of all the effects which do not depend on our free will do not persuade me that he is just as much the cause of those which do depend on it. From his sovereign perfection it follows necessarily that he could be this cause, and that he could have never given free will to human beings. But since we feel ourselves to have it, it seems that it is repugnant to common sense to think it dependent on God in its operations as well as in its being.

If one is well persuaded that the soul is immortal, it is impossible to doubt that it will not be more happy after its separation from the body (which is the origin of all the displeasures of life, just as the soul is the origin of all great contentments), despite the opinion of M. Digby,[88] whose teacher[89] (whose works you have seen) made him believe in the necessity of

322

323

---

88. See above, note 48.

89. While he was at Oxford Digby was under the tutelage of Thomas Allen (1542–1632), the mathematician. Allen's works are all in manuscript form, so it is not clear how Descartes would have seen them. Allen was a colleague of Thomas Harriot (1560–1621). Harriot's *Artes analyticae praxis* was published posthumously in 1631, and Descartes might well have read that work. Elisabeth might be conflating the two here.

purgatory, by persuading him that the passions, which have held dominion over reason during the life of a man, leave some vestiges in the soul after the death of the body. These passions torment the soul all the more in that they find no means of satisfying themselves in a substance so pure. I do not see how this accords with its immateriality. But I have no doubt that even though life is not bad in itself, it ought to be abandoned for a condition which we will know to be better.

By that special providence which is the foundation of theology, I understand that by which God has for all eternity prescribed means so strange as His incarnation for a part of creation that is so inconsiderable compared with the rest, as you represent this world in your physics. He has done this in order to be thereby glorified, which seems a very undignified end for the creator of this grand universe. But I have here been presenting more the objection of our theologians than my own, having always believed it very impertinent for finite persons to judge the final cause of the actions of an infinite being.

You do not think that we need an exact knowledge of how much we should reasonably interest ourselves for the public, because insofar as each person relates everything to himself, he will also work for others if he is served by prudence. Of the whole of this prudence I only ask of you a part. For in possessing it, one could not fail to do justice to others and to oneself. A lack of prudence can cause a person at liberty sometimes to lose the means to serve her country because she abandons herself too easily for her interest, and a timid person to lose herself along with her country, for failing to risk her good and her fortune for her conservation.

I have always been of a condition which rendered my life quite useless to persons I love, but I seek its conservation with much more care since I have had the good fortune to know you, because you have shown me the means to live more happily than I did before. I am only lacking the satisfaction of being able to show you how much this obligation is felt by

Your affectionate friend at your service,

Elisabeth.

AT 4:330

DESCARTES TO ELISABETH

Egmond, 3 November 1645

Madame,

I encounter good reasoning so infrequently, not only in the conversations I have in this desert, but also in the books I consult, that I cannot read what is in the letters from your Highness without drawing from them a feeling of extraordinary joy. I find your reasoning so strong that I would prefer to admit I am beaten than to undertake to resist it. For even though the comparison that your Highness refuses to make to her benefit can be verified well enough by experience, it is all the same a very praiseworthy virtue to judge favorably of others, and it accords so well with the generosity which prevents you from wanting to measure the capability of the human mind by the example of the common man, that I cannot fail to esteem extremely highly both the one and the other.

I also would not dare to contradict what your Highness writes about repentance, seeing as it is a Christian virtue, and one which serves to make one correct oneself, not only of mistakes committed voluntarily but also of those made through ignorance, as when some passion interfered with our knowing the truth.

I know well that the sadness of tragedies would not please as it does, if we feared that it would become so excessive that we would be inconvenienced by it. But when I said that the passions are the more useful the more they incline toward excess, I meant to speak only of those which are altogether good, which is why I added that they must be subject to reason. For there are two sorts of excess, one which, insofar as it changes the nature of the thing and thereby makes something good bad, prevents it from remaining subject to reason; the other which, insofar as it augments only its quantity, thereby makes something good better than it is. Thus, an excess of daring is temerity when it goes beyond the limits of reason. But when it does not pass those limits, it can still have another excess, which consists in being accompanied by neither irresolution nor fear.

I have thought over the past days of the number and order of all the passions, in order to be able to examine their nature in more detail. But I have not yet digested my opinions concerning this subject enough to dare to write them to your Highness, and I will not neglect to acquit myself of them as soon as it is possible for me.

As far as free will is concerned, I confess that in thinking only of ourselves we cannot but take it to be independent. But when we think of the infinite power of God, we cannot but believe that all things depend on Him and, by consequence, that our free will is not exempt from this. For it implies a contradiction to say that God created men of such a nature that the actions of their will do not depend on His. For this is the same as saying that his power is at the same time finite and infinite: finite since there is something that does not depend on it at all, and infinite since He was able to create this independent thing. But, just as the knowledge of the existence of God

331

332

333 ought not to hinder us from being assured of our free will, since we experience it and feel it within ourselves, so too that of our free will ought not to make us doubt the existence of God. For the independence that we experience and feel in us and that suffices for rendering our actions praiseworthy or blameworthy is not incompatible with a dependence that is of another nature, according to which all things are subject to God.

As for the state of the soul after this life, I have much less knowledge of it than M. Digby. For leaving aside what faith teaches us, I confess that, by natural reason alone, we can make many conjectures to our benefit and have some high hopes, but no assurance. And since the same natural reason teaches us also that we always have more goods in this life than evils, and that we ought never to leave the certain for the uncertain, it seems to me to teach us that we ought not to truly fear death, but also that we ought never to seek it out.

I do not need to respond to the objection that the theologians might make, concerning the vast extent that I attributed to the universe, since your Highness has already responded for me. I add only that, if this vast extent could render the mysteries of our religion less believable, the size that the astronomers have always attributed to the heavens ought to be
334 able to do the same, since they have considered the heavens so great that the earth is, by comparison, only a point. And yet this objection is never leveled at them.

As for the rest, if prudence were mistress of events, I do not doubt that your Highness would achieve all she wanted to undertake. But all men would have to be perfect sages in order to for us be assured of what they will do given the knowledge of what they ought to do. Or we would need to know the particular humor of all those with whom we have something to work out. Even that would not be enough, since they have, apart from this, their free will, whose movements are known only by God. Since we ordinarily judge what others will do by what we would want to do if we were in their place, it often happens that ordinary and mediocre minds, being similar to those with whom they interact, penetrate better into their motives, and succeed more easily in what they undertake, than do those who are more refined. For the latter interact only with those who are greatly inferior in knowledge and in prudence and judge altogether differently than they do in these matters. This ought to console your Highness when fortune is opposed to your plans. I pray to God that he favors them, and I am, Madame,

Your Highness's very humble and very obedient servant,
Descartes.

The Hague, 30 November 1645

M. Descartes,

You must be surprised that, after you told me that my reasoning does not appear altogether ridiculous to you, I have waited so long to take advantage of your responses. It is with shame that I confess to you the cause, since it has reversed all that your lessons had seemed to establish in my mind. I thought that a strong resolution to seek true happiness only in things that depend on my will would render me less sensitive to those things that come to me from elsewhere, before the folly of one of my brothers apprised me of my weakness. His folly has troubled the health of my body and the tranquility of my soul more than all the misfortunes that have already come my way. If you take the trouble to read the newspaper, you could not fail to know that he has fallen into the hands of a certain group of people who have more 336 hatred for our house than affection for their religion, and he has let himself be taken in by their traps to such a degree as to change his religion and make himself a Roman Catholic, without having made the least grimace which might have persuaded the very credulous that he did so for the sake of his conscience.[90] I must see someone whom I loved with as much tenderness as I know how to have, abandoned to the scorn of the world and the loss of his soul (according to my belief). If you did not have more charity than bigotry, it would be impertinent of me to speak with you on this matter. This would still not excuse me, if I were not in the habit of telling you all my faults, as if to that person in the world most capable of correcting them for me.

I confess to you as well that even though I do not understand how the independence of our will is no less contrary to the idea we have of God than its dependence is to its freedom, it is impossible for me to square them, it being as impossible for the will to be at the same time free and attached to the decrees of Providence as for divine power to be both infinite and limited at once. I do not see at all the compatibility between them of which you speak, or how this dependence of the will can have a different nature than its freedom, if you do not take the trouble to teach this to me.

With regard to contentment, I confess that the present possession of it is much more assured than the expectation of it in the future, no matter

90. Elisabeth is here adverting to the conversion of her brother Edward to Catholicism. His conversion allowed him to marry Anne of Gonzaga, princess of Mantua, an alliance no doubt helpful to the exiled Palatine house. Elisabeth herself refused to convert in order to effect a marriage between herself and Wladislaw IV of Poland.

how good the reason on which that expectation is founded. But I am having
337   trouble persuading myself that we will always have more goods in life than
evils, since it takes more to make the former than to make the latter; that is,
since man has more occasions on which to receive displeasure than pleasure,
since it takes an infinite number of mistakes to get one truth, since there are
so many means to go astray for every one which takes one along the right
path, and since there are so many persons who have the intent and the power
to harm and few who have either one or the other to help. Finally, all that
depends on the will and the course of the rest of the world is capable of un-
settling one. And according to your own belief, nothing but what depends
absolutely on our will is sufficient to give us a real and constant satisfaction.

As for prudence in matters that concern human society, I do not expect
an infallible rule, but I would be very pleased to see those you would suggest
to one who, in living only for himself, in whatever profession he might have,
would not leave off working for others also, if I dare to ask you to shed more
light, after having so poorly employed that which you have already given to
Your very affectionate friend at your service,
Elisabeth.

AT 4:339

ELISABETH TO DESCARTES

[The Hague] 27 December [1645]

M. Descartes,

The son of the late Professor Schooten[91] today gave me the letter[92] you
had written me in his favor, in order to prevent me from favoring his rival. I
told him that not only had I no intention of harming him, but I was willing
to help him as much as I could, since you had charged me to like him and
be receptive to him. He then asked me to recommend him to the curators.[93]
340   Knowing only two, M. de Wimenom and M. Bewen, and the latter being
out of town, I spoke to the first, who promised to work for M. Schooten,
even though he had intended to abolish this post as superfluous. This seems

91. Frans van Schooten (1615–60) was a candidate for a professorship in mathematics and
architecture at the University of Leiden, a post left open by the death of his father. In 1643,
Schooten became his father's assistant. Schooten had met Descartes in 1637 and was a great
promoter of Cartesian geometry.

92. We do not have this letter.

93. Elisabeth is here referring to the University of Leiden. In 1645 there were three curators:
Gerard Schaep, master of Kortenhoef, Amelis Van den Bouckhorst, master at Wimmenum (Wimenom, above) and Cornelius van Beveren (Bewen, above), master at Strevelshouck.

to be the only difficulty which he would have to combat, his competitor not being considered to be anywhere near him, except by a few scrupulous men who fear that he would introduce the errors of his Arminian religion into his lessons on mathematics. If he had given me the time to ask him to come see me so that he might learn the success of my recommendations, I would have had the means of informing him of some things which I think ought to serve him in his efforts. But he was in such great haste to leave that I was forced to follow him all the way to the door in order to ask him to whom I should address my recommendations for him. I know that if he had considered me only as your friend, without thinking of titles that embarrass those who are not accustomed to them, he would have acted otherwise, as then he would have certainly judged that in a matter that I know you to favor, I would act with more than ordinary care. I ask you to believe that I will never lose an occasion to show you in deeds that I am truly, M. Descartes,

Yours very affectionately at your service,
Elisabeth.

27 December

I am afraid that you have not received my last letter of the thirtieth of last month, since you have not made any mention of it.[94] I would be upset if it came into the hands of one of these critics who condemn as heresies all the doubts that can be raised about received opinions.

341

DESCARTES TO ELISABETH

AT 4:351

Egmond, January 1646

Madame,

I cannot deny that I was surprised to learn that your Highness was annoyed to the point of having her health ill affected by a thing that most of the world would find good, and that many sound reasons would render excusable to others. For all those of my religion (who are, without doubt, the greater number in Europe) are obliged to approve of it, even if they were to see circumstances and apparent motives there that were blameworthy. We believe that God uses diverse means to attract souls to him, and though some enter the cloister with a bad intention, they still lead a very saintly life there afterward. As for those of another faith, if they speak ill of such a person, one

94. Presumably, she means that he did not mention it in the lost letter conveyed through Schooten.

352   can take issue with their judgment, for, as in all matters involving differing parties, it is impossible to please some without displeasing others. If they consider that they would not be of the religion they are had they or their fathers or their grandfathers not left the Roman church, they will not have reason to mock or to call inconstant those who leave their church.

As regards the wisdom of these times, it is true that those who have fortune resting with them are right to remain near her and to join their forces together so that she does not escape. But those whose home she has fled are, it seems to me, not at all ill served in directing themselves to follow different paths, so that even if not everyone can find her, there will be at least someone who meets up with her. At the same time, since we think that each one of them has several resources, having friends in different places, they make a more considerable search party than if they were all to engage as one. This prevents me from imagining that the authors of this advice intended to harm your house by it. But I do not pretend that my reasons could abate the resentment of your Highness. I hope only that time will diminish it before this letter is presented to you, and I would fear refreshing it if I were to elaborate more on this subject.

353   This is why I move to the difficulty your Highness proposed concerning free will, the dependence and liberty of which I will try to explain by a comparison. If a king who has prohibited duels and who knows very certainly that two gentlemen in his kingdom, living in different towns, are quarreling and are so worked up against one another that nothing could prevent them from fighting one another if they were to meet; if, I say, this king orders one of them to go on a certain day toward the town where the other is, and he also orders the other to go on the same day toward the place where the first is, knowing quite assuredly that they would not fail to meet each other and to fight each other, and thus to violate his prohibition, he thereby does not compel them. His knowledge, and even his will to determine them there in this manner, do not alter the fact that they fight one another just as voluntarily and just as freely as they would have done if he had known nothing of it, and it was by some other occasion that they had met. They can also justly be punished, since they violated the prohibition. So what a king can do in this matter concerning the free actions of his subjects, God, who has infinite prescience and power, does infallibly concerning all those of men. Before He sent us into this world, He knew exactly what would be the inclinations of our will. It is He Himself who put them in us. It is also He who disposed all

354   the other things outside of us, in order to bring it about that such objects are presented to our senses at such and such a time, on the occasion of which he knew our free will would determine us to such and such a thing. And he wills

things this way, but he does not will thereby that our will be constrained to choose a certain way. As one can distinguish in this king two different degrees of will, the one by which he willed these gentlemen to fight one another, since he made it so they would meet, and the other by which he did not will it, since he prohibited duels, so do the theologians distinguish in God an absolute and independent will by which he wills that all things happen such as they happen, and another which is relative, and which is related to the merit or demerit of men, according to which he wills that they obey his laws.

I must also distinguish two sorts of goods to defend what I wrote before (that is, that in this life we always have more goods than evils) against your Highness's objection to me concerning all the inconveniences of life. When we consider the idea of the good to serve as a rule for our actions, we take it to consist in all the perfection that can be in that thing which we call "good," and we compare it to a straight line, which is unique among an infinity of curves to which we compare evils. It is in this sense that the Philosophers are accustomed to saying that *bonum est ex integra causa, malum ex quouis defectu.*[95] But when we consider the goods and the evils that can exist in one and the same thing to find out how we should value it, as I did when I spoke of how we should value this life, we take the good to consist in anything that one can find advantageous, and one calls evil only that from which one can receive some inconvenience. Thus, when one offers work to someone, he considers from one side the honor and the profit he can attain from it as goods, and from the other side the pain, the peril, the loss of time, and other such things as evils. Comparing these evils with these goods, according to which he finds the former greater or lesser than the latter, he accepts it or refuses it. So what made me say earlier that there are always more good things than evil ones in this life is that I think we ought to make very little of all the things which are outside of us and do not depend on our free will, in comparison with those which do depend on it. The latter we can always render good when we know how to use our free will well. We can prevent, by this means, all the evils that come from elsewhere, as great as they may be, from entering into our soul any further than does the sadness excited there by the comedians when they represent some very tragic events before us. But I admit that one must be very philosophical to arrive at this point. However, I also think that even those who let themselves be carried away more by their passions always judge, inside them, that there are more goods than evils in this life, even though they do not perceive them themselves. For even if they sometimes call death to their aid when they feel great pains, it is only insofar

355

356

---

95. The good is from the whole entire cause, the bad from any defect whatsoever.

as it helps them to carry their burden, just as it is in the fable. But they do not want to lose their life for that. Or better, if there are some of them who do want to lose their life, it is by an error of their understanding and not by a well-reasoned judgment or by a belief that nature imprinted on them, as is that which brings it about that one prefers the goods in this life to its evils.

The reason I believe that those who do nothing that is not for their particular utility ought also, just as much as others, to work for others and try to bring pleasure to each, as much as is in their power, if they want to be prudent, is that one commonly sees that those who are deemed officious and prompt in bringing pleasure also receive a number of good favors from others, even from those who do not owe them anything. They would not have received these favors had they been thought by others to be of some other humor, and the pains they take in bringing pleasure are not as great as the conveniences afforded by their friendships. For others expect from us only the services we can perform easily, and we don't expect any more from others. But it often happens that what costs them little profits us a lot, and even can be worth our life. It is true that sometimes our efforts to do good aren't worth the trouble, and, on the contrary, that we gain in doing badly. But this cannot change the rule of prudence, which relates only to those

357   things that happen most often. For me, the maxim that I have observed most in all the conduct of my life has been to follow only the common path and to believe that the principal finesse is to avoid using finesse. The common laws of society, which all tend to make people treat each other well, or at least not to do any ill to each other, are, it seems to me, so well established that whoever follows them honestly, without any dissimulation or artifice, leads a much happier and more assured life than those who seek their own utility by other routes, though, in truth, they succeed sometimes through the ignorance of other men and by the favor of fortune. But it happens much more often that they fail and that in thinking to establish themselves, they ruin themselves. It is with this ingenuity and this frankness, which I profess to observe in all my actions, that I also profess particularly to be, &c.

AT 4:403

ELISABETH TO DESCARTES

[The Hague] 25 April [1646]

404   M. Descartes,

The treaty that my brother Philip just reached with the Republic of Venice has given me, since just after your departure, an occupation much less agreeable than the one you left me, concerning a matter which is beyond my knowledge, and to which I am drawn only to quell the impatience of the young man it concerns.[96] This has prevented me up to now from exercising the permission you gave me to lay out for you the obscurities my own stupidity leads me to find in your *Traité des passions*. These are few in number, since one would have to be senseless not to understand that the order, definition, and distinctions you give to the passions, and indeed all the moral part of this treatise, surpass all that anyone has ever said on this subject.[97]

But the part of it involving physics is not so clear to the ignorant, for I do not see how one can know the diverse movements of the blood which cause the five primitive passions, because they are never alone. For example, love is always accompanied by desire and joy, or by desire and sadness, and as it grows stronger, the others grow as well.[98] . . . How is it possible to observe the difference in the beating of the pulse, the digestion of meats, and other changes of the body that serve in discovering the nature of these movements? Also as you note, in each of the passions the motions are not the same for all temperaments.[99] Mine is such that sadness always takes away my appetite, as long as it is not mixed with some hate which comes only from the death of some friend.

405

When you speak of the exterior signs of these passions you say that wonder, joined to joy, makes the lungs expand in an irregular way, thereby causing laughter.[100] I ask you to add in what way wonder (which, according to your description, seems to operate only in the brain) can open the orifices of the heart so promptly to bring about this effect.[101]

The passions you note as the cause of sighs do not always seem to be so, since custom and the fullness of the stomach produce the same effects.[102]

But I find it much less difficult to understand all that you say on the passions than to practice the remedies you prescribe for their excesses. For how is one to foresee all the accidents that can come upon one in life, as it

96. Elisabeth's brother Philip had agreed to lead a regiment in a war against the Turks waged by a united Venice and Poland. This seems to have been negotiated by the Venetian plenipotentiary to the congress at Münster, the ambassador Contarini. See AT 4:670.

97. Descartes has clearly made significant progress on the *Passions* since his letter of 6 October 1645, and it seems as though he has now enumerated the passions much as he does in part 2 of that work.

98. See *Passions* aa.96–106. The ellipsis that follows indicates that there is a gap in the manuscript.

99. See *Passions* a.136.

100. See ibid., a.124.

101. See ibid., a.71f.

102. See ibid., a.135.

is impossible to enumerate them? And how are we to prevent ourselves from desiring with ardor those things that necessarily tend to the conservation of man (such as health and the means to live), but that nevertheless do not depend on our free will? As for knowledge of the truth, the desire for it is so just that it exists naturally in all men. But it would be necessary to have infinite knowledge to know the true value of the goods and evils which customarily move us, as there are many more such things than a single person would know how to imagine. Thus, for this it would be necessary to know perfectly everything that is in the world.[103]

406   Since you have already told me the principal maxims concerning private life, I will content myself with now hearing those concerning civil life, even though civil life often leaves one dependent on persons of so little reason that up to this point I have always found it better to avail myself of experience rather than reason, in matters that concern it.

I have been interrupted so often in writing you that I am constrained to send you my rough draft and to use the Alkmaar messenger, since I have forgotten the name of the friend to whom you wanted me to address my letters.[104] I do not dare return your treatise to you until I know it, since I am not willing to risk putting in the hand of a drunk such a great prize, which has given so much satisfaction to

Your very affectionate friend at your service,

Elisabeth.

AT 4:406   DESCARTES TO ELISABETH

May 1646 (A)

407   Madame,

I have found out by experience that I was right to number glory among the passions,[105] for I could not prevent myself from being moved in seeing the favorable judgment that your Highness made of the little treatise I wrote on them. I am also not at all surprised by the faults she pointed out therein, since I did not doubt in the least that there were a great many there, the

---

103. Elisabeth here seems to be taking issue with the remedies Descartes adverts to in *Passions* aa.138, 144–48. Given the content of Elisabeth's remarks here, it seems that at this point Descartes had shared with her a draft of part 2 of the *Passions*: Of the Number and Order of the Passions and the Explanation of the Six Primitives. He also had shared with her a section of what was to become part 1 of the work. It is not clear he has completed part 3.

104. See AT 4:390. Descartes, in a letter to a lawyer requests that correspondence be directed to M. Adam Spucker in Alkmaar.

105. See *Passions* aa.66, 204.

passions being a matter that I had never before studied and on which I have but drawn the first pencil sketch, without adding to it the colors and the ornaments which would be required to have it appear before eyes less clear-sighted than those of your Highness.

I have also not yet put in all the principles of physics which I made use of in enumerating the movements of the blood that accompany each passion, since I do not know how to deduce them without explaining the formation of all the parts of the human body. This is something so difficult that I would not yet dare to undertake it, although I myself am just about satisfied concerning the truth of the principles I supposed in this writing. These principles are: that the duty of the liver and the spleen is always to contain some reserve blood, less purified than what is in the veins; and that the fire in the heart needs to be continually fired, either by the juice of meats, which comes directly from the stomach, or, without that, by this blood that is in reserve, since the other blood which is in the veins expands too easily; and   408
that there is such a link between our soul and our body that the thoughts which have accompanied some movements of the body, from the beginning of our life, still accompany them in the present, so that, if the same movements are excited a second time by some exterior cause, they excite in the soul the same thoughts, and reciprocally, if we have the same thoughts, they produce the same movements;[106] and finally, that the machine of our body is made such that a single thought of joy, or of love, or another similar one is sufficient to send the animal spirits through the nerves to all the muscles which are required to cause the different movements of the blood that I said accompany the passions. It is true that I had difficulty in distinguishing those that appertain to each passion, since they never occur alone. But nevertheless, since the same ones are not always joined together, I tried to observe the changes that happened in the body when they were changing company. Thus, for example, if love was always joined with joy, I would not know to which of the two ought to be attributed the heat and the dilation which they make us feel around the heart. But since it is also sometimes joined with sadness, and then we still feel this heat, and no longer this dilation, I judged that the heat appertains to love, and the dilation to joy. Even if desire were almost always with love, they are nevertheless not always together to the same degree. For even if one loves a lot, one desires little when one does   409
not conceive any hope. And since one has none of the diligence and the

---

106. See ibid. aa.44, 50, 107, 136, 211. In aa.136 Descartes identifies this as "the principle on which everything I have written about this [i.e., the passions] is based." AT 11:428. See also the letter to Chanut of 1 February 1647, AT 4:603–6, CSMK 306–8, and the letter to Elisabeth of 8 July 1647 below. Descartes does modify this principle slightly but importantly in aa.44, 50, and 211, as he there maintains that we can change these natural associations by habit.

readiness then that one would have if the desire were greater, one can judge that it is from desire that those things come and not from love.

I believe very much that sadness takes away the appetite in many, but since I have always found that it augments it in myself, I have based my account on that. I think that the difference that occurs here comes from the fact that the first subject of sadness some people had at the beginning of their lives was that they did not receive enough food, and that others first felt sadness when the food they received was harmful to them. In the latter the movement of the spirits that destroys the appetite has ever since remained joined with the passion of sadness. We see also that the movements that accompany the other passions are not entirely similar in all men, and this can be attributed to a similar cause.

For wonder, even though it has its origin in the brain, and though the temperament of the blood alone cannot cause it, as it can often cause joy or sadness, all the same, it can, by means of the impression it makes in the brain, act on the body as much as any of the other passions, or even more in a certain way, because the surprise that it contains causes the quickest 410 movements of all. And as one can move the hand or the foot almost at the same instant that one thinks of moving them, since the idea of this movement that is formed in the brain sends the spirits into the muscles which serve to achieve this effect, in this way, the idea of a pleasant thing which surprises the mind sends the spirits just as quickly into the nerves that open the orifices of the heart. Wonder, by its surprise, simply augments the force of the movement which causes joy. Since the orifices of the heart are dilated all of a sudden, the blood which enters into the lungs by the vena cava and leaves them by the arterial vein inflates them suddenly.

The same exterior signs that usually accompany the passions can also sometimes be produced by other causes.[107] Thus, flushing of the face does not always come from shame, but it can also come from the heat of the fire, or even because one is exercising. The laughter called sardonic is nothing else but a convulsion of the nerves of the face. Similarly one can sigh sometimes from custom, or from a malady, but this does not prevent sighs from being exterior signs of sadness or of desire, when passions cause them. I had never heard said or observed that they were also sometimes caused by the fullness of the stomach, but when this does happen I think it is a movement nature uses to make the juice of meats pass more promptly through the heart, so that the stomach is emptied sooner. For sighs, in agitating the lungs, make the blood they contain descend more quickly by the venous 411 artery on the left side of the heart, so that the new blood, composed of the

107. See *Passions* aa.113–36.

juice of meats, which comes from the stomach through the liver and the heart just to the lung, can be easily received there.

For the remedies against the excesses of the passions, I admit that they are difficult to practice, and even that they cannot suffice for preventing disorders of the body, but only for making it such that the soul is not troubled and can retain its free judgment. In regard to which I do not judge it necessary to have exact knowledge of the truth of each thing, or even to have foreseen in particular all possible accidents, which would no doubt be impossible. But it is enough to have imagined in general things more troubling than those which have come, and to be prepared to suffer through them. I also do not think that one ever sins by excess in desiring those things necessary to life. It is only bad or superfluous desires that need to be regulated. For those which tend to the good are, it seems to me, all the better the greater they are. Even though I may have wanted to flatter my own failing in putting a certain sort of languor among the excusable passions, I nevertheless value much more the diligence of those who always carry themselves with ardor in doing those things which they believe to be in some way their duty, even if they do not hope for very much fruit there.

I lead a life so retired, and I have always been so distant from the management of affairs, that I would not be less impertinent than the philosopher who wanted to instruct on the duty of a captain in the presence of Hannibal[108] if I were to undertake to write here the maxims one ought to observe in civil life. I do not doubt that those your Highness proposes are the best of all: that is, that it is better to regulate oneself in this regard according to experience rather than according to reason, since we have rarely come across people who are as perfectly rational as all men ought to be, to the extent that one could judge what they will do solely by considering what they ought to do. Often the best advice is not the happiest. This is why one is constrained to take a chance and to put oneself in the power of fortune, which I hope is as obedient to your desires as I am, &c.

412

DESCARTES TO ELISABETH

AT 4:413

Egmond, May 1646 (B)

Madame,

414

The opportunity I had to give this letter to M. de Beclin, who is a very close friend, and whom I trust almost as much as myself, leads me to take

---

108. Hannibal (247–183 BCE), the Carthaginian general, was one of the great military leaders of antiquity. He commanded the Carthaginian forces against Rome in the Second Punic War.

the liberty to confess to a very glaring error I made in the treatise on the passions. To flatter my own negligence, I put among the number of the emotions of the soul that are excusable, a certain sort of languor which sometimes prevents us from executing those things which are approved by our judgment.[109] What gives me the most concern here is that I remember that your Highness noted this point in particular, as showing that I did not disapprove of having this passion in a matter where I cannot see its usefulness. I admit that we have good reason to take the time to deliberate before undertaking important matters, but once a project has begun, and when we are in accord with the main aim, I do not see that there is any profit in looking for delays in disputing over whether the conditions are right. If the

415   project succeeds despite this, all the little advantages one might perhaps have acquired by this means are less serviceable than the disgust usually caused by these delays is harmful. If it does not succeed, all this will serve only to show the world that one had plans that have failed. Apart from that, it happens more often when the project one undertakes is very good than when the project is bad that the opportunity for it disappears while one puts off doing it. This is why I am persuaded that resolution and promptness are virtues very necessary for matters already begun. One does not have cause to fear what one does not know, for often things about which we have been the most apprehensive before knowing them turn out to be better than those we desired. Thus, the best thing in this case is to trust oneself to divine providence and to let oneself be led by it. I assure myself that your Highness understands my thought very well, even though I explain it very badly, and that she pardons the extreme zeal that obliges me to write this. For I am, as much as I can be, &c.

AT 4:447   ELISABETH TO DESCARTES

[The Hague, July 1646]

448   M. Descartes,

Since your voyage is delayed until the 3rd/13th of this month, I must remind you of the promise you made me to leave your agreeable solitude to give me the happiness of seeing you, before my departure from here makes me lose the hope of doing so for six or seven months. That is the longest term

---

109. See *Passions* a.170 on irresolution. Descartes there incorporates the point he makes here: that irresolution can benefit us in providing us with time to weigh a decision, but that when the time for action comes we must be decisive.

of seclusion that the Queen my mother, Monsieur my brother,[110] and the sentiment of the friends of my house have prescribed for my absence.[111] But it would be again too long if I were not assured that you will continue there the charity of allowing me to profit from your meditations by your letters, since, without their assistance, the cold winds of the north and the caliber of people with whom I would be able to converse would extinguish the small ray of common sense that I take from nature and which I remember how to use by your method. They promise me that in Germany I will have enough leisure and tranquility to study it, and I will not bring there any greater treasure, from which I hope to take more satisfaction, than your writings. I hope that you will permit me to take the work on the passions, even though it was not able to calm those that the last piece of misfortune has excited. It must be that your presence brought the cure to them, since neither your maxims nor my reasoning had been able to. The preparations for my voyage and the affairs of my brother Philip, along with the polite kindness of attending to the pleasure of my aunt, have prevented me until now from giving you the thanks you deserve for the usefulness of your visit; I ask that you receive them now from

  Your very affectionate friend at your service,

   Elisabeth.

449

M. Descartes,

I am obliged to send this letter by messenger, since its timeliness is more necessary to me at this moment than its security.

DESCARTES TO ELISABETH

Egmond, September 1646

AT 4:485

Madame,

  I read the book about which your Highness commanded me to write her my opinion,[112] and I found there many precepts which seem very good

486

110. Charles Louis (Karl Ludwig) was the head of the Palatine house at this time, as Frederick, king of Bohemia, had died in 1632 and the oldest son, Frederick Henry, had died in 1629.

111. Elisabeth and her brother Philip were forced to leave Holland as Philip, with Elisabeth's knowledge, killed François d'Espinay in broad daylight in The Hague. D'Espinay, who already had a bit of a reputation as a ladies' man, apparently had been courting their mother, and then their sister, Louise Hollandine. Elisabeth was to go to stay with her aunt, the electress of Brandenburg, in Berlin.

112. Elisabeth seems to have made this specific request to comment on Machiavelli's *The Prince* in person, though it follows on her earlier effort to receive Descartes' thoughts on maxims for guiding civil life. See the letter of 25 April 1646. It is unclear in what language Descartes read

to me, among them those in chapters 19 and 20: *that a prince must always avoid the hate and contempt of his subjects, and that love of the people is worth more than fortresses.* But there are several others of which I cannot approve. I think that what the author has missed most is that he has not drawn enough of a distinction between princes who have acquired a state by just means, and those who have usurped power by illegitimate means, and that he has given to all in general the precepts that are proposed only to these latter ones. For just as in building a house on foundations so bad that they cannot support high and thick walls, one is obliged to make those walls thin and low, so too those who have begun by establishing themselves through crimes are ordinarily constrained to continue to commit crimes and would not be able to maintain themselves in power were they to want to be virtuous.[113]

It is with regard to such princes that he could say in chapter 3 that *they will not fail to be hated by most,* and that *they often gain more benefit from doing more harm than from doing less, since light offenses suffice to engender the will to avenge oneself, and great ones destroy the power to do so.*[114] Then, in chapter 15, he says that, *if they wanted to be good men, it would be impossible for them to avoid ruin among the great number of evil people found everywhere.*[115] And in chapter 19 he writes that *one can be hated for good actions just as well as for bad ones.*[116]

On these foundations, he rests some very tyrannical precepts: *that one should ruin a whole country in order to become master of it; that one should exercise great cruelty, so long as it is done promptly and all at once; that one should try to appear to be a good man, but that one should not be one truly; that one should keep one's word only for so long as will be useful; that one should dissimulate; that one should betray; and finally that to rule, one should strip oneself of all humanity, and that one should become the fiercest of all the animals.*[117]

But it is a very sorry matter to make books that undertake to present such precepts, which, at the end of the day, cannot give any assurance to those to whom it offers them. For, as he himself admits, *these princes cannot guard themselves from the first person willing to risk his life to take revenge on them.*[118] Instead,

487

The Prince. Adam and Tannery give good reason to think he read it in Italian. See AT 4:493. Descartes' paraphrasings and quotations are in French in this letter. For a contemporary English translation see Machiavelli, *The Prince,* ed. Quentin Skinner and Russell Price (Cambridge: Cambridge University Press, 1988).

113. The architectural metaphor is familiar from Descartes' *Meditations,* the First Meditation in particular, and the Replies to the Seventh Objections (of Bourdin). See AT 7:536–37, CSM 2:366–67.

114. See Machiavelli, *Prince,* ed. Skinner and Price, 9.

115. Ibid., 54.

116. Ibid., 68.

117. Ibid., 30–34 (chap. 8) and 61–63 (chap. 18).

118. Ibid., 69–70 (chap. 19).

in order to instruct a good prince, however newly he has come to power, it seems to me one should propose to him altogether contrary maxims; and it should be supposed that the means he used to establish himself in power were just, as in effect I believe they almost always are, when the princes who practice them think them to be. For justice between sovereigns has different limits than that between individuals, and it seems that in these cases God gives the right to those to whom he gives force. But the most just action becomes unjust when those who do them think them so.

One must also distinguish between subjects, friends or allies, and enemies. With regard to the last, one has permission to do almost everything, provided that one can draw from it some advantage for oneself or for one's subjects. And I do not disapprove, on this occasion, of coupling the fox with the lion, and joining artifice to force. I even include, under the name of enemy, all those who are not friends or allies, since one has the right to wage war on them when one finds it in one's interest, and since, when they start to become suspect or fearsome, one has a basis to distrust them.[119] But I take exception to one kind of deception, which is so directly contrary to society that I do not think it is ever permissible to use it, even if our author approves of it in various places and it is all too common: it is to feign to be the friend of those one wishes to defeat in order to be better able to surprise them. Friendship is something too sacred to abuse in this way. Those who would be able to feign loving someone in order to betray him deserve that those whom they later want to befriend truly believe nothing of what they say and hate them.

As for allies, a prince ought to keep his word to them exactly, even when this is disadvantageous to him. For the reputation of always doing what he promises can never be more disadvantageous than useful, and he can only acquire this reputation through those occasions when he has something to lose. In those situations in which he will be completely ruined, the right of man frees him from his promise. He must also use great circumspection before promising, in order to be able always to keep his faith. And even if it is good to have friendships with most of his neighbors, I nevertheless think that the best thing is not to have any close alliances except with those who have less power. For no matter how loyal one intends to be, one ought not

119. Descartes here seems to be following Hugo Grotius's discussion of the just causes of war in book 2 of *On the Law of War and Peace*. That work was first published in 1625 in Paris. Grotius (1583–1645) pioneered natural rights theory. He was Dutch, though he received his doctorate of law from the University of Orleans in 1625. He lived in Paris in exile from 1625 to 1631. In 1635 he was appointed Sweden's ambassador to Paris, and in this capacity he helped to negotiate a treaty to end the Thirty Years' War. He was, however, recalled from that position in 1644, before a full peace was negotiated.

to expect the same from others, but to arrange one's affairs as if one will be cheated whenever one's allies find it to their advantage. And those who are more powerful can find it to their advantage when they want to, but not those who are less powerful.

As for subjects, there are two sorts of them: the great and the common people. I understand by the great all those who can form parties against the prince. Of their loyalty he ought to be very sure. Or if he is not sure, all those in politics are in agreement that he ought to employ all his care to abase them, and that insofar as they are inclined to cause trouble to the state, he ought to consider them only as enemies. But for the other sort of subjects, he above all ought to avoid their hatred and their contempt, which I think he can always do so long as he observes exactly their way of justice (that is to say, in accordance with the laws to which they are accustomed), without being too rigorous with punishment or too indulgent with pardons, and so long as he does not put himself completely in the hands of his ministers. Rather he should leave his ministers in charge only of the most odious condemnations and show himself to be concerned with the rest. Then also, he should retain his dignity sufficiently so that he does not forsake any of the honors and the deference the people believe are due him, but he should not demand any more. And he should perform publicly only the most important actions, or those which can be approved by all, reserving to keep his pleasures to himself, and never at anyone else's expense. Finally, he should be immovable and inflexible. I do not mean in the first plans, formed on his own, for since he cannot see everything for himself, it is necessary that he ask for advice and listen to the reasons of several people before being resolved. But he ought to be inflexible about those things he has shown himself to be resolved on, even if they are harmful to him. For they cannot be as harmful as the reputation of being light and variable.

Thus I disapprove of the maxim of chapter 15 which claims that, *as the world is very corrupt, it is impossible that one will not ruin oneself if one always wants to be a good man, and that a prince, in order to maintain himself, must learn to be wicked when the occasion requires it.*[120] That is, unless maybe by a good man, he means a superstitious and simple man who does not dare to go to battle on the Sabbath, and whose conscience can be at rest only if he changes the religion of his people. But thinking that a good man is he who does everything true reason tells him to, it is certain that the best thing is always to try to be one.

I also do not agree with what is said in chapter 19: that one can be hated just as much for good actions as for bad ones,[121] unless envy is a species of

490

120. See Machiavelli, *Prince,* ed. Skinner and Price, 54–55.
121. Ibid., 68.

hate. But this is not the sense of the author. And princes are not usually envied by most of their subjects; they are so only by the great, or by their neighbors, in whom the same virtues that cause envy also cause fear. This 491 is why one should never abstain from acting well, to avoid this sort of hate. There is no hate that can destroy these princes but what arises from injustice or the arrogance which the people judge to be in them. One sees that even those who are condemned to death do not ordinarily hate their judges when they think their punishment deserved. One also suffers wholly undeserved evils with patience when one believes that the prince, from whom one has received them, is in some way constrained to inflict them, and that he was displeased to do so, since one judges that it is just to prefer the public utility to that of individuals. It is only difficult when one is obliged to satisfy two parties who judge differently what is just, as were the Roman emperors who had to keep both soldiers and citizens content.[122] In this case it is reasonable to grant something to each, and one need not try to bring instantly to reason those who are not accustomed to listen to it. But it is necessary to try little by little, either by public writings or by the voice of preachers, or by some other means, to make them see reason. For in the end the people suffer all that one can persuade them is just and are offended by all they imagine to be unjust. The arrogance of princes, that is to say, the usurping of some authority or some rights or some honors the people do not think are deserved, is odious to them only because they consider it a kind of injustice.

As for the rest, I am also not of the opinion of this author in what he 492 says in the preface: *that as it is necessary to be in the plains to see the shape of the mountains when one wants to sketch them, so too one must be a private citizen in order to know well the duties of a prince.*[123] For the sketch represents only those things which are seen at a distance, but the principal motives and actions of princes are often such particular circumstances that one can imagine them only if one is a prince oneself, or perhaps if one has been party to their secrets for a very long time.

This is why I would deserve to be mocked if I thought myself able to teach something to your Highness on this matter. This is not my intent; I intend only that my letters give her some sort of distraction different from those that I imagine she is having on her trip. I hope that trip is perfectly happy, as without a doubt it will be if your Highness is resolved to practice those maxims which teach that the felicity of each depends only on oneself, and that it

---

122. Descartes is adverting to Machiavelli's own discussion of the Roman emperors Commodus, Severus, Antoninus Caracalla, and Maximinus in chapter 19. See ibid., 68–70.

123. See ibid., 4.

is very necessary to carry oneself outside the rule of fortune so that, while one does not miss the occasions to take the advantages it can give, one does not let oneself become unhappy when it refuses them. Since in all worldly affairs there are some reasons for and some against, one should consider principally those that make one approve of what happens. What I think are the most in-

493 evitable are the maladies of the body, which I pray God preserves you from, and I am with all the devotion that I can have, &c.[124]

AT 4:495

DESCARTES TO SOPHIE[125]

Egmond, September 1646

496 Madame,

I count among the number of obligations I have to the Princess Elisabeth, your sister, that having asked me to write her, she wanted it to be sent through your Highness. Knowing how much she cherishes you, I hope that my letters will be less importunate as she receives them in the company of yours, and that they will give her more joy than they would have if they were sent all alone. Also this gives me the occasion to be able to assure you in writing that I am, &c.

AT 4:519

ELISABETH TO DESCARTES

Berlin, 10 October [1646]

M. Descartes,

You are right to believe that the diversion that your letters bring me is different from that I have had while away, since it gives me a greater and more lasting satisfaction. Although I've found in the latter all that the friendship and the caresses of those close to me could give me, I consider them as something

520 which could change, while the truths that the former bring me leave impressions in my mind which will always contribute to the contentment of my life.

124. Adam and Tannery speculate that this letter is incomplete. There should be a postscript in which Descartes proposes a code for their continued correspondence. See Elisabeth to Descartes, 10 October 1646.

125. This letter accompanied the previous letter of Descartes to Elisabeth. There has been some dispute about whom it was addressed to; Clerselier indicates it was to Elisabeth's sister, Louise Hollandine. But Adam and Tannery remark upon a note inserted in one edition that states that Louise Hollandine denied the letters were addressed to her and asserted that they were addressed to Sophie, Elisabeth's youngest sister. Adam and Tannery give good reason to find this claim credible. Sophie would have been about sixteen years old. She would go on to correspond with Leibniz and other leading intellectual figures in her own right as the electress of Hanover.

I have a thousand regrets at not having brought by land the book you have taken the trouble to examine so that you might tell me your thoughts on it. I was persuaded that the baggage I sent by sea at Hamburg would be here sooner than we would be. It is not here yet, even though we arrived here 7/17 September. For this reason I can consider the maxims of this author only as much as a very bad memory can provide me of a book that I have not looked at once in six years. But I recall that I approved of a few, not because they are good in themselves, but because they bring about less evil than those used by a number of ambitious imprudent persons I know, who tend only to stir things up and leave the rest to fortune. Those of this author tend all of them toward stability.

It seems to me as well that to teach how to govern a state, he starts from the state which is the most difficult to govern, where the prince is a new usurper, at least in the opinion of the people. In this case, his own opinion of the justice of his cause could serve to ease his conscience, but it will not ease his affairs where the laws oppose his authority, the great undermine him, and the people curse him. When the state is so disposed, a great violence causes less evil than a small one, because the latter offends as much as the former and gives occasion for a long war, while the former destroys the courage and the means of the great ones who could undertake such a war. Also, since the violence comes promptly and all at once, it annoys less than it surprises and is also more supportable by the people than a long chain of miseries that civil wars bring.

It seems to me that he added there, or better taught, by the example of the nephew of Pope Alexander whom he puts forward as a perfect politician,[126] that the prince should use a minister to perform these great cruelties, one whom he can afterward sacrifice to the hatred of the people. Even though it appears unjust of the prince to bring about the loss of a man who obeyed him, I find those persons who want to be employed as executioner of a whole people so barbaric and unnatural, no matter how great the compensation, that they do not merit any better treatment. As for me, I would prefer the condition of the poorest peasant in Holland to that of the minister who would want to obey similar orders or to that of the prince who would be constrained to give them.

When the same author speaks of allies, he supposes them, in a parallel way, to be as evil as they can be, and matters to be in such an extreme state that it is necessary either to lose an entire republic or to break one's word to those who keep it only so long as it is useful to them.

But if he is wrong to have made these general maxims from those cases which occur in practice on very few occasions, he errs equally in this with all

521

126. See *The Prince*, chap. 7, especially Skinner and Price, 24–29.

the Church Fathers and the ancient philosophers who do this as well. And I believe that this comes from the pleasure they draw from putting forward paradoxes that they can later explain to their students. When this man here says that one will be destroyed if one always wants to be a good man, I do not think he means that to be a good man it is necessary to follow laws of superstition. Rather he means this common law by which one should do unto others as one would like done to oneself: a law which princes are almost never able to observe with regard to one of their subjects, who must be sacrificed each time public utility requires it. Since, before you, no one has said that virtue consists in following right reason, but have only prescribed laws or more particular rules, one should not be surprised that they have failed to define it well.

I find that the rule you observe in his preface is false because the author has never known a person who sees clearly all that he sets about doing, as you do, and who by consequence, in private and retired from the confusion of the world, would nevertheless be capable of teaching princes how they should govern, as seems to be the case from what you have written.

For myself, who have only the title of prince, I study only so that I might apply the rule that you put at the end of your letter, and try to present events to myself in as agreeable way as I can. Here I do not encounter much difficulty, being in a house where I have been cherished since my childhood and where everyone conspires to take care of me.[127] Even though some of these efforts distract me sometimes from more useful occupations, I easily support this inconvenience through the pleasure there is in being loved by those closest to one. There you have, Monsieur, the reason that I did not have the leisure to give you sooner an account of the fortunate success of our voyage, since it is has passed without a single inconvenience, with the promptness that I wrote of above, and of the miraculous spring[128] of which you spoke to me at The Hague.

I have only been to a little place away from here, to Cheuningen, where we met the whole family of the House, who were there. The elector[129] wanted to bring me to see the spring, but since the rest of our company preferred

127. Elisabeth is writing from her aunt's house in Berlin. Elisabeth Charlotte, her father's sister, had married George William of Brandenburg. It was here that she was brought, along with her brother Charles Louis (Karl Ludwig), by her grandmother Juliana upon the losses of her father, Frederick V, at White Mountain. They remained there for several years, until they were sent for in The Hague, where their parents had set up a court in exile.

128. The salt water of the springs at Hornhausen, about 180 km south of Berlin, were reputed to have curative powers. See also the letter of 29 November 1646 below.

129. Frederick William, elector of Brandenburg (1620–88). He became elector in 1640 and remained so until his death. He came to be known as the Great Elector.

another diversion, I did not dare to contradict them and satisfied myself by seeing and tasting the water, of which there are different sources with different tastes. Only two are generally used, the first of which is clear, salty, and a strong purgative; the other is a bit white, tasting of water mixed with milk, and is, or so they say, refreshing. They speak of a quantity of miraculous cures they have brought, but I wasn't able to hear of one from any person worthy of trust. They are right in saying that this place is full of poor people who claim to have been born deaf, blind, lame, or hunchback and found their cure in this spring. But since these are mercenary types, who find themselves in a nation that is rather credulous with respect to miracles, I do not believe that this should persuade reasonable people. In the whole court of the elector, my cousin, there was only his great esquire who discovered this curative power for himself. He had a wound under his right eye, from which he had lost the vision on one side, because of a little skin that had grown under this eye. The salty water from this spring, being applied to the eye, dissolved the aforementioned skin so much that he can now see people while closing his left eye. On the other hand, as he is a man of such a strong complexion and bad diet, a good purge could not harm him as it might many others.

524

I examined the code that you sent me and found it very good, but too long to write a whole thought. And if one writes only a bit of a word, one would figure it out by the number of letters. It would be better to make a key of words by alphabet and then to mark a distinction between the numbers that signify letters and those that signify words.

I have so little leisure to write here that I am constrained to send you this draft, in which you can see from the difference in pens all the times I have been interrupted. But I prefer to appear before you with all my faults than to give you a basis for thinking that I have a vice so removed from my nature as that of forgetting my friends in absence, especially a person whom I would not know how to cease feeling affection for, without ceasing also to be reasonable, like you, Monsieur, to whom I will be all my life,

Your very affectionate friend at your service,
Elisabeth.

DESCARTES TO ELISABETH

AT 4:528

November 1646

Madame,

I received a great favor from your Highness in her wanting me to learn, through her letter, of the success of her voyage and that she arrived happily in a place where it seems to me that she has as many goods as one can reasonably hope to have in this life, since she is highly esteemed there and cherished by those near her. Knowing the condition of human affairs, it would be asking too much of fortune to expect so many favors from her that we could not even imagine finding anything to complain about. When there is nothing present that offends the senses, or any indisposition of the body that troubles it, a mind that follows true reason can easily content itself. For this it is not necessary that one forget or neglect things far away. It is enough that one try to have no passion for what can displease. And this does not go against charity, since one can often better find remedies for ills that one examines dispassionately than for those that afflict us. But as the health of the body and the presence of agreeable objects help the mind greatly in chasing away all the passions which participate in sadness and allow those which participate in joy to enter, so, reciprocally, when the mind is full of joy this serves well to make the body carry itself better and present objects appear more agreeable.[130]

I even dare to think that interior joy[131] has some secret power to make fortune more favorable. I would not write this to people who have weak minds, for fear of introducing them to some superstition, but with regard to your Highness I only fear that she will mock me for having become too credulous. All the same, I have an infinity of experiences, and with that the authority of Socrates, for confirming my belief.[132] That is, I have often noticed that things I have done with a happy heart and without any interior repugnance have usually succeeded well for me. Even in games of chance, where fortune alone reigns, I have always had more favorable experiences when I have come to the game with reasons for joy than when I have done so with reasons for sadness. And what is commonly called the "daimon"[133] of Socrates was without doubt nothing else but that he was accustomed to following his interior inclinations and thought that the outcome of what he undertook would be happy when he had some secret feeling of gaiety, and, on the contrary, that it would be unhappy when he felt sad. It is true, however, that it would amount to being superstitious to believe as strongly in this

---

130. Descartes here reiterates the view he outlined earlier in his letter of May or June 1645, AT 4:218ff.

131. Descartes also writes of interior passions at *Passions* a.147, AT 11:440–41, though he does not there make the claim he does here.

132. See Plato, *Euthydemus* 277d–282e. There Socrates identifies wisdom with good fortune.

133. The word Descartes uses here is *genie*, the same word used in the French translation of the First Meditation: "Je supposerai donc qu'il y a, non point un vrai Dieu, qui est la souveraine source de verité, mais un certain mauvais genie" (AT 9:17).

as it is said he did. For Plato tells us of Socrates that he even remained in his lodgings when his daimon did not counsel him to go out.[134] But concerning the important actions of life, when they present themselves so unclearly that prudence cannot teach us what we ought to do, it seems to me that we have good reason to follow the advice of our "daimon" and that it is useful to have a strong belief that the things we undertake without repugnance and with the freedom which ordinarily accompanies joy will not fail to succeed for us.

So I dare here to exhort your Highness that, since she finds herself in a place where the objects before her give her only satisfaction, it is also in her interest to make her own contribution to the efforts to achieve her content-ment. She can do this easily, it seems to me, by keeping her mind only on present things and by never thinking of business except in those hours when the courier is about to leave. And I think that it is a good thing that your Highness's books were not brought to her as soon as she expected. For read- ing them is not so likely to engender gaiety as to bring on sadness, especially reading that book by the Physician of Princes,[135] who represents only the difficulties princes have in maintaining themselves and the cruelty or perfidy he recommends they undertake, so that those who read it have fewer reasons to envy the condition of princes than to feel sorry for it.

Your Highness has noted perfectly well its faults and my own. For it is true that it was his plan to praise Cesare Borgia that led him to establish general maxims for justifying particular actions which could have been diffi-cult to excuse. I have since read his discourses on Titus Livy where I noticed nothing evil.[136] His principal precept, which is to eliminate one's enemies entirely or else to make them one's friends, without ever taking the middle way, is without doubt always the surest. But when one has nothing to fear, this is not the most generous way to proceed.

Your Highness has also noted very well the secret of the miraculous spring,[137] in that there are many poor people who pronounce publicly on its virtues and who are perhaps hired by those who hope to make a profit from it. For it is certain that there is no remedy at all which can be used for all maladies. But of the many who have used that remedy, those who have found

531

---

134. See Plato, *Apology of Socrates,* 31d. Socrates here argues that his daimon, or inner voice, pre-vented him from taking part in public affairs, and he offers an account of how it was justified in doing so. It is not clear that this is Descartes' point. For one, Socrates claims that his daimon only forbade and never urged him to do anything, whereas Descartes' daimon does direct him to act. Plato, *Complete Works,* ed. John M. Cooper, assoc. ed. D. S. Hutchinson (Indianapolis: Hackett, 1997), 29.

135. That is, Machiavelli, author of *The Prince.*

136. Machiavelli, *Discourses on the First Decade of Titus Livius.*

137. The spring at Hornhausen. See Elisabeth's letter of 10 October 1646.

532   themselves cured speak well of it, and no one talks about the others. In any case, the purgative quality in one of these springs, and white color, with the softness and refreshing quality of the other, makes me think that they pass through deposits of antinomy or mercury which are two awful drugs, especially mercury. This is why I would not want to advise anyone to drink from them. The acid and the iron in the waters of Spa give much less reason to fear, and since they both shrink the spleen and chase away melancholy, I value these waters.

If your Highness will please permit me to finish this letter where I began it, I will wish her principally satisfaction of mind and joy, as they are not only the fruits which attend all other goods but also often a means for increasing the grace one has been given for acquiring them. Although I may not be capable of contributing anything to your service except my wishes, I dare nevertheless to assure you that I am more perfectly than is anyone else in the world, &c.

AT 4:533

DESCARTES TO SOPHIE [138]

November 1646

Madame,

The letter that I had the honor to receive from Berlin makes me aware that I have a great obligation to your Highness, and considering that those letters I write and those I receive pass through such dignified hands, it seems to me that your sister imitates the divine sovereign, who has the habit of using the intermediary of angels to receive the submissions of men who are greatly inferior to them, and to make them aware of his commandments. Since I am of a religion which does not forbid me from invoking angels, I ask you to find it agreeable that I compare you to them and that I express here that I am with great devotion, &c.

AT 4:577

ELISABETH TO DESCARTES

[Berlin] 29 November [1646]

578   M. Descartes

I am not accustomed enough to favors of fortune to expect an extraordinary one; it is enough for me that she does not too often send me accidents

138. This letter accompanied the previous letter, from Descartes to Elisabeth, as Sophie served as messenger.

that would give cause for sadness to the greatest philosopher in the world. Since nothing similar has come to me during my stay here and everything around me is quite agreeable and the country air does not disagree with my complexion, I find myself in a state where I can practice your lessons concerning gaiety, even though I do not expect to find the effects you have experienced in games of chance in the conduct of my affairs. For the good luck you found then when you were inclined to joy from some other source apparently proceeded from your playing all your hands more freely, which usually makes one win.

But if I were to have occasion to do as I like, I would not put myself again in a hazardous state, if I were in a place where I had found such contentment as in the place I have come from. As for the interests of our house, I long ago abandoned them to destiny, seeing that even prudence would not be worth the trouble if it is not helped by other means. One would have to have a greater "daimon" than Socrates to succeed in that matter; for since he was not able to avoid either imprisonment or death, he has no reason to brag about it very much. I have also observed that those matters where I follow my own inclinations succeed better than those where I let myself be guided by the advice of those more sage than I am. But I do not attribute this as much to the felicity of my mind as to the fact that since I have more concern for that which affects me than anyone else, I have examined the paths that could harm or benefit me better than have those on whose judgment I rely. If you want me still to assign some role to the occult quality of my imagination, I believe that you do so in order to accommodate me to the humor of the folk of this country here and particularly to the learned who are even more pedantic and superstitious than those I knew in Holland. This comes from the fact that all the people here are so poor that no one studies or reasons except about what is required to live.

I have taken all the pains in the world to wrest myself from the hands of the doctors, in order not to suffer from their ignorance. And I haven't been ill, except that the change of air and diet has given me, instead of impetigo, some abscesses on my fingers. From these symptoms, these men judge that there is still some bad substance hidden away that is too large to pass through that region and which it is necessary to oppose with purges and bleeding. But feeling otherwise so well that I am noticeably gaining weight, I have used stubbornness when reason was useless and have taken none of their remedies. I am more apprehensive about the medicine here because everyone uses extracts from chemistry, the effects of which are immediate and dangerous.

Those who have searched for the ingredients of the spring at Hornhausen believe that the salty source contains only ordinary salt, and about

579

580

the other they do not agree at all. They (principally the Lutherans)[139] also attribute their effect more to a miracle than to the composition of the water. As for me, I will take the safest course, according to your opinion, and will not make use of it at all.

I also hope never to be in a state where I need to follow the precepts of the Physician of Princes, because violence and suspicion are things contrary to my nature. Even so, I blame the tyrants only for their initial plan to usurp a country and for the initial undertaking of it; for afterward the path which establishes them in power, however harsh it is, will always lead to less public harm than would a rule contested by battle.

This study also does not occupy me enough to leave me chagrined, for I use the little time left me after the letters I have to write, and the pleasantries I owe those close to me, to reread your works, from which I profit more in one hour in cultivating my reason than I would in my whole life with other readings. But there is no one else here who is reasonable enough to understand them, even though I have promised this old duke of Brunswick, who 581 is at Wolfenbuttel,[140] to give them to him in order to adorn his library. I do not believe that he will use them to adorn his feeble brain, as it is already thoroughly occupied with pedantry. I am here letting myself run on for the pleasure of entertaining you, forgetting that I am sinning against the human race by wasting your time (which you employ for its benefit) with the silliness of

Your very affectionate friend, at your service,

Elisabeth.

AT 4:588

DESCARTES TO ELISABETH

Egmond, December 1646

589   Madame,

Never have I found such good news in any of the letters I have heretofore had the honor of receiving from your Highness as I have in the last of 29 November. For that letter leads me to believe that you now are in better health and feel more joy than I have seen before. After virtue, which you

---

139. See above, note 128 and related text, where this spring is first mentioned. The area in which the spring is located lies in the heart of territory in Germany that became Lutheran, which may explain why Lutherans commented upon it when it became a phenomenon of some interest from March 1646 at least through the remainder of that year.

140. August, duke of Brunswick-Lunenburg, then duke of Wolfenbuttel in 1634 (1579–1666). He would have been sixty-six years old at this time.

have never lacked, I believe that these are the two principal goods we can have in this life. I do not put any stock in this little ailment the doctors have made up so that you might employ them. Though it might sometimes be a little uncomfortable, I come from a country where it is so common in those who are young and are otherwise quite healthy that I do not consider it so much an illness as a mark of health and a prophylactic against other maladies. Practical experience has taught our doctors certain remedies for curing this problem, though they do not advise that one take them in any other season but spring, since at that time the pores are more open and one can better destroy the cause. Thus, your Highness is very right not to want to use the remedies for this illness, especially at the beginning of winter, which is the most dangerous time. If this trouble lasts until spring, then it will be easier to chase it away with some light purgatives or with a refreshing broth to which there is nothing added but some herbs used in cooking, while refraining from eating meat that is too salted or otherwise spiced. Being bled may be of great use, but since it is a remedy involving some danger and the frequent use of it shortens one's life, I do not at all advise her to make use of it unless she is accustomed to it. When one is bled in the same season three or four years in a row, one is almost obliged thereafter to have it done every year at the same time. Your Highness also does very well in not wanting to use any of the remedies of the chemists. It is useless to have long experience with their power, as the least little change that one makes in their preparation, even when one thinks one is making things better, can entirely change their qualities and make what was once medicinal into something poisonous.

Almost the same thing can be said about science, when it is in the hands of those who try to apply it without knowing it well. For in thinking they are correcting or adding something to what they have learned, they change it into a mistake. I find evidence of this in the book of Regius, which has finally come out in print.[141] I would note here some points about it, if I thought that he had sent a copy to your Highness. But it is so far from here to Berlin that I think he will have waited for you to return to offer it to you. And I will wait as well to tell you my views about it.

I am not surprised that your Highness does not find any learned men in the country where she is who are not entirely preoccupied with the opinions of the Schools. For I see that in Paris itself and all the rest of Europe there are so few others that, if I had known this beforehand, I would perhaps never

141. Henricus Regius, *Fundamenta Physica*. Recall that her study with Regius served as impetus to Elisabeth to begin to correspond with Descartes. See Elisabeth's letter to Descartes of 16 May 1643, note 3 above, and Descartes' letter of March 1647 below, as well as his letter to Mersenne of 5 October 1646 (AT 4:510–11, CSMK 295–96).

have had anything published. All the same, I have this consolation, that even if I am assured that most people did not lack the will to attack me, no one as yet has entered the lists against me.[142] I have even received compliments from the Jesuit fathers, who I always thought were those most concerned with the publication of a new philosophy, and who would be the least likely to excuse me if they thought they had reason to find fault there.

I count among the number of obligations I owe your Highness, the promise she made to the duke of Brunswick, who is at Wolfenbuttel, to give him my writings. For I am sure that before you were where you are, I did not have the honor of being known there at all. It is true that I am not interested in being known to many people, but my principal ambition is to be able to express that I am with an entire devotion, &c.

DESCARTES TO SOPHIE [143]

AT 4:592

Egmond, December 1646

Madame,

The angels cannot leave more wonder and respect in the minds of those to whom they deign to appear than the letter I have had the honor of receiving, with that of your sister, has left in mine. Rather than diminishing the opinion I had, on the contrary, it assures me that it is not only the face of your Highness that merits being compared with that of angels. For just as painters can draw a model from your face with which to represent angels well, so too the graces of your mind are such that the philosophers have reason to wonder at them, and to judge them similar to those of these divine "daimons" who are drawn only to good actions and who do not fail to favor those who are devoted to them. I thus beg you to believe that it is with a very particular zeal that I am, &c.

ELISABETH TO DESCARTES

AT 4:617

Berlin, 21 February 1647

M. Descartes,

618   I value joy and health as much as you do, although I prefer your friendship as much as virtue. For it is from your friendship that I draw joy and health, joined with the satisfaction of the mind which surpasses even joy,

142. Descartes is taking consolation that his works had not been entered in the *Index librorum prohibitorum,* the list of books prohibited by the Catholic Church. The censorship list was established in 1557 and not suppressed until 1966. Descartes' works were added to the list in 1663.

143. Again, this letter served to transmit the previous letter of Descartes to Elisabeth.

since it has taught me how to possess these things. I can no longer fail in my resolution to take no remedy at all for the little ailments that remain with me, since this resolution has met with your approval. I am at this hour so well cured of these abscesses that I do not think that there is any need for me to take medicaments to purge the blood in the spring, having discharged enough of the bad humors from my body and emptied it, or so I believe, of the fluxions that the cold and the stoves would have otherwise given me.

My sister Henriette[144] was so ill that we thought we had lost her. It is this that prevented me from responding sooner to your last letter, as I needed to be near her all the time. Since she is doing better, we have been obliged to attend the Queen Mother of Sweden,[145] every day in her train, and in the evenings at festivities and balls. These are very annoying distractions to those who are able to give themselves to better things, but they annoy less insofar as one does it for and with those people whom one has no grounds to resent. This is why I am more at ease here than I ever would be at The Hague.

619

I would be happier all the same to be able to spend my time in reading the book of Regius and your sentiments on it. If I do not return to The Hague in the coming summer (I am not yet able to determine whether I will, even though I have not changed my resolution, because whether I will depends in part on the will of others and public affairs), I will try to have the book sent to me by the ships which go from Amsterdam to Hamburg. I hope that you will do me the favor of sending me your sentiments on it by courier. Every time I read your writings, I cannot imagine how you can, in effect, regret having had them printed, since it is impossible that in the end they will not be received by and be useful to the public.

A little while ago I met one single man who has read some of your writings. He is a medical doctor named Weis, and he is very wise as well. He told me that Bacon[146] first made him suspicious of the Aristotelian philosophy and that your method made him reject it entirely and convinced him

---

144. One of Elisabeth's younger sisters, she was born in July 1626. In 1651 she was married to Sigismond Ragoczy, prince of Transylvania, who died that same year. Elisabeth seems to have been instrumental in negotiating this marriage.

145. Marie Eleanor of Brandenburg, daughter of the Elector Georg Wilhelm, and mother of Queen Christina of Sweden. In 1640, she moved to Denmark, and she remained in Brandenburg until 1648, when she returned to Sweden. She died in 1655.

146. Francis Bacon (1561–1626). In all likelihood Weis would have been influenced by Bacon's *Novum Organum*, first published in 1620, in which Bacon outlines a new method to replace that of the Aristotelians.

of the circulation of the blood,[147] which destroyed all the old principles of
their medicine. This is why he admits that he consented to the new theory
620   with regret. I have just presented him with a copy of your *Principles*, and he
promised to tell me his objections to it. If he finds any, and they are worth
the trouble, I will send them to you, so that you can judge the capability of
the one I find to be the most reasonable of the doctors here, since he has a
taste for your reasoning. But I am sure that no one knows how to esteem you
to a higher degree than does

Your very affectionate friend at your service,
Elisabeth.

AT 4:624

DESCARTES TO ELISABETH

The Hague, March 1647

Madame,

The satisfaction I see your Highness receives where she is makes me
not dare to wish for her return, even if I have great trouble stopping myself
from doing so, especially since now I find myself in The Hague. And since I
note, from your letter of 21 February, that we cannot expect you here before
the end of summer, I propose to make a trip to France to handle my private
matters, and plan to return near winter. I will not leave for two months, so
that before I go I can have the honor of receiving the commandments of
your Highness, which will always have more power over me than anything
else in the world.

625   I praise God that you now are in perfect health, but I beg you to pardon
me if I dare to contradict your opinion that you should not use remedies,
since the malady you had on your hands is gone. For I fear as much for your
Highness as for your sister that the humors which have been purged were
stopped by the cold of the season and that in spring they will bring back
the same malady or put you in danger of some other malady if you do not
remedy them by a good diet, using only meats and beverages which refresh
the blood and which purge without any effort. As for drugs, whether from
the apothecaries or the empirics, I hold them both in such low esteem that
I would never dare advise anyone to use them.

I do not know what I could have written your Highness concerning the
book of Regius that gives you occasion to want to know what I observed
there. Maybe I did not give my opinion, in order not to prejudice your judgment in case you already had the book. But since I learn that you do not yet

---

147. Weis would have been so persuaded by part 5 of Descartes' *Discourse on the Method*.

have it, I will tell you here artlessly that I do not think that it is worth your trouble to read it. It contains nothing concerning physics, unless you include my claims, improperly ordered and without their true proofs, so that they appear to be paradoxes, and so that what is put in the beginning cannot be proven except by what is near the end. He has included almost nothing of his own, and few things that I have not published. But he has not neglected to omit what he owes to me, in that professing to be my friend and knowing well that I would not want what I have written regarding the description of animals to be divulged—so much so that I did not want to show it to him and excused myself by saying that he would not be able to prevent himself from talking about it with his disciples if I showed it to him—he has not failed to appropriate for himself several things from there. Having found a means to acquire a copy of it without my knowledge, he has transcribed the whole part where I talk about the movement of the muscles, where I consider, for example, two of the muscles which move the eye, from which there are two or three pages which he has repeated twice, word for word, in his book, it pleased him so much. All the same, he has not understood what he has written. For he has omitted the principal thing, which is that the animal spirits running from the brain to the muscles cannot return through the same channels by which they come. Without this observation all that he writes is worth nothing. And because he did not have my illustration, he made one that shows his ignorance clearly. They told me that he has at present yet another book on medicine [148] in press, where I expect he will have put all the rest of my writings insofar as he has been able to digest them. He without doubt would have taken many other things from them, but I know that he only got a copy when his own book was done being printed. But just as he blindly follows what he believes to be my opinions in all that regards physics or medicine, even though he does not understand them, so too does he contradict them blindly in all that concerns metaphysics. I have begged him to write nothing about metaphysics, [149] since this does not concern his topic at all, and since I was sure that he was not able to write anything on it that was not bad. But I have obtained nothing from him. For, not planning to satisfy me in this regard, he was no longer worried to disoblige me in other matters.

I will not fail tomorrow to bring to the P.S. [150] a copy of his book, whose title is *Henrici Regij fundamenta Physices*, with another little book of my good

148. *Utrajectini Fundamenta Medica* (Amsterdam: Theodorum Ackersdycium, 1647).

149. See Descartes to Regius, May 1641 (AT 3:371–72, CSMK 181–82), December 1641 (AT 3:454–55, CSMK 199), December 1641 (AT 3:460, CSMK 200–201), January 1642 (AT 3:491, CSMK 491–92).

150. No doubt P.S. adverts to the Princess Sophie, who was serving as intermediary in this portion of the correspondence.

friend M. de Hogelande,[151] who has done the complete opposite of Regius. While Regius has written nothing which was not taken from me, and which, despite that, is against my views, the other has written nothing which is properly from me (for I do not think he has ever even read my writings well) and all the same he has written nothing which is not in my favor in that he has followed the same principles. I will ask Mme. L.[152] to add these two books, which are not heavy, to the first packets it pleases her to send through Hamburg, to which I will add the French version of my *Meditations*, if I have it before leaving here, for it has already been long enough since they sent word that the printing is done.[153] I am, &c.

628

AT 4:628

ELISABETH TO DESCARTES

Berlin, 11 April 1647

M. Descartes:

I had not regretted my absence from The Hague until you wrote me of your being there and I felt myself deprived of the satisfaction that I would have surely had from your conversation during your stay. It seems to me that I always come away from your conversation more reasonable, and even though the repose that I find here, among those who have affection for me and who esteem me much more than I merit, surpasses all the goods I could have elsewhere, they do not even begin to approach those of your conversation. I am nevertheless obliged to stay here a few months. It is impossible to predict the number, since I do not at all see the electress, my aunt,[154] being in the mood to permit my return. I have no basis on which to ask her for permission before her son[155] is near her, which, according to him, will not be until September, though maybe his affairs will require him to come sooner or to stay longer. Thus, I can hope, but cannot be assured, that I will have the good fortune to see you again during the time you have proposed for your return from France. I hope that your trip will be successful, and if I had not

629

151. The book was dedicated to Descartes. See *Cogitationes, quibus Dei existential, item animae spiritalitas, et possibilis cum corpore unio demonstratur; nec non brevis historia oeconomiae corporis animalis preponitur atque mechanice explicatur* (Amsterdam: Ludovicus Elzevirium, 1646).

152. Perhaps Princess Sophie, or another sister, Princess Louise Hollandine.

153. See AT 4:563–64. The French edition of the *Meditations*, translated by the duke of Luynes and approved by Descartes, was published in 1647 in Paris by Jean Camusat and Pierre le Petit.

154. Elisabeth Charlotte, Electress Dowager of Brandenburg, widow of Elector Georg Wilhelm. She was the sister of Elisabeth's father, Frederick.

155. Friedrich Wilhelm, elector of Brandenburg, in December of 1646, had married Louise Henriette of Nassau, daughter of the prince of Orange, Frederick Henry.

experienced the constancy of your resolutions, I would fear that your friends would require you to stay there. I ask you in the meantime to give an address to my sister Sophie, so that I can have news of you from time to time, for such news does not cease to be agreeable to me, however long it takes to arrive.

After Easter, we will go to Crossen, the home of my aunt, on the border of Silesia, for a stay of three weeks to a month. There the solitude will give me 630 more leisure to read, and I will employ it all on the books you have had the goodness to send me. For them I thank you. I had more desire to see the book of Regius for what is yours in it than for what is his. Other than the fact that he goes a little fast, he has helped himself to the assistance of Doctor Jonson,[156] as he himself said to me. This is capable of getting him into even more trouble, as he has a mind so confused in itself that he does not have the patience to understand the things he has read or heard. But even though I would excuse all the other faults of the aforementioned Regius, I would not know how to pardon him the ingratitude he shows you, and I take him to be altogether cowardly, since conversing with you has not given him other sentiments.

M. Hogelande will no doubt succeed with what he has published since he followed your principles, which I could not get even one of the doctors from Berlin to listen to, so preoccupied are they with the Schools. The one I mentioned in my last letter has not seen me at all since I gave him your physics. This is a sure sign that everyone here is well, since he is one of the house doctors.

When I told you that I did not want to use any remedies for the abscesses I had in the fall, I meant remedies from the apothecary, because I use those herbs which refresh and purge the blood as an aliment in the spring, as I do not usually have an appetite in this season for other things. I plan as well 631 to be bled in a few days, because that has become a bad habit and I cannot change it without getting a headache. I would fear giving you a headache with this annoying account of myself, if your concern for my health had not brought me to it. It would make me quite vain if I could find any other cause but the extreme good will that you have for

Your very affectionate friend at your service,
Elisabeth.

DESCARTES TO ELISABETH   *AT* 5:15

Egmond, 10 May 1647

Madame,

Though I can find reasons why I would be pleased to stay in France while I am there, so long as I am alive and healthy there will nonetheless be

156. See above, note 51.

none with the force to prevent me from returning before winter, since the letter I had the honor of receiving from your Highness gives me hope that you will return to The Hague near the end of summer. Indeed I can say that this is the principal reason why I prefer to stay in this country rather than others. I foresee that from now on I will be unable to get the peace I had previously sought here as completely as I desire, for I have not yet received proper redress for the injuries I suffered at Utrecht,[157] and I see that those are attracting further insults. There is a troop of theologians, men of the Schools, who seem to have formed a league with the aim of crushing me by calumny. They scheme all they can with the aim of destroying me, and if I do not rise to defend myself, it will be easy for them to injure me in some way.

In proof of this, for three or four months, a certain Regent of the College of Theologians of Leiden, named Revius,[158] has raised four different theses in disputation against me. In doing so he has perverted the sense of my *Meditations* and made people believe that I said things in it which are quite absurd and contrary to the glory of God—for instance, that I doubt that there is a God, and even that I want people to deny absolutely for a period of time that there is one, and similar things. But since this man is not competent, and since even the majority of his students made fun of his attacks, the friends that I have at Leiden didn't even bother to alert me to what he was doing, until other theses were put forward by Triglandius,[159] their leading professor of theology, which included these words: *Eum esse blasphemum, qui Deum pro deceptore habet, ut male Cartesius.*[160] At this my friends, even though they too are theologians, judged that the intention of these people, in accusing me of so great a crime as blasphemy, was nothing less than to try to condemn my views as very pernicious. First, they would try me by some synod on which they would be the most powerful, and then they would make the magistrates, who believe in them, attack me. To prevent this, it is necessary that I oppose myself to their plans. All of this is the reason that for the past eight days I have been writing a long letter to the curators of the Academy of Leiden[161] to demand justice against the calumny of these two theologians. I do not yet know the response that I will get. But insofar as I know the temper of the people of this country and how they revere not probity and virtue, but rather the beard, the voice and the brow of theologians, and how those

157. See above, note 13.

158. Jacobus Revius (1586–1658) not only raised early criticisms of Cartesian philosophy but was also a poet and was involved in translating the Bible into Dutch. In 1979, his poem "Noah's Ark" was translated into a children's book by Peter Spier and illustrated.

159. Jacob Trigland (1583–1654).

160. It is blasphemy to take God as a deceiver, as Descartes has evilly done.

161. See AT 5:1–15, 4 May 1647.

who are the most insolent and who cry the loudest have the most power here (as is ordinarily the case in all states run by the people), even though they have the least reason, I expect only some superficial remedy that will serve only to make this whole thing longer and more importunate insofar it does not remove the cause of the evil. Instead, I think I am obliged to do my utmost to get complete satisfaction for these injuries and also, at the same time, for those of Utrecht. In the event that I cannot obtain justice (and I foresee it will be very difficult to obtain), I think I am obliged to leave these provinces altogether. But since everything here happens very slowly, I am sure that it will be more than a year before this comes to pass.

I would not take the liberty to engage your Highness with these little things, if her favoring me by wanting to read the books of M. Hogelande and Regius, because of what they said there concerning me, did not make me think that you would not find it disagreeable to know what concerns me from me myself. In addition, the obedience and the respect that I owe you demands that I keep you informed of my actions.

I praise God that this doctor to whom your Highness presented my *Principles* has been such a long time without returning to see you, since this is a sign that there are no sick persons at all at the court of the electress. It seems that one is more perfectly healthy when it is the general state of the place where one resides than when one is surrounded by sick people. This doctor will have had all the more leisure to read the book it pleased your Highness to present him and afterward will be better able to tell you his judgment.

While I write this, I received letters from The Hague and Leiden informing me that the assembly of the curators was postponed[162] and that they have not yet given them my letters. I see that an annoyance is being made into a big affair. They say that the theologians want to be the judges, that is to say, to subject me to an inquisition here that would be more severe than that in Spain ever was, and to make me the adversary of their religion. They want me to draw on the credit of the ambassador of France, and the authority of the prince of Orange, not to obtain justice but to intercede and prevent my enemies from going further. I nonetheless think that I will not follow this advice.[163] I will only demand justice, and if I cannot obtain it, it seems to me that the best course will be for me to prepare very quietly to leave. But no matter what I think or what I do, in

18

19

---

162. These letters are lost. Adam and Tannery speculate that the letters from The Hague were from Constantijn Huygens (1596–1687), David le Leu de Wilhem (1588–1658), or Henri Brasset (1591–after 1657), those from Leiden from Adrianus Heereboord (1614–61) or Cornelis van Hogelande (1590–1662).

163. Descartes does seem to have consulted the French ambassador. See Verbeek, *Descartes and the Dutch*, 34–51, especially 47.

whatever part of the world I go, there will never be anything more dear than to obey your orders and tell you with how much zeal I am, &c.

AT 5:46

ELISABETH TO DESCARTES

Crossen, May 1647

M. Descartes,

It has been three weeks since I was sent the impertinent corollary of Professor Triglandius, along with word that those who argued for you were not defeated by reason but were constrained to silence themselves by the tumult excited in the academy, and of the plan of Professor Stuard[164] (a man who has read a lot but with very mediocre judgment) to refute your *Metaphysical Meditations*. I thought that this would give you the same pain the calumny of the student of Voetius did,[165] but I did not think it would make you resolve to leave Holland, as you said in your letter of the tenth of this month. It would not dignify you to cede the place to your enemies, and your leaving would appear as a kind of banishment. This would garner more prejudice against you than the theologians could muster, for calumny is not of much consideration where those who govern can neither exempt themselves from it nor punish those who spread it. The people there pay this great price solely for freedom of speech, and as the speech of theologians is privileged everywhere, it knows no restraint in a democratic state. This is why it seems to me that you have reason to be content if you obtain what your friends in Holland advise you to request, though you need not follow their advice to make the request, and the resolution you have made is better suited to a free man assured of his actions. But if you continue on the course of leaving the country, I would rescind the resolution I have made to return there, if the interests of my family do not call me back, and I will wait here until the outcome of the treaties of Munster[166] or some other treaty brings me back to my country.

The estate of the electress is in a place that does not suit my complexion badly, two degrees closer to the sun than Berlin, surrounded by the River Oder and a land that is extremely fertile. The people there have recovered

47

---

164. See Samuel Sorbière, *Lettres et discours de M. de Sorbière* (Paris: F Clousier, 1660), 687–88, quoted at AT 5:49–50. Sorbière refers to the gentleman as "Stuart, a Scottish professor, . . . who knew only the old ways in philosophy. "

165. Elisabeth is referring to the matter of Martin Schoock. See Elisabeth's letter of 22 June 1645 and Descartes' of June 1645 above.

166. The Peace of Westphalia, negotiated at Münster and Osnabrück, brought an end to the Thirty Years' War. It was signed on 24 October 1648.

from the war better than the people here, although the armies were there for a longer time and damaged more by fire. In several villages there are now so many mosquitoes that quite a few men and animals have died or become deaf and blind. They arrive in the form of a cloud and leave in the same way. The inhabitants think that this comes from a spell. But I attribute it to the extraordinary flooding of the Oder which lasted all the way to the end of April this year, and it has already been very hot.

Two days ago I received the books of M. Hogelande and Regius, but some news prevented me from reading anything more than the beginning of the former. In that work, I would have greatly valued the proofs for the existence of God, if you had not accustomed me to demand them from the principles of our knowledge, but the comparisons by which he shows that the soul is united to the body and constrained to accommodate itself to its form, in order to partake of the good or bad which comes to it, do not yet satisfy me.[167] For the subtle matter, which he supposes to be enveloped in a coarser one by the heat of fire or by fermentation, is nevertheless corporeal and receives its pressure or its movement by the quantity and surfaces of its small parts. The soul, which is immaterial, could not do this.

My brother Philip, who brought me the said books, told me that there are two others en route, and since I had not requested any, I think that these will be your *Meditations* and *Principles of Philosophy* in French.[168] I am most impatient to receive the latter, since you have there added some things that were not in the Latin. I think they must be in the fourth part, since the others seemed to be as clear as it is possible to make them.

The doctor I mentioned before has told me that he had some objections concerning minerals, but that he did not dare to send them to you before he had examined your principles one more time. However, his practice prevents him from doing so. The people here have an extraordinary faith in his profession. Without the great dirtiness of the commoners and the nobility, I think that they would have less need of his profession than any people in the world, since the air here is so pure. I am here in much better health than I ever was in Holland. But I would not want to have been here always, since there is nothing but my books to prevent me from becoming completely stupid. I would have a complete satisfaction if I could express to you the esteem I have for the good will you continue to have for

Your very affectionate friend at your service,

Elisabeth.

167. Elisabeth is still concerned with the philosophical issues she raised in the letters of 1643.

168. French translations of both works were published in 1647.

DESCARTES TO ELISABETH

The Hague, 6 June 1647

Madame,

As I pass through The Hague on my way to France, since I cannot
there have the honor of receiving your orders and paying you reverence, I
feel obliged to write these lines to assure your Highness that my zeal and
my devotion will not change at all even though I change ground. Two days
ago I received a letter from Sweden from the Resident of France there,[169] in
which he proposed a question to me on behalf of the queen,[170] to whom he
had shown my response to his previous letter. From the way he describes
this queen, with his reports of her addresses, it seems to me that you would
be well suited to conversing with one another. Since there are so few people in the rest of the world who are so suited, it would not be awkward
for your Highness to start a very close friendship with her. Beyond the
contentment of mind that you would have from it, this could be desirable
for diverse reasons. I had written earlier to my friend the Resident of Sweden, in responding to a letter in which he spoke of her, that I did not find
what he said to me of her unbelievable, because the honor I have had of
knowing your Highness had made me understand how much persons of
great birth are able to surpass the others, etc.[171] But I do not remember
whether this was in the letter he showed her or in a preceding one. Since
it seems to be the case that from now on he will show her the letters he
receives from me, I will always try to put in something that will give her
reason to hope for friendship with your Highness, if you do not forbid me
to do so.

The theologians who wanted to destroy me have been silenced, but
by flattering them and by taking care not to offend them as much as was

60

---

169. Hector-Pierre Chanut (1601–62) was a French diplomat. He was also the brother-in-law
of Descartes' friend Claude Clerselier, the first editor of Descartes' letters. For Chanut's letter
of 11 May 1647 see AT 5:19–22, and for Descartes' reply of 6 June 1647 see AT 5:50–58,
CSMK 319–23.

170. Descartes here adverts to the beginning of his exchange with Queen Christina. Chanut was posted to Sweden, to which he became ambassador in 1649. Descartes wrote a
letter on love to Chanut (1 February 1647, AT 4:600–617, CSMK 305–14). Christina
had been shown this letter by her physician, M. de Rier. Her comments, however, were
not focused on Descartes' view of love. Christina had asked Descartes to explain his view
that the universe was not finite, but infinite, and how it remained consistent with Christian
doctrine.

171. See Descartes to Chanut, 1 November 1646, AT 4:536, CSMK 299. This is not the letter
Christina remarked upon.

possible, which is a sign of the times.[172] But I am afraid that these times will last always and that the theologians will be allowed to hold so much power that they will be insufferable.

The printing of my *Principles* in French is being completed. Since they will print the letter last, I am sending your Highness a copy of it here[173] so that if there is something that is not agreeable to her and which she judges should be put otherwise, she will please do me the favor of alerting me, who will be all his life, &c.

DESCARTES TO ELISABETH

AT 5:89

Egmond, 20 November 1647

Madame,

Since I have already taken the liberty of telling your Highness of the correspondence I have begun to have with Sweden, I think I am obliged to continue and tell her that a little while ago I received some letters from the friend[174] I have in that country. In them, he informs me that the queen, when she was in Uppsala where the academy of the country is, wanted to listen to a lecture on elocution by a professor[175] whom he esteems to be the most able and most reasonable of this academy. She asked him to discourse on the subject of the sovereign good in this life. But after having listened to this lecture, she said that these men only skim the surface of these matters, and that it was necessary to know my opinion on this topic. To this he replied to her that I was very reticent in writing on such matters, but that, if it pleased her Majesty, he would ask on her behalf, and he did not think that I would neglect to try to satisfy her. Upon this, she very expressly charged him to ask it of me and made him promise that he would write to me by the next post. On this he counsels me to reply to him and to address the letter to the queen, to whom he will present the letter, and he says that he is sure that the letter will be well received.

I believed I ought not to neglect this opportunity. Considering that when he wrote this letter he could not yet have received the letter[176] in

90

---

172. Descartes was vindicated of the charges leveled by Triglandius, Heereboord, and Stuart by the curators of the University of Leiden (AT 5:29–30).

173. Descartes is no doubt referring to the letter in which he dedicates the work to Elisabeth.

174. See AT 5:79–81 for summaries of Chanut's letters of 21 September 1647 and 9 November 1647.

175. Johann Freinsheim (1608–60), a professor of politics and eloquence at Uppsala University, and also librarian to the Queen.

176. This letter from Descartes to Chanut has been lost.

which I spoke of those I had the honor of writing to your Highness concerning the same matter, I thought that the plan I had had in this matter had failed and that it was necessary to take another tack. This is why I wrote a letter to the queen[177] in which, after having briefly laid out my opinion, I added that I omitted a lot of things, because in considering the number of matters which present themselves in running a great kingdom and of which her Majesty is herself taking care, I did not dare demand a longer audience of her. I also added that I sent M. Chanut some writings in which I laid out my thoughts concerning the same matter at greater length, so that if it pleased her to see them he could present them to her.[178]

The writings I sent to M. Chanut are those letters I had the honor of writing to your Highness concerning Seneca's *De vita beata,* up through the majority of the sixth letter, where after having defined the passions in general, I write that I find it difficult to enumerate them. In addition to this, I also sent him the little *Treatise on the Passions,* which I transcribed with great trouble from a very confused draft of it I had kept. And I told him that I in no way wanted him to present these writings to her Majesty first, since I would fear not showing as much respect as I ought to her Majesty if I were to send her letters I wrote for another rather than what I could judge would be agreeable to her. If he thought it good to speak of this to her, he should say that I sent the letters to him, and if she wanted to see them after that, I would be free of this scruple. I told him that I was convinced that it would be more agreeable for her to see what had already been written for another than to see something addressed to her, since she could assure herself all the more that I had changed or disguised nothing for her sake.

I decided in this matter not to include anything more about your Highness, or even to state her name, which all the same he could not fail to know because of my earlier letters. Although he is a very virtuous man and a good judge of persons of merit, and I do not doubt that he honors your Highness as much as he ought, he has all the same spoken only rarely of her in his letters even though I say something about her in each of mine. So I thought that he would have scruples about talking of her with the queen, since he does not know if this will be pleasing or displeasing to

177. See Descartes to Christina, 20 November 1647, AT 5:81–86, CSMK 324–26.

178. In his letter of 20 November 1647 to Chanut (AT 5:86–88, CSMK 326–27), Descartes attached his letters to Elisabeth and her responses concerning the basis of morality and the regulation of the passions, that is, their letters from 21 July 1545 through 28 October 1645. Note that he seems to have done so without Elisabeth's permission.

those who have sent them. But if I have an occasion to write to her herself in the future, I would not need an interpreter. The aim I have this time in sending these letters is to afford her the opportunity of considering these thoughts, and if they please her, as I have reason to hope they will, she would have the occasion to confer with your Highness. To whom I am all my life, &c.

ELISABETH TO DESCARTES

Berlin, 5 December 1647

M. Descartes,

As I received the French translation of your *Meditations Metaphysiques* a few days ago, I am obliged to thank you with these lines, even though I cannot express my recognition of your goodness without asking you also to have the goodness to excuse the trouble I give you of reading and responding to my letters, which turn you away so often from useful meditations to subjects which would not be worthy of consideration without the partiality of friendship. But I have received so many proofs of that friendship you have for me that I presume there is enough there for me to relay without difficulty the degree of satisfaction with which I read the above-mentioned translation. I am more in possession of your thoughts, now that I have seen them   97
so well expressed in a language I use regularly, even though I thought I had understood them before.

Each time I reread the objections that were raised, my wonder increases at how it is possible that people who have spent so many years in meditation and study do not know how to understand things that are so simple and so clear. Most of them, in disputing over the true and the false, do not know how to distinguish them, and M. Gassendi,[179] who has such a reputation for knowledge, made, after the Englishman,[180] the least reasonable objections of all.

This shows you how much the world needs the *Treatise on Erudition* which you once wanted to write. I know that you are too charitable to refuse some-

---

179. Pierre Gassendi (1592–1655) was author of the Fifth Objections. Gassendi was a philosopher and scientist in his own right and a great force behind the revival of Epicurean philosophy.

180. Thomas Hobbes (1588–1679), the author of the Third Objections, is most famous as the author of *Leviathan*. Both Hobbes and Gassendi were materialists about thought, and so opposed Descartes.

thing so useful to the public and that, for this, I have no need to remind you that you gave your word to

> Your very affectionate friend at your service,
> Elisabeth.

AT 5:111

DESCARTES TO ELISABETH

Egmond, 31 January 1648

Madame,

I received your Highness's letter of 23 December[181] at almost the same time as the earlier one, and I admit that I am having trouble knowing how I ought to respond to this earlier one, since your Highness there expresses that she would like me to write the *Treatise on Erudition* about which I once had the honor of speaking to her. There is nothing that I wish for with more zeal than to obey your orders, but I will state here the reasons why I laid aside the plan for this treatise, and if they are not satisfactory to your Highness, I will not fail to take it up again.

112

The first is that I did not know how to arrange all the truths that ought to be there without arousing the men of the Schools too much against me, and I do not find myself in a position where I can entirely disdain their hatred. The second is that I already touched on some of the things I would have wanted to put there in a preface to the French translation of the *Principles*, which I think your Highness has now received. The third is that I am in the midst of another piece of writing, one which I hope can be more agreeable to your Highness: the description of the functions of animals and of man. Since what I have had in draft for twelve or thirteen years now, and which was seen by your Highness, has come into the hands of several who have badly transcribed it, I thought myself obliged to make it more precise, that is to say, to rewrite it. I have even ventured there (but only for the past eight or ten days) to want to explain the way in which an animal is formed from the beginning of its origin. I say an animal in general since I would not dare to undertake this for man in particular, as I do not yet have enough evidence for this effort.[182]

For the rest, I think of what remains of this winter as possibly the most tranquil time I will have in my life. This is the reason why I prefer to use it

113

---

181. This letter has been lost.

182. Descartes, in response to what he took to be Regius's plagiarism of the draft *Treatise of Man*, sets about writing a *Description of the Body and the Formation of the Foetus*. Neither was published until after Descartes' death.

on this study rather than on another that does not require as much attention. The reason I fear having less leisure after this is that I am obliged to return to France next summer and to spend next winter there. My personal affairs and other reasons will keep me there. Also, I have been honored with an offer there of a king's pension, without my having asked for it. This will not be capable of holding me there, but many things can happen in a year. There is nothing, however, which could happen that would prevent me from preferring the good fortune of living in the same place as your Highness, if the occasion presented itself, to that of living in my own country or in any other place I might be.

I am still waiting for a response to my letter concerning the sovereign good, since it stayed for almost a month in Amsterdam, due to the fault of the person to whom I had sent it to be mailed.[183] But as soon as I have some news of it, I will not fail to let your Highness know. The letter did not contain anything new that merited being sent to you. I have received, since then, some letters from that country that indicate that mine are awaited, and according to what is written to me about this princess, she must be extremely disposed toward virtue and capable of judging things well. They also indicate that the version of my *Principles* will be presented to her, and I have been assured that she will read the first part with satisfaction, and that she will be very capable of reading the rest, if business does not interfere with her leisure.

I send with this letter a pamphlet of little importance,[184] and I do not enclose it in the same packet because it is not worth the cost. The insults of M. Regius constrained me to write this, and it was printed before I knew it would be. They even added some verses and a preface which I disapprove of, although the verses are by M. Hey[danus],[185] but he did not dare to put his name to them, as he ought not to have.

I am, &c.

---

183. Descartes had entrusted his friend Brasset to mail his letter to Chanut, but Brasset did not do so until 20 December 1647. See AT 5:109. Henri Brasset (1591–1654) was a French diplomat and the French Resident in the Hague from 1648 to 1654.

184. Descartes encloses his *Comments on a Certain Broadsheet* (*Notae in Programma quoddam*), written in response to a broadsheet published anonymously by Regius at the end of 1647 in response to Descartes' repudiation of Regius' *Fundamenta Physica*. Descartes' *Comments* was published in 1648 by Elzevier in Amsterdam, initially without Descartes' approval. The text of the *Comments* is found at AT 8B:336ff., CSM 1:294ff.

185. It is not clear who the author of this verse is. Adam and Tannery speculate that the "Hey. " of the Clerselier edition might be better read "Huy. " and so refer to Huygens. See AT 8B:340.

ELISABETH TO DESCARTES

Crossen, 30 June 1648

195   M. Descartes,

The inflammation of my right arm, caused by the mistake of a surgeon who cut part of a nerve in bleeding me, prevented me from responding sooner to your letter of 7 May.[186] In it you presented me with a new effect of your perfect generosity in regretting having to leave Holland because you are there able to hope to give me the pleasure of the benefit of your conversation. Such conversation truly is the greatest good I could await, and the only reason that I dream of the means of returning to Holland, whether by the settlement of affairs in England or by the despair of such a settlement in Germany.

Meanwhile, people are talking of the trip you once proposed, and the mother of the person[187] to whom your friend has given your letters has received the order to make it succeed without it being known in her country that it is not her own doing. It was a bad choice to trust the good woman with a secret, since she had never had one before. All the same, she accomplishes the rest of her commission with great passion and wants a third party to want it. This was not at all part of the plan, but he has put it in the hands of his family, who will no doubt be in favor of the voyage. If they send the necessary money, he is resolved to undertake it, since in this liaison he would be able to render service to those to whom he owes it and to return with the above-mentioned good woman, who does not intend to

196   stay there either. There is only this consideration to alter the reasoning you have offered against the said voyage. The death of this woman (who is sick enough), or her having to leave before the response of the other's family arrives — these are the two most obvious events which could prevent it. Three weeks ago I received a very obliging letter from the place in question, full of goodwill and protestations of friendship, but which makes no mention at all of your letters, or of that which has been said above. Also, it was only sent to the good woman by word of mouth through a messenger.[188]

---

186. Descartes' letter is now lost.

187. That is, the mother of Queen Christina of Sweden, to whom Chanut presented Descartes' exchange with Elisabeth concerning the sovereign good. Elisabeth is here referring to an effort to have her join the party of the Queen Mother of Sweden. See above, note 145, for more details about the Queen Mother. Elisabeth in what follows speaks of herself in the third person masculine.

188. Elisabeth suggests here that she has had some communication from Queen Christina herself, though not one that could be preserved. There is some reason for her discretion here, as

I have not yet given you an account of my reading of the French version of your *Principles of Philosophy.* There is something in the preface that I need you to explicate, but I will not go into that here, since it would make my letter too long. But I will undertake to do so another time, and promise myself that in changing your residence you will conserve the same charity for

Your very affectionate friend at your service,

Elisabeth.

DESCARTES TO ELISABETH

AT 5:197

Paris, June or July 1648

Madame,

Even though I know well that the place and the condition I am in could not possibly give me any occasion to be useful to your Highness, I would not fulfill my duty or my zeal if, after having arrived in a new residence, I neglected to renew the offers of my very humble obedience. I have found myself here amidst a conjunction of events that all human prudence could not possibly have predicted.[189] The Parlement, joined with the other sovereign courts, are assembling now every day in order to make a decision concerning some orders they claim ought to be put in the management of finances. This is done at present with the permission of the queen, and it appears that this matter will go on for a long time. But it is not easy to judge what will come of it. It is said that they propose to find money sufficient to continue the war and to raise great armies without trampling on the people. If they take this course, I am convinced that this will be the means of coming at last to a general peace. But in waiting to see if this will happen, I would have done well to take myself to a country where the peace has already been made. If these clouds do not dissipate soon, I propose to return toward Egmond in six weeks or two months and to stay there until the sky over France is more serene. Meanwhile, holding myself as I do with one foot in

198

---

the Peace of Westphalia was still being negotiated. Sweden was a principal in these negotiations and the Palatine family certainly had something at stake, their former kingdom.

189. Descartes refers here to the events of the Fronde, during which Parlement was trying to limit the fiscal authority of the king (at the time Louis XIV was in his minority). The date of the Notice of the Union of Parlement with the other Sovereign Courts was 13 May 1648. Anne of Austria, regent and mother of Louis, was originally opposed to the notice, but her opposition ended 22 June. The government responded in August 1648 by arresting some members of Parlement, but it was forced to yield by popular protest. The Peace of Westphalia in October 1648 allowed for royal troops to act against the Fronde, which they did. A peace between Parlement and the crown was reached in March 1649.

one country and the other in another, I find my condition a very happy one in that it is free. And I think that rich people differ from others more in that the unpleasant things which happen to them are felt more by them than in that they have more enjoyment of pleasant things, since all the contentment they can have is commonplace to them, not touching them as much as afflictions, which come to them only when they expect them least and when they are not at all prepared for them. This ought to serve as consolation to those whom fortune has accustomed to its disgraces. I would want her also to be as obedient to all your desires as I will be all my life, &c.

ELISABETH TO DESCARTES

Crossen, July 1648

M. Descartes,

You could not be anywhere in the world where the trouble you take to send me your news would not provide me with satisfaction. For I am persuaded that what is happening with you will always be to your advantage and that God is too just to send you troubles so great that your prudence would not know how to draw something from them. Take, for instance, the unexpected disorders in France which conserve your liberty in requiring you to return to Holland: otherwise, the Court would have captured you, no matter what care you could have taken to oppose yourself to it. As for me, I receive the pleasure of being able to wish for the good fortune of seeing you in Holland or elsewhere.

I think you will have received the letter that spoke of another voyage that ought to be taken if friends approve, thinking that it would be useful in this situation. Since then they have asked for it and provided the necessary funds. Nevertheless, those with whom this must begin are prevented day after day from the tasks necessary for this, for reasons so weak that even they do not dare to confess them. Meanwhile, at this hour there is so little time to do this that the person in question cannot be ready.[190] From one side, she[191] will be unwilling to break her word; and from the other, her friends will think that she did not have the will or the courage to sacrifice her health and her repose for the interest of a house for which she would still give up her life if it were required. This upsets her a bit, but it does not succeed in surprising her since she is well accustomed to suffering blame for the faults of others

---

190. The Queen Mother of Sweden arrived in Stockholm on 19 August 1648, so her departure must have been imminent.

191. Elisabeth is now referring to herself in the third-person feminine.

(even on those occasions where she would not want to rid herself of it) and of seeking her satisfaction only in the expression that her conscience gives her of her having done what she must. All the same, this sometimes turns her thoughts away from more agreeable matters. Even though you are right 211 to say that those who are rich differ more from others in that they are more sensible of the displeasures which befall them than in that they enjoy good things more, because there are few who have true objects of their pleasures (but if this were to involve benefiting the public and particularly persons of merit, a condition that would provide great means of doing so would also give more pleasure than those to whom fortune refuses this advantage could have), I would never ask for any greater pleasure than to be able to express to you the esteem I have for your goodwill for

Your very affectionate friend at your service,
Elisabeth.

ELISABETH TO DESCARTES

AT 5:224

Crossen, 23 August 1648

M. Descartes,

In my last letter I spoke to you of a person who, without having erred, was in danger of losing the good opinion and perhaps the good wishes of most of her friends. Now she finds herself delivered from this danger in a quite extraordinary way. This other of whom she had asked for the time necessary to get to her, responds that she would have waited if her daughter[192] had not changed her resolve, judging that it would have been bad had she been approached so closely by persons of a different religion. This is a development which, in my opinion, does not agree with the praise that your friend[193] had for her, at least if it is entirely hers and does not come, as I suspect it does, from the weak mind of her mother who, since this matter has been on the table, has been accompanied by a sister who gains her subsistence from a party contrary to the house of the person mentioned above.[194]

---

192. That is, Queen Christina.

193. Pierre Chanut, who was serving as intermediary between Descartes and Queen Christina.

194. Marie Eleanor of Brandenburg, the Queen Mother of Sweden, had two sisters. The first, Catherine, married first Bethlen Gabor, prince of Transylvania, and then after his death the duke of Saxe-Lauenberg. She died August 1649. Catherine's two husbands were both Protestant. The second sister, Anne Sophie, was married to Frederick Ulrich, duke of Wolfenbuttel. At his death in 1634, his estate passed to Auguste of Brunswick-Luneberg. She died in 1660. Her husband took the part of the king of Denmark in the Thirty Years' War, and so Elisabeth must be referring to her here.

226   Your friend can clarify things for you, if you find you need to send him something else. Or maybe he will write to you of his own accord, since they say that he governs entirely the mind he praises so much. I do not know what else to add to this, except that I do not judge this above-mentioned accident to be among the misfortunes of the person to whom it arrives, since it keeps her from a voyage where the bad that would revisit her (like the loss of health and rest, joined to those annoying things she must suffer in a brutal nation) was very certain, and the good that others would have hoped for very uncertain. And if there is something offensive in the affair, I find that it will fall back entirely on those who did it, since it is a mark of their inconstancy and lightness of mind, and that all those who have knowledge of this know also that she has not contributed a thing to this silliness.

As for me, I intend to remain here still, just until I learn the state of affairs of Germany and England, which seem now to be in crisis. We had an amusing encounter three days ago, though very inconvenient nonetheless. While we were walking through an oak wood, the electress with those in her train, we were overcome in an instant by a sort of redness over the whole body, except for the face, and without fever or other ill besides an insupportable itch. The superstitious believed themselves under a spell, but the peasants told us that there is sometimes a certain venomous pollen on the trees, which in descending infects those passing by. It is to be remarked that all the different remedies each imagined for an illness so new, like baths, bleeding,

227   cupping glasses, leeches, and purgatives, served for nothing. I give you this account because I presume that in it you can find something to confirm some of your doctrines. I am perfectly, M. Descartes,

Your very affectionate friend at your service,
Elisabeth.

AT 5:231

DESCARTES TO ELISABETH

Egmond, October 1648

232   Madame,

I have had the good fortune to receive at last the three letters that your Highness has done the honor of writing me, and they have not fallen into bad hands. But the first, of 30 June, was brought to Paris when I was, in the meantime, already on my way back to this country. Those who received it for me waited until they had news of my arrival before sending it on to me, and so I was only able to get it today, when I also received the latest letter of 23 August, through which I learn of an insulting proceeding, at which I wonder. I want to believe, with your Highness, that it does not come from the person to whom it is attributed. Whatever it happens to be, I do not think that one ought to be so put out, since, as your Highness notes quite well, the inconveniences of such a voyage would be unavoidable and the advantages very uncertain. As for me, by the grace of God, I finished what I was obliged to do in France. I am not sorry to have gone there, but I am all the happier to have returned. I saw no one whose condition seemed to me worth desiring as one's own. Those who had the most flashy appearance seemed to me those most worthy of pity. I could not have gone there at a time more advantageous for reminding me of the felicity of a tranquil and retired life and the richness of the most mediocre fortunes. If your Highness compares her condition with that of the queens and the other princesses of Europe, she will find there the same difference as that between those who are in port, where they relax, and those who are on the high sea, stirred up by the winds of a tempest. Even if one is thrown into port by a shipwreck, so long as one does not there lack those things necessary for life, one ought not to be less content there than if one had arrived there in another way. The aggravating encounters which befall people who are in the thick of things and whose felicity depends wholly on others penetrate all the way to the base of their heart, whereas this venomous vapor that fell from the trees where your Highness was peacefully walking touched only, I hope, the exterior of her skin, where, I think, it shouldn't have done any harm at all if it was washed within an hour with a little alcohol.

I have not received any letters in the last five months from my friend about whom I had written before to your Highness.[195] Since in his last letter he let me know very pointedly the reasons that had prevented the person to whom he had given my letters from responding to me, I judge that his silence comes only because he is still waiting for this response, or maybe even because he is a little embarrassed at not having anything to send me, even though he imagined he would. I am restraining myself from writing him first, in order not to seem to be reproaching him for this by my letter. I did not neglect to hear news of him often when I was in Paris, through those near to him who received it every eight days. But when they let him know that I am here, I do not doubt that he will write me here, and that he will let me know what he knows of the proceedings which concern your Highness, for he knows that I take great interest in them. But those who have never had the honor of seeing you, and who have no firsthand knowledge of your virtues, could not conceive that one could be as perfectly as I am, &c.

195. The most recent letter from Chanut to Descartes was dated 4 April 1648.

DESCARTES TO ELISABETH

Egmond, 22 February 1649

281   Madame,

Of the several disturbing pieces of news I received at the same time from different places,[196] the one that affected me most deeply was the illness of your Highness.[197] Even though I also learned of her recovery from it, that did not stop me from retaining some vestiges of sadness, which cannot be so quickly erased from my mind. The inclination your Highness had during her illness to write some verse reminds me of Socrates, who, according to Plato, felt a similar desire while he was in prison. I think that this mood to write verse comes from a strong agitation of the animal spirits, which can completely overtake the imagination of those who have a very soft brain but only warms firm ones a little more and disposes them to poetry. I take this latter comportment as a sign of a soul that is stronger and of more grace than the common one.

If I did not know yours to be such a soul, I would fear that you were ex-
282   traordinarily afflicted by learning of the disastrous conclusion of the English Tragedies.[198] But I swear to myself that your Highness, being accustomed to the disfavor of fortune, and having seen herself so recently in the greatest peril of her life, would be neither so surprised nor so troubled to learn of the death of one of her relations as she would have been had she not previously received other afflictions. And even though this very violent death seems more awful than the one waiting in one's own bed, all the same, to under-stand it properly, it is more glorious, more happy, and more gentle. For in this case what would particularly afflict the common man ought to serve as consolation to your Highness. For it is a great glory to die on an occasion that makes one universally pitied, praised, and missed by all those who have any human feeling. And it is certain that without this experience the mercy and the other virtues of the late dead king would never be as remarked upon or as valued as they are and will be in the future by those who read his story. I am sure also that during the last moments of his life his conscience gave

196. Descartes had learned of the deaths of two of his friends, the abbot of Touchelaye and a M. Hardy, master of Contes, who had housed Descartes while he was in Paris. See AT 5:279–80.

197. In all likelihood, Elisabeth informed Descartes of an illness in a letter that is now lost.

198. The English Civil War had escalated, and Charles I, Elisabeth's uncle, was beheaded on 9 February 1649.

him greater satisfaction than indignation—the only sad passion which they say was noticed in him—caused him upset. As for what is painful, I do not figure that in at all. For the pain lasts for so short a time that if the murderers could have used fever or some other malady that nature usually uses to remove men from the earth, we would have reason to deem them crueler than they are when they kill with the stroke of an axe. But I do not dare to rest for a long time on a subject so disastrous. I add only that it is much better to be delivered entirely from a false hope than to be caught up in it uselessly.

283

While writing these lines, I have received letters from a place from which I have had none for seven or eight months, one of which is from the person to whom I had sent the treatise on the passions a year ago, who has written in her own hand to thank me for it.[199] Since she remembered, after such a long time, someone so insignificant as myself, it is to be thought that she will not forget to respond to the letters of your Highness, even if she has delayed four months in doing so. The letter informs me that she has charged one of her people to read my *Principles*, in order to facilitate her own reading of it. Nevertheless, I do not think that she finds enough leisure to apply herself to it, even if she seems to have the will to do so. She thanks me directly for the treatise on the passions, but she makes no mention of the letters to which it was joined, and the letters let me know nothing from that country which concerns your Highness. I can infer nothing else but that, as the conditions of the German peace were not as advantageous to your house as they might have been,[200] those who contributed to this fact are in doubt as to whether you wish them ill, and restrain themselves for that reason from expressing friendship toward you.

284

Since the conclusion of this peace, I have always been troubled that I learned nothing about whether your brother the elector[201] had accepted it, and I would have taken the liberty to write of my feelings earlier to your Highness if I had been able to imagine that he would consider this in his deliberations. But since I know nothing about the particular reasons that move him, it would be temerity for me to make any judgment. I can only say, in general, that when it is a question of the restitution of a state which

---

199. See letter from Christina of 12 December 1648, AT 5:251, and that from Chanut, of the same date, AT 5:252.

200. The Peace of Westphalia did return Heidelberg and the surrounding area to the Palatine house, but these lands formed but a small portion of their former holdings.

201. Charles Louis (Karl Ludwig) was the Elector Palatine. For insight into the dispute amongst the siblings over lands and wealth that followed soon after, see Foucher de Careil, *Descartes et la princesse Palatine, ou de l'influence du cartésianisme sur les femmes au XVIIe siécle*, appendix.

is occupied or disputed by others who have power in hand, it seems to me that those who have only equity and the right of men pleading for them ought never to count on obtaining all they hope for. They have much better reason to thank those who enable them to be given some part of it, no matter how small it is, than they have to wish ill to those who retain the rest of it. Even though no one would say it was wrong for them to dispute their right as much as they can while those who have power deliberate on it, I think that once these conclusions are reached prudence obliges them to express that they are content, even if they are not so, in order to maintain their standing. They also ought to thank not only those who have given them something but also those who did not destroy them completely, and by this means to acquire the friendship of each of them, or at least to avoid their hate. In addition, there still remains a long road from the promises to their effect. And if those who have power agree among themselves alone, it is easy to find reason to partition among themselves what they might have been willing to give to a third because of the jealousy between them and to prevent the one enriched by his spoils from being too powerful. The smallest part of the Palatinate is worth more than the whole empire of the Tartars or the Muscovites, and after two or three years of peace, a stay there will be as agreeable as one in any other place on earth. For me, who is not attached to living in one place, I would have no difficulty in exchanging these Provinces, or even France, for that country, if I had the power of finding there an equally secure peace, even if the only reason that made me go there was the beauty of the country. But there is no place on earth so rough and inconvenient that I would not deem myself happy to pass the rest of my days there if your Highness were there and I were capable of rendering her some service. Since I am entirely and without any reservations, &c.

AT 5:330

DESCARTES TO ELISABETH

Egmond, 31 March 1649

Madame,

It has been almost a month since I had the honor of writing to your Highness and of telling her that I had received some letters from Sweden. I have just received some others, and through these I am invited by the queen to voyage there this spring so I might return before winter. But I responded this way: even though I do not refuse to go there, I think that I will not

leave here until the middle of summer.[202] I asked for this delay in light of several considerations, and particularly in order that I can have the honor of receiving your Highness's orders before leaving. I have already declared so publicly the zeal and the devotion that I have to your service that it would give more reason to form a bad opinion of me if it is remarked that I am indifferent to what concerns you than it would if it seemed that I search pointedly for occasions to acquit myself of my duty. So I plead your High-   331
ness very humbly to do me the favor of instructing me as to all she judges I can do to render service to her or to those close to her, and of being assured that the power she has over me is as if I had been her house servant all my life. I entreat her also to let me know how it would please her for me to respond, if it happens that your Highness's letters concerning the sovereign good, of which I had made mention last year in my letters, are remembered, and there is curiosity to see them. I am counting on passing the winter in that country and returning only next year. It is believable that there will be peace by then in all of Germany, and if my desires are fulfilled I will take a course back through the place where you will be, in order that I can more personally express that I am, &c.

DESCARTES TO ELISABETH   *AT 5:359*

Egmond, June 1649

Madame,

Since your Highness desires to know what I have resolved regarding the voyage to Sweden,[203] I will tell her that I persist in planning to go there, insofar as the queen continues to express that she wants me to go there, and   360
as M. Chanut, our Resident in that country, who passed through here eight days ago on his way to France, spoke so positively to me of this marvelous queen that the trip there no longer seems to me to be so long or so troublesome as it did before. But I will not leave until I receive news from that country one more time, and I will try to wait for the return of M. Chanut to make the voyage with him, since I hope that he will be sent back to Sweden. In other matters, I would esteem myself fortunate, if, while I am there, I could render some service to your Highness. I will not neglect to seek out assiduously opportunities to do so, and I will not fear writing openly

202. See Descartes to Chanut, 31 March 1649, AT 5:323–29, CSMK 370–71.
203. Elisabeth's letter to which this letter is responding is lost.

all that I do or think regarding this subject. For I cannot have any intention that would be prejudicial to those to whom I am obliged to show respect. I hold as a maxim that the just and honest paths are the most useful and most sure, and so even if the letters I will write were to be seen, I hope that they could not be interpreted badly or fall into the hands of persons who are so unjust as to find it bad that I perform my duty and make an overt profession of being, &c.

AT 5:429

DESCARTES TO ELISABETH

Stockholm, 9 October 1649

Madame,

I arrived four or five days ago in Stockholm, and I take one of the first of my duties to be to renew the offers of my very humble service to your Highness, so she can know that the change of climate and of country can change nothing or diminish my devotion and my zeal. I have so far had the honor of seeing the queen only twice, but it seems that I already know her well enough to dare to say that she has no less merit and more virtue than her reputation assigns her. With the generosity and majesty that shine in all her actions, one sees a gentleness and a goodness that oblige all who love virtue and who have the honor to approach her to be entirely devoted to her service. One of the first things she asked of me was whether I had news of you, and I did not hesitate to tell her immediately what I think of your 430 Highness. For remarking the force of her mind, I did not fear that this would arouse any jealousy in her, just as I am sure that your Highness feels none when I write her freely of my feelings about this queen. She is extremely drawn to the study of letters. But, since I do not know anything about what she has already seen of philosophy, I cannot judge what her taste might be there or whether she will be able to spend some time studying it. Nor, as a result, can I judge if I will be capable of satisfying her and being useful to her in some way. This great ardor she has for the knowledge of letters incites her now more than anything to learn the Greek language and to collect many old books. But this might change. If it does not change, the virtue I remark in this princess obliges me always to prefer the usefulness of service to her to the desire to please her. Thus this will not prevent me from telling her frankly of my feelings. If they fail to be agreeable to her, which I don't think they will, I will at least draw the benefit of having fulfilled my duty. This will give me the opportunity to be able to return before too long to my solitude, without which it is difficult for me to advance in the search for truth. And it is in this that my principal benefit in this life consists. M. Freinsheimius[204] has led her Majesty to find it good that I should go to the castle only during those hours when it pleases her to give me the honor of talking with her. Thus, I will not be too put out by being at court, and this is quite suited to my disposition. Nevertheless, even though I have a very great veneration for her Majesty, I do not think anything is capable of keeping me in this country for longer than next summer, but I cannot absolutely predict what the future holds. I can only assure you that I will be all my life, &c.

431

ELISABETH TO DESCARTES

AT 5:451

4 December 1649

M. Descartes;

Your letter of 9 October was brought though Cleve, and although old it does provide a very agreeable and very obliging proof of the continuation of your goodwill toward me. It assures me also of the fortunate success of your voyage, since it was worth the trouble and you find still more marvels in the queen of Sweden than her reputation brings to light. But I must say that you are more capable of knowing them than those who proclaimed them before. It seems to me that I know more of them, by the little that you have said of them, than by all of what I have learned elsewhere. Do not believe, however, that a description so advantageous gives me reason to be jealous. Rather it leads me to esteem myself a little more than I did before she gave me the idea of a person so accomplished, who defends our sex from the imputation of imbecility and weakness that the pedants would have given it. I am sure that once she has tasted your philosophy one time she will prefer it to their philology. But I wonder how it is possible for this princess to apply herself to study as she does and to the affairs of the kingdom as well, two occupations that are so different, each of which demand an entire person. The honor she did me of remembering me in your presence, I attribute entirely to a plan to oblige you, for it gave you occasion to exercise a charity that you have expressed on many other occasions. I owe you this benefit as well as I do if I obtain some part of her approbation, which I will be all the more able to conserve because I will never have the honor of being known to her Majesty except as you represent me. I feel myself, all the same, guilty of a

452

204. See above, note 175.

crime against her service, as I am glad that your extreme veneration for her will not require you to remain in Sweden. If you leave there this winter, I hope that it will be in the company of M. Kleist,[205] with whom you will find the best means of giving the happiness of seeing you again to

your very affectionate friend at your service,
Elisabeth.

205. Ewald von Kleist, ambassador of Brandenburg to Denmark and Sweden in 1649. Thanks to Jeroen van de Ven for insight into Kleist's identity.

APPENDIX
ADDITIONAL CORRESPONDENCE OF PRINCESS ELISABETH OF BOHEMIA

INTRODUCTION

In this volume, I have also included transcriptions of Edward Reynolds's dedication to Elisabeth of his *Treatise on the Passions and Faculties of the Soule of Man*, and Elisabeth's correspondence with the Quakers Robert Barclay and William Penn.

Nothing is known of how Reynolds came to dedicate his work to Elisabeth, other than what he writes, or of how the two came in contact with one another. According to the dedicatory letter, Reynolds published his *Treatise* at Elisabeth's request. He himself is not enthusiastic about it. While his apologetic tone may be a matter of convention, the work does differ substantially from his published sermons. Still, in some ways, Reynolds's work prefigures the treatise on the passions Elisabeth was to commission from Descartes. The work treats of the passions as bodily motions that give rise to thoughts, and draws a distinction between rational and sensitive passions and those that fall in between. Reynolds considers three aspects under which the passions might be considered, the natural, the moral, and the civil, and we might think that whereas Descartes focuses on the natural aspect, Reynolds focuses on the moral. Like Descartes, Reynolds parts company with the neo-Stoic moralists and denies that the eradication of the passions should be the goal of any regulation of the passions. Rather, both theorists of the passions take it that the passions are conducive to human happiness and virtue so long as they are subject to reason.

It is also not known how Elisabeth, as abbess at Herford, came in contact with the Quakers. One thought is that Francis Mercury van Helmont, who both served as Elisabeth's physician and had dealings with English Quakers, facilitated their interaction. The question then arises as to how Elisabeth came in contact with van Helmont. It is also very likely that Elisabeth became connected with Barclay through familial political interests. Robert

Barclay's father, David Barclay of Ury, supported the Scottish engagement with the king in the English Civil War, and his alignment with the royalist cause might well have brought him into contact with Elisabeth's brother Rupert. His first letter to her in this series does imply he knows Rupert.

Elisabeth's exchange with Robert Barclay begins just about the time of the publication of his *Theologiae Vere Christianae Apologia*, or *Apology for the True Christian Religion*, first published in 1676. It constituted the first substantial defense of Quakerism. Barclay had already articulated the basic tenets of Quakerism two years earlier in his *Theses theologicae*. Barclay's enthusiasm for Quakerism is clear in this exchange, and he presses upon Elisabeth the possibility of her experiencing the true divine light. While Elisabeth is initially receptive to Barclay's apparent efforts to convert her, her letters are short and skeptical of her own ability to have the divine light revealed to her. She is, nonetheless, uniformly polite and concerned for Barclay's well-being, particularly with regard to his imprisonment at Aberdeen. In addition, it is remarkable just how much the correspondence with Barclay is colored by political matters in Scotland and England in the aftermath of the English Civil War. Elisabeth does seem to be concerned to preserve good relations with someone who had been a royalist supporter.

Elisabeth's correspondence with William Penn immediately following his trip through the Rhine Valley has a similar flavor. Penn initially wrote to Elisabeth upon learning that she had welcomed the Labadists into Herford. Penn viewed Labadie as a false Quaker and took it upon himself to introduce the true Quakerism to Elisabeth. Penn clearly hopes to convert Elisabeth and her friend Anna Maria van Hoorn to Quakerism. While Elisabeth is receptive to his entreaties, she does not count herself as being illuminated by divine light.

One might initially think there is a connection between Elisabeth's early interest in Cartesianism and her later interest in Quakerism. Just as Descartes, in the *Meditations*, insists that each individual must withdraw from the senses and meditate along with him in order to clearly and distinctly perceive those truths which constitute first philosophy, so too is it a basic tenet of Quakerism that each individual must, in Barclay's words, "chain down" his or her imagination in order to have that intensely personal experience through which divine truth is grasped. Elisabeth's skepticism about Quakerism, however, contrasts with her embrace of Cartesianism. While this may well indicate a shift in her view, it need not. Elisabeth's attraction to Descartes' philosophy was due to its method as much as to its metaphysical and natural philosophical positions. For Descartes, we are able to perceive clearly and distinctly because we have undertaken to break down systematically the problem at hand, and then to construct a solution based on an intuitive grasp of the relations of the parts. While Quakerism too relies on our faculty of intuition, it does not say much about the method for accessing that intuition properly. By Elisabeth's exacting standards, it might be that Quakerism simply does not go far enough. Nonetheless, it is interesting that she continues to be receptive to positions which champion alternative ways of finding the truth that human beings naturally seek.

LETTER OF DEDICATION OF *A TREATISE OF THE PASSIONS AND FACULTIES OF THE SOUL OF MAN,* BY EDWARD REYNOLDS

To her Highness the Princess Elizabeth, Princess Palatine of the Rhine, Duchess of Bavaria, and eldest daughter to her Majesty the Queen of Bohemia.
May it please your Highness;

What the great philosopher has observed of men's bodies, is, upon so much stronger reasons, true of their minds, by how much our intellectual maturity is more lingering and sluggish than our natural, that the too early conceptions and issues of them do usually prove but weak and useless. And we shall seldom find, but that those venturous blossoms, whose over-hasty obedience to the early spring does anticipate their proper season, and put forth too soon, do afterwards for their former boldness suffer from the injury of severer weather, except at least some happy shelter, or more benign influence redeem them from danger. The like infelicity I find myself obnoxious unto at this time. For I know not out of what disposition of mind, whether out of love of learning (for love is venturous, and conceives difficult things easier than they are) or whether out of a resolution to take some account from myself of those few years wherein I had then been planted in the happiest of all soils, the Schools of Learning; whether upon these, or any other inducements, so it has happened, that I long since have taken boldness in the minority of my studies to write this ensuing treatise: that before I adventured on the endeavour of knowing other things, I might first try whether I knew myself. Least I should justly incur the censure, which that sour philosopher passed upon the grammarians: that they were better acquainted with the evils of Ulysses than with their own.[1] This hasty resolution having produced so untimely an issue, it happened by some accident to be like Moses in his infancy exposed to the seas. Where I made no other account, but that its own weakness would there

---

1. I have not been able to identify the source of this remark.

have revenged my former boldness, and betrayed it unto perishing. But as he then, so this now, has had the marvellous felicity to light on the view, and fall under the compassion of a very gracious Princess. For so far has your Highness vouchsafed (having happened on the sight on this tractate) to express favour thereunto, as not only to spend hours in it, and require a transcript of it, but further to recommend it by your gracious judgement unto public view. In which particular I was not to advise with my own opinion, being to express my humblest acknowledgement to your Highness.

This only petition I shall accompany it withal unto your Highness' feet, that since it is a blossom which put forth so much too soon, it may therefore obtain the gracious influence of your Highness' favour, to protect it from the severity abroad which it otherwise justly fears.

God Almighty make your Highness as great a mirror of his continual mercies, as he has both of his graces and of learning.

Your Highness' most humble servant,

Edward Reynoldes.

ROBERT BARCLAY TO ELISABETH

London, 24 April 1676

Dear friend,

The sense and constant remembrance which I entertain in my spirit of that good opportunity which it pleased the Lord to minister unto us when together would long here now have engaged me to write unto thee but that I was not willing to do any thing in the forwardness of my own spirit, yea not in the forwardness of the affectionate part. Therefore I have waited for this season wherein I might transmit unto thee (as by these I do) a salutation of love in the sense of that life that alone makes every means conveyed in the sense of it, to the benefiting and bettering the soul.

I hope the Lord, yea, I am confident, the Lord's at work with thee and is near to reveal himself to thee as thou waits still and abides faithful in that which he hath manifested in and unto thee. Therefore sink down more and more to feel after it and be not disobedient to the least manifestation of his appearance, however cross it may be not only to thy own inclinations but to thy present station and condition in the world. There is nothing lets more the manifestation of God's power in the soul in that fullness of glory wherein he doth reveal himself to his children than disobedience to the least of his requirings, and there is no snare more incident to man than through an expectation of great and glorious things, either to despise or forget to obey in these little and small things which are revealed, by which nevertheless God often tries our faithfulness and resignation. He that is faithful in a little shall be ruler over much, therefore be faithful to the least appearances of God's light in thy heart, and thereby thou shalt receive what more is requisite for thee and the real enjoyment of that inward peace that will follow. Such inward waiting upon the Lord is beyond the highest notions and speculations of mortification and self-denial. I can say in that fullness of assurance in which I have received a full share in the ministry of the gospel of peace, this love of God is to thee and is near to gather thee to himself. O that thou may be made willing to receive him and may not stick to lay thy outward crown and glory at the foot of Jesus. Neither refuse the shame and reproach that attends his blessed work and testimony in this world, for which though thou may suffer for a season, yet if thou be found faithful unto the obedience of the cross, generations to come shall call thee blessed as being of the first of the great of this world who has been found worthy to receive Christ in his spiritual appearance. O how my soul travels that this may be thy lot. I am often near thee in spirit and in the sense of that precious seed which God hath sown both in thee and in the Countess of Hornes.[2] I am often bowed down before the Lord and I hope my travel shall not be in vain, for many of God's faithful messengers upon the hearing of what past have the same sense with me and have been concerned upon their account and have travelled for you, I doubt not. But as any of them are drawn in the love of God (as I hope they may) to visit thee either personally or by writing, they will be ready to answer it. Neither shall I question but they will find with thee good acceptance. As for my part, the Lord seems to have laid a particular care and concern upon me which I am very willing to answer, for he hath kindled that love in my heart for thee which I shall not adventure to express lest I might seem to exceed. It is manifest to him who hath begotten it by my daily breathings and cries unto him in thy behalf and it shall not be unknown unto thee as thou lives more and more in that in which thou can be sensible of it. I shall be glad to hear from thee as thou finds true freeness to let me know how things are with thee. Let these transmit the remembrance of my true and unfeigned love to the Countess of Hornes. I hope she hath held her resolutions of learning to read and understand English, which it may please the Lord to bless unto her. I delivered thy letter to thy brother,[3] who was civil to me. I also took occasion from then to employ him to be of assistance to me in an address I intend to make the King in behalf

2. Anna Maria van Hoorn. Little is known about her other than that she was a daughter of a Dutch merchant. In this correspondence it becomes clear that she was a close companion of Elisabeth at the convent at Herford.

3. In all likelihood, Prince Rupert.

of my Father and about forty more of our friends that are about some months ago imprisoned in Scotland for conscience sake, in which he promised his concurrence. If it proves successful it is well; if not, it is well also. We must be content to suffer and I shall go home cheerfully, willing to partake with them of their bonds. I intend to send thee some books which I hope may be useful unto thee, but above all I recommend thee to that inward word of grace in which thou can read thyself and learn to know the Lord, in which pure and fruitful knowledge that thou may more and more advance is the earnest desire of

Thy assured friend in the love of Jesus,

Barclay.

ELISABETH TO ROBERT BARCLAY

21/31 *July 1676*

My dear friend in our Saviour Jesus Christ.

I have received your letter dated the 24th of June this day and since I am pressed to take this opportunity to make a certain address unto your brother Benjamin Furly,[4] I must give you that abrupt answer. Your memory is dear unto me, so are your lines and your exhortations very necessary. I confess myself still spiritually very poor and naked. All my happiness is that I do know that I am so, and that whatsoever I have studied and learned heretofore is but dirt in comparison to the true knowledge of Christ. I confess also my infidelity to this light heretofore by suffering myself to be conducted by false politick lights. Now that I have sometimes a small glimpse of the true light I do not attend it as I should, being drawn away by the works of my calling, which must be done, and (as your swift English hounds) I often over-run myself, being called back when it is too late. Let not this make you less earnest in prayers for me, you see, I need them. Your letters will be always welcome to me, so will your friends if any please to visit me. I should admire God's providence if my brother could be a means of releasing your father and forty more in Scotland. Having promised to do his best I know he will perform it. He has ever been true to his word and you shall find me with the grace of our Lord a true friend.

Elizabeth[5]

4. Benjamin Furly (1636–1714) was a merchant in Rotterdam. He was Penn's estate agent there. Furly is also known for housing John Locke upon his stay in the Netherlands in 1687.

5. Since this portion is a transcription, I have followed the Anglicized spelling of Elisabeth's name in the original text.

P.S. The Countess of Hornes sends you her most hearty commendations. She has not had time to learn English having employed it in more necessary works since God has visited this family with many sick of small pox and contagious fevers of which she has had a care not considering the infection. Amongst the rest there was a servant of hers very desperately sick of whom she had a special care deeming her to be also a sister in Christ who did draw great comfort out of the books you left here.

ROBERT BARCLAY TO ELISABETH

Edinburgh, 6 September 1676

Dear Friend,

Last night thy acceptable letter came to my hands, in which my spirit was refreshed, in a sense that the Lord continueth his love to thee, which I hope shall never cease until it accomplishes the desired end. It is good thou retain a sense of thy own poverty, for it is the humble the Lord regardeth. He filleth the hungry with good things but sendeth the fully empty away. It is good how poor we be of ourselves, that having no confidence in ourselves nor in the fruits of self, we may seek for that heavenly treasure which God hath placed in our earthen vessels, even that saving divine light which makes all things manifest, which though it be small and contemptible in its first appearance, yet as it is heeded and regarded doth shine more and more until it fill the soul with its brightness and glory. Nothing hinders it more than the fertility of activity of the natural spirit in its thoughts and imaginations, which must be chained down. As the mind is freely resigned and willing to part with its own thoughts by sinking down into a profound stillness and silence, there is a secret power that will be revealed to help the soul to retain itself and go through this chief work of mortification. I doubt not but as thou abides faithful and single to the Lord but thou will feel his strength revealed in thee and his light will more and more shine to teach thee how to order thy steps in thy present calling so as to separate between the precious and the vile. I doubt not but thy brother would have kept his word in speaking to the king in my behalf but it is so happened that at that time he had a sore leg (of which he is since recovered) so that I could not make use of him. With no small difficulty I obtained a kind of a recommendation from the king to the council of state, but such is the opposition and enmity of the world's spirit against us and the influence of the chief bishops who sit in council that no release for the prisoners could be obtained so that they must patiently suffer till the Lord in his own time work their deliverance, who will suffer them to continue no longer there than is good for their souls and his own glory. And indeed they have great reason to be contented, for the glory and heavenly majesty of the Lord doth singularly every day appear among them and the virtuous life of Jesus doth often flow among them as a mighty stream. That the praises of the Lord is often sounded forth through young boys and girls to the astonishment of many and streams of joyful tears are almost always running down the cheeks of the aged and oftentimes it is with them as with the disciples in the day of Pentecost. They seem (through the overflowing power of God) to the dark world as men reeling and drunk with new wine. Thus are shut up together 42 men in one great room who not of self-will nor their own choice but by the providence of God are pleased for a time together in a heavenly community as joint sufferers for the testimony of Jesus. I this day take my journey towards them not doubting but I shall be taken and shut up with them and with all cheerfulness of spirit am prepared to partake with them of their bonds not doubting but I shall also share of their joys. I hope neither I nor they shall there be forgetful of thee, but as we have access breath to the Lord that thou may come to witness the glorious liberty of the sons of God. It will be very refreshful and comfortable to me in my prison to hear of thee for thy prosperity and increase in the truth is desired by me as that of my own soul. My love to thee in the Lord is great which does and shall still oblige me to continue

  Thy faithful friend,
   Barclay.

ELISABETH TO ROBERT BARCLAY

6 October 1676

My friend,

  In your letter dated the 6th of September you approve the sense I have of my poverty, which continueth still. But I see no way to grow rich in this present condition. The silent waiting is no more in my power than flying through the air. Since my calling gives me some diversions, I scarce have an hour of the day to myself. The night is my best time in which I endeavour to practice your lesson but cannot brag of much progress. The Countess of Hornes doth outgo me far. Having stronger ties and more liberty, she hath sent to Benjamin Furly an essay of her translation out of English into low Dutch. It is a treatise in which I have found great satisfaction. I am sorry that my brother's affection and the king's order have both proved useless to you for the release of your joyful prisoners. It is a happiness indeed to partake of such bonds and be free of the fetters that tie to the world by ceremonies and inventions of many kinds which are not to be withstood by one that hath not more grace than is felt at this present by

Your true friend,

Elizabeth.

P.S. Your books are not yet come into my hands, but though I send to the Elector of Brandenburg and my brother-in-law I am certain neither of them both will vouchsafe to read it, but my brother the Elector will and perchance my nephew the Duke of Hanover, who is a Papist but curious of outward knowledge.

ROBERT BARCLAY TO ELISABETH

Ury, 28 October 1676

Dear friend,

I did write to thee about 7 weeks ago from Edinburgh at what time I presented a paper from the King to the Council here in behalf of the prisoners in which I acquainted thee of its proving unsuccessful. The Council refused to release them unless they would pay certain fines and promise not to meet to worship God again unless according to the religion approved by law, neither of which because for conscience sake they cannot do, they must remain and patiently wait until the Lord, in whose hand are the hearts of men, work their deliverance who will not suffer this exercise to continue any longer than it is needful for us. Therefore I, being in daily expectation to hear from thee of the receipt of that letter wherewith, I also wrote one in French to Anna.[6] Do forbear to enlarge at this time only thou may know that thou are daily in my remembrance. And my breathing is that the Lord may not suffer his seed to be unfruitful in thee but raise it, and thee by it, over all difficulties that stand in the way until thou arrive at the blessed end, which is more desirable than all the glory of this world. My mentioning of your condition to several of my brethren and sisters did raise great love in their hearts towards you and frequent breathings for you which, though at a great outward distance, I hope are not without virtue and service towards you. Among others, one singular woman found herself drawn to write this foregoing letter to Anna, which I hope will be useful to you both. She is a

6. The countess of Hornes.

woman of great experience and tenderness of heart and who through great tribulation both of body and mind hath attained the earnest of the kingdom. She is also deeply engaged in the present trial: both her husband son and son-in-law being prisoners. Let these remember my dear love to Anna to whom I forbear to write apart expecting a particular answer from her of mine. I was glad to hear of thy reception of our friend from Amsterdam[7] and owe thee so much the more love for it that meeting her at London I did much press upon her to make that visit. My heart bleeds and breathes for Ernestus[8] that the Lord may make way for his deliverance and therefore I have written to him by this post. The Lord of his mercy keep you all sensible until his work be accomplished. My love salutes all in thy family whose faces are towards Zion and I remain

Thy assured friend in the Lord,
Barclay.

ELISABETH TO ROBERT BARCLAY

1/11 December 1676

My dear friend,

I have received your letter from Ury dated the 28th of October and at the same time information from Benjamin Furly that you have been clapped up, though I am sure that the captivers are more captive than you are being in the company of him that admits no bonds and is able to break all bonds. It is a comfort to me that I shall not want your prayers and that other true members of Jesus Christ join with you therein for the raising of that which is still very small and weak in me though it be not without some manifestation. I have translated or rather read L.S.[9] letter unto Anna for she is now able to translate any English into her native language but not to read an English hand with abbreviations. You will see by her answer (which perchance will need another interpreter) what sense this letter raised in her. I doubt not but your letter to Ernestus will be of as good use to him as the copy of it (sent by Benjamin Furly) has been to me but there are still great mountains in our

---

7. Benjamin Furly.

8. Ernestus is in all likelihood Ernst August, duke of Brunswick-Lüneburg (1629–98), the husband of Elisabeth's youngest sister, Sophie, and so the brother-in-law mentioned in the postscript of her previous letter. The Latin form of his name is Ernestus Augustus. Sophie married him on 30 September 1658. He became the first elector of Hanover in 1692.

9. Lillias Gillespie Skene (1626–97), a Quaker poet and wife of Alexander Skene.

way, which God in his infinite mercy will remove, in his due time. That he may break all our bonds is the sything[10] of

Your true friend,

Elizabeth.

ROBERT BARCLAY TO ELISABETH

Aberdeen Prison, 24 October 1676

Dear friend,

Thy letter in answer to mine of the 6th of September came yesternight to my hand and was very acceptable unto me in my present bonds. My fervent desires always remain for thee to hear that thou continueth under a sense of thy present condition and seeth the need thou has to partake of the spiritual riches of Christ's kingdom, which are more desirable than all the world. This is good in its place but thou must not satisfy thyself to abide here, but must apply thyself to that divine grace and light that hath shown thee thy poverty in which there is power to make thee rich, if thou can receive and suffer it to dwell richly in thee. I confess that so needful inward silence is hard to the natural mind especially to those who have enriched their spirits with great variety of notions and have laboured to deck themselves with the wisdom and knowledge of this world. Thy eminency wherein though it commended thee to the world, renders now that which is most needful so difficult for thee and makes that thy friend because of her greater simplicity and less attainments in these things has a readier access to possess and enjoy the naked truth, which for this cause of old was more readily received by poor fishermen and simple women than by the great rabbis and wise Greeks. Yet thy difficulties are not so great, nor thy encumbrances so invincible. But that the grace of God which has appeared unto thee and has really touched thee with a sense of thy condition is sufficient for thee. Therefore beware that the enemy does not betray thee (after the Lord has thus awakened thee), as if sufficient grace were not given thee to deliver thee from all thy temptations. For God as he is powerful, so he is willing thou should overcome, and his grace will not be to thee in vain unless thou make it so by unfaithfulness. In that seed and light that has appeared to thee, there is strength to deliver thee from all. Though the appearance of it be small, yet there is might in it as it is received. Therefore it is compared to a grain of mustard seed: remember that parable. I know no calling (however it were lawful otherwise) that ought

10. I take this to be an alternate spelling and a form of *to sithe,* meaning "to say with a sigh."

to divert thee from this so necessary a business. The kingdom of God ought to be sought after in the first part though it were with the neglect of other matters which will be abundantly made up other ways and caring for the better part. It matters not though other matters be disregarded for a season for this man was commended of the Lord Jesus, and indeed when the Lord touches the heart of any to draw them out of the spirit of this world, there is a great retirement and abstraction both of mind and body necessary for a season, because of the soul's weakness at such a time and its capacity to be entangled with any diversion. Therefore let me not only seriously advise thee but likewise obtest [11] thee in the bowels of our Lord Jesus for thy soul's sake to draw near to the Lord in the small appearance of his seed in thy heart and for that end, abstract thyself from the multiplicity of thy outward affairs though thou should leave undone not only all things that are superfluous but even some things that may appear to thee at present to be needful in that respect. Afterwards when through such retirement to be more acquainted and so more distinctly to perceive and discern the witness of God in thy soul and to feel the power thereof, thou will be the more capable clearly to distinguish between the precious and the vile and more enabled to forsake the one and follow the other. If upon a pressing outward business or to visit a relation or friend after the flesh thou can retire thyself for a season from these outward diversions, far more ought thou to disentangle thyself when the Lord calls for it by the awakening of his seed in thy heart for the redemption of thy soul. Two things are therefore absolutely needful even to the entry as well as accomplishment of this work, to wit, faith and obedience. Faith in the measure and manifestation of the light and grace that hath appeared so as not to be befooled by the enemy and kept under his bonds through a faithless persuasion. That the temptations and difficulties are too great or too strong for any grace already obtained and obedience in the things already clearly discovered especially in acts of forbearance, in whatever is seen not so profitable or acceptable and not a deferring to obey in things already seen through a hope and foolish desire to see and understand more. This is to resemble the unprofitable servant that hid his talent, and judged God a hard master. It is needful then to believe in the power and virtue of God's grace received not doubting but as more is needed, it will be added, and to obey in all things already manifested, not meddling in things as yet not seen. I am doubtful that thy missing herein renders the silent waiting so uneasy to thee and makes

---

11. This word, now obsolete, means "to call upon in the name of something sacred," or "to beseech or implore."

thy progress so slow; whereof bear with me to give thee an example out of a holy jealousy I have of thee and earnest desire of thy soul's salvation. I know the Lord has abundantly shown thee the emptiness and unprofitableness of that customary worship and service which is offered in the strength of man's natural spirit and will (which is a discovery yet hid from many). Thinks thou then that thou are not unfaithful to his manifestation while thou openly countenance to this unallowable service, yea, and entertains one to perform that which thou are persuaded in thy heart God accepts not. How can thou then judge that God will give thee to partake of his spiritual worship in thy chamber while thou openly before the world countenances that which is natural and carnal and so concurs to keep up that which God is pulling down and will pull down not by carnal weapons or human policy but by his own spirit and power. Now all the reasons that may weigh with thee in this particular such as the fear to give offence, to appear singular, to bring thyself under outward reproach or shame are not sufficient in the sight of God to excuse thee. Therefore, the not answering God's love in this discovery may justly provoke him both to withhold more grace and light until thou answer what is already received. He that is faithful in a little shall be made ruler over much. Try thyself therefore by the light of Christ Jesus in this one particular and it may be useful unto thee. Let thy resignation be really manifest to the Lord in freely answering his will according as he makes it known unto thee. So shall thou approve thyself a follower of him who embraced the cross and despised the shame. For thy seeing the necessity of self-denial unless thou apply thyself to practice, it will not avail thee. I hope thou will take in good part my freedom herein which proceedeth from pure love and an earnest desire I have that thou may go on so as not to lose the glorious prize that is set before thee which is better than an earthly crown. My soul breathes to the Lord for thee that this may be thy portion, for the obtaining whereof I with my brethren do at present contentedly suffer these bonds though we see no way of outward deliverance, not doubting but the Lord will bring it about in his own time. In the belief whereof is at present patiently satisfied

    Thy assured friend,

        Barclay.

P.S. As for the sending of my books to those persons, I leave to do therein as thou shall find true liberty in the Lord and useful for his glory and the advancement of righteousness in the earth for which end I wrote them. I hope by now thou has received my last with that of our dear sister (now very weak) to Anna.

ELISABETH TO ROBERT BARCLAY

9/19 February 1676

Dear friend,

I have received two of your letters. The last came to my hands this day somewhat late, which makes it impossible for me to send the letters you desired to my Lady Lauderdale [12] but I shall do it by the next. Though I have no kind of acquaintance with her, and, as Helmont [13] tells me, her husband is no friend of my brothers, therefore all which comes that way is like to want effect. Yet I cannot in conscience neglect anything that is thought conducting his children's release, I will rather appear impertinent than be wanting therein. I am both afflicted and comforted by the relation of your present condition and give you many thanks for the good counsel you impart in your former letter here mentioned. Faith and obedience are two precious gifts. I cannot say that I have them, though I long and pray for them. But this I am certain, that any action that comes not from thence would be sinful though it was materially good. Therefore I must not do anything upon persuasion of others nor out of my own opinion until I have the light of faith for my conduct, which I suppose you will not require from

Your true friend,

Elizabeth.

ROBERT BARCLAY TO ELISABETH

Aberdeen Prison, 5 March 1677

Dear and well beloved Elizabeth,

By thine of the 19th of the last month I received with gladness the renewed testimony of thy love and friendship. Not because of any great expectation I have, that this essay will produce my outward liberty, but because it hath pleased God to raise and beget in thee that love and regard to his precious truth and testimony and that compassion towards his despised witnesses that for their sakes thou not only willingly undergoes this trouble

---

12. Either Anne, wife of Scottish royalist John Maitland, earl of Lauderdale, or her daughter, but in all likelihood the mother. The Lauderdale home passed to the daughter upon her death, and the house was bought by German Ireton and sold shortly thereafter to William Mead in 1677. Mead was an associate of George Fox, a leading Quaker.

13. Francis Mercury van Helmont (1614–98), son of the alchemical philosopher Jean Baptiste van Helmont.

but runs the hazard of incurring the Court censure and of bearing a part of the reproach which hath been and always will be the lot of the faithful from such as are acted and guided by the spirit of this world. The Lord God Almighty of his infinite goodness reward thee sevenfold therefore in thy bosom by causing the light of his son more clearly and powerfully to shine in thee and by giving thee a willing mind fully to resign thyself unto him and grace and strength to follow and obey him in all his requirings at thy hands. For certainly that observable preservation of thee even unto this time from these snares and evils that do so commonly and easily beset and follow persons of thy quality, that singular light and discovery he has given thee of the vanity of the perishing glory and splendour of this world, not only in mere opinion and notion, but by a living impression and sense upon thy soul which hath begot in thee a disgust, distaste, and as it were a weariness of these things are signal testimonies of his special love and regard to thee and evident tokens of his purpose of good towards thee. As thy condition in this is singular with respect to thy circumstances, so thou needs be the less startled if thou should find the Lord drawing thee either to the forbearance of or practising of anything not only unusual unto, but in some respect almost inconsistent with thy station and dignity in the world, which will nothing add to the better part, for thy being a Princess may well let, will never further thee to be a Christian and (however the world think otherwise) it is far more honourable as well as advantageous in the end to be a Christian than the other and they are wise indeed (though they may be esteemed fools) that do choose the better part. I would not be understood to suppose that these kind of dignities materially considered are utterly inconsistent with Christianity, since it is promised that such shall be nursing fathers and mothers in the church, but by reason of that general corruption that has overspread not only mankind generally, but even the Christian world so called. There are certain ceremonies and circumstances offered unto such places that belong no ways to the being of them, which, I may boldly say, in certain respects render those that enjoy them almost incapable to be Christians. Yet is most incident to fallen man so to adhere to these additional superfluities, that he will commonly rather dispense with the substance than with them which is the natural fruit of cursed self always more prone to idolize its own inventions and productions than the ordinance and institution of God. Beware therefore lest thou fall in this evil through an unwillingness to suffer the reproach or contempt that might befall thee from such as might accuse thee either for forbearing or doing things that may seem not to suit with thy station and dignity. Therefore wait seriously in the silent place in a mind willing to obey for light from the Lord rightly to distinguish betwixt these things that are good and necessary and these things that are hurtful and unnecessary, that thou may neither omit to do anything of thy duty with respect to the answering of thy present calling in the service of thy generation and yet may not do anything as such (which are but circumstantial superfluities of human invention added under the notion of decorums) that may prove hurtful or destructive to thee in the progress of Christianity. This ought to be narrowly inquired to by all, even such as are inwardly convinced in their minds that do allowably continue in the exercise of such employments. For it may be the place of some to lay aside that which is materially lawful which yet with respect to them, the condition of their soul chiefly to be minded, and God's requirings of them may be both hurtful and pernicious for them to continue in. Thus Abraham was called from his father's house, Moses and David from their flocks, Peter and John from their lawful employments, Matthew from the receipt of custom, and Mary from helping her sister in the lawful management of her house, which thing I judge also may well deserve thy serious consideration. What thou says that the performance of things materially good ought to proceed not from the persuasion of others or mere opinion but from the light of faith is true, and I agree well to it. As also it is far from me to require any far less of thee to do anything merely upon my persuasion, for I am a great enemy to implicit faith, and the end of my labour and ministry is to bring all to the anointing that they may know that to lead them and be the bottom of their obedience so as to do what they do in faith. Yet such as come here know that the admonishing and instructing one another and the subjection of the spirits to the prophets is in no way inconsistent with it, but there is a great difference betwixt the not practicing of things materially good until the light of faith be known for the motive of obedience and the forbearing of things either materially evil or consequently pernicious and destructive to the condition of my soul. Concerning this I signified some remarkable scripture testimonies in my last to Anna, which I desire thou may weigh in the fear of the Lord, to be passive needs less than to be active. If I were fully persuaded I am out of my way, I need nothing further to make me halt and stand still and go no further wrong, though perhaps I may need some further information to put me right again. Therefore if once God has shown me and persuaded me that I am in the practice of anything that is displeasing to him and hurtful and unprofitable to my own soul, this is the light of faith sufficient to authorize me to forbear these things, to stand still and not dare to advance further in that acceptable path. Otherwise might not Ernestus plead the same excuse for his idolatrous bowing to the mass wanting the light of faith though convinced the thing is wrong. And this is the more seriously to be considered if the things be of that nature that the forbearing of them be uneasy to that part that is unwilling to undergo sufferings from, or the reproach of the world. Therefore an inward tenderness of heart and holy awe and fear upon the mind with a jealousy over the deceitfulness of our own hearts is very precious upon such occasions, lest these scruples proceed rather from a mind that would save self and shun the cross, then an unwillingness to be found forwardly doing anything in our own wills without the light of faith, especially if in doing these things thus seen to be unprofitable we dare not say we follow the light of faith, and that likewise when we impartially examine our hearts we are secretly convinced that had not the forbearing of these things such uneasy consequences we would not be so scrupulous to let them alone. My dear friend, the Lord give thee a clear understanding of these things who knows I use this freedom with thee not to overdrive thee but of pure love and a desire thou may not fall short in anything to the hindering of thy growth in righteousness. That thou may receive light and grace from God more and more to wax strong therein is the earnest and daily prayer of

Thy assured friend,
Barclay.

P.S. Mind my dear love to Anna and if thou have occasion at any time to write to Ernestus show him I am not unmindful of him. George Keith,[14] my dear brother and fellow companion in bonds, salutes thee and Anna.

ROBERT BARCLAY TO ELISABETH

Aberdeen Prison, 16 March 1677

Dear friend,

Having written to thee somewhat largely two weeks ago in answer to thy last, I intended not to have so soon troubled thee with anything further. For it is, and hath been always, my care not to be officiously importunate to any, far less to one of thy quality, with respect even to human discretion and civility but much more not to be forward in my own spirit to labour in the work of the Lord without the allowance and concurrence of his life and power. But as the testimony of his spirit in my heart does at present secure me from the fear of the latter, so I presume thy love and friendship for me

---

14. George Keith (1638–1716) was a Scottish preacher who joined the Quakers in 1663. He was closely associated with Robert Barclay and George Fox. In 1692, he was denounced by William Penn for starting a separate faction of Christian Quakers in America.

together with thy good nature will excuse the former, in case I have failed
therein and that so much the rather as my love to thee and earnest desire for
thine and Anna her progress in that which is most excellent has as it were
constrained me to this address. For a certain dear sister having found it in her
heart from the Lord to salute thee and Anna and to transmit unto you somewhat of the counsel of the Lord very needful for you, I could not forbear to
use all diligence to convey it to your hands, knowing that words in season
are like apples of gold in pictures of silver. I will not add any recommendation to this epistle, not doubting but it will recommend itself to the witness
of God in thy conscience. She is wife to my dear brother George Keith and
albeit but a young woman, yet one, who through great inward exercises and
a sound work of judgement in her heart, hath attained not only an excellent
understanding but also a good measure of discerning and a sound and steady
place in the truth. She is also a gentlewoman of good condition, who yet
for the truth's sake hath not refused to bear much reproach. Being a woman
very serious, she is far from being forward to do any thing of this kind in her
own will, and her forbearance in that respect will in part appear in the letters
themselves. I am not a little eased and refreshed when I find the Lord doth
thus in so great simplicity, and yet life draws forth any of his servants thus
to salute thee, taking it as a certain token for good from the Lord towards
thee. I have often thought and seen that there are many in these parts who
were but prejudices removed and they come to an inward converse and feeling with some of us, would quickly, laying aside all impediments, flee and
take hold of this standard of the Lord, which he has raised and is raising by
his own power. Among whom I question not but thy old friend Anna Maria
Shurman would be one, if yet in the body. O how has my soul compassion-
ated her as well as the other simple hearts there with her in whom I have
seen that the simplicity is betrayed, and they miserably misled, and a selfish
spirit mightily exalting itself among them under the specious presence and
notion of self-denial and mortification. Therefore in that love that longs for
the redemption of all these that sincerely seek the Lord, I have waited for
a seasonable opportunity in which I might write to her in particular and to
the other honest hearted among them. But then should the Lord give me a
season so to do, I should be partly at a loss how to transmit it unto them as
they might not be robbed of the benefit of it by such as I fear seek dominion
over their faith and love to have pre-eminency among them, who I know will
be loath to part with their crown, having, I doubt, by preaching the denying
of self and mortification thereof to others, received more plentiful occasion
to feed and gratify it in themselves than they should have got had they
continued in their former stations among those they account the unchristian

world. Perhaps if I find a place or anything to signify to them, thou might assist me in the right address of it. In the meantime, I found freedom to offer thee that in case hitherto neither thou nor Anna has acquainted them of your correspondence with us, thou might take occasion to communicate to them some of those letters, especially of the woman's and signify to them that these are some salutations you have received from these true Christians in Britain of which thou formerly advised Anna Maria Shurman of that so she or such as are tender among them being really reached and touched in their hearts with the life that will be savoured in these letters may be forced to acknowledge that it proceeds from such who are led by the anointing and are in the truth. Indeed, not perhaps imagining that it comes from Quakers, and then afterwards when they may come to understand from whom it is, the former sense of the heart may help to wipe away these prejudices that have hitherto clouded their understandings and bring them or some of them to make a more serious search and inquiry without partiality. I leave thee to do herein as the circumstances of the case will bear and as by the direction of the Lord thou shall find most convenient. Let these transmit the salutation of my dear love to Anna not forgetting any other in thy family whose faces are towards Zion, but especially to the young maid of whom I understand by Anna's letter to Lillias Skene that she is seriously seeking the Lord. The earnest breathing and prayers remains for thee of him who is and always hopes to approve himself to be

 Thy most affectionate friend,

   B.

P.S. I had forgotten to signify to thee that my dear brother George Keith and husband to the author of these letters upon the seeing of thy last to me hath found in his heart to write a small treatise for thine and Anna's sake of the discerning of what proceeds merely from a natural conviction or opinion and what from a principle of faith, which because it would have swelled this packet too great, is reserved for another occasion.

ROBERT BARCLAY TO ELISABETH

London, 15 June 1677

Dear friend,

 I understand by Benjamin Furly, who is here at present, that there came a letter from thee to me, which it seems by going into Scotland has missed me. How providentially I am at liberty, I suppose by him thou has understood, and since notwithstanding of that unexpected freedom, the malice and fury of our persecutors doth continue both to those that are behind and to us that are here so far as they are capable to express it, I offered to use some endeavours here if possible to mitigate if not to remove it, but as yet without any probable expectation of success. I have spoke to the Lady Lauderdale who is only like to return thee a court complement by conveyance of thy brother. It troubles me thou should meet with such a reply from her, not for the want of success as to us who must freely accept of sufferings in this world but for thy honour's sake, yet I hope thou will take it patiently as some small part of that reproach of the cross which all must bow to that thereby expect to receive an entrance into the kingdom. George Keith, I hope, will ere long be with thee and I also understand from Scotland that his wife and L.S. who formerly wrote to Anna have it in their hearts from the Lord to give you both a visit, but whether they be yet set forward I cannot determine. I hope they come in that which will minister strength to thee and that the purpose of God's love to thee in sending such to thee through the difficulties of so tedious a travel and from so remote a corner shall not be in vain. Thy friend Helmont is here and about 2 or 3 weeks ago found himself under a necessity so as he could not forbear with peace of conscience and without disobeying of God to come under the contemptible appearance of one of us by keeping his hat upon his head and laying aside those other ceremonies which truth has obliged us to depart from. His so doing did not a little surprise thy brother and the Lord Craven[15] with whom he had occasion to meet the other day, the last of whom telling him he would write it for news to thy sister Sophia. Helmont himself was willing I should prevent thy knowing it by any other hand. I should be glad to understand from thee the receipt of this letter because I know nothing as yet of my seeing thee at this time but am likely in a few weeks to return to Scotland where I expect I shall very quickly be shut up again in prison in which place it will be comfortable to me to hear from thee because of the unquenchable love which the Lord hath begotten in my soul for thee and that continual care that lives in my heart concerning thee, which obliges me often to remember thee before the Lord and earnestly to breath for thee that thou may not sit down by the way but by a full and perfect resignation and obedience to the Lord in all things thou may obtain the travel of thy soul, even the peace that passeth understanding,

15. William, Lord Craven, Earl of Craven (1606–97), was a great defender of the Stuart cause, devoting resources to supporting Charles I as well as helping the family Palatine. He was an early member of the Royal Society. The brother of Elisabeth referred to here is no doubt Rupert.

which is more desirable than an earthly crown, which is the sincere cry of him for thee who is

Thy most assured friend,
Barclay.

ELISABETH TO ROBERT BARCLAY

6/16 July 1677

Dear friend,

Benjamin Furly hath sent me your letter dated the 15th of June in which you mention that mine is gone astray and that you did employ that liberty which God hath given you to endeavour the procuring the like to your friends but in vain. And that I was like to receive only a court compliment from the Lady Lauderdale and that I should bear this dishonour as a cross which all must bear that expect an entrance in the kingdom of heaven. I confess I do not find any such thing therein because I do not seek honour from man but it is a cross to me that you will not make use of the liberty which God miraculously gave you but will return to Scotland to be clapped up again in prison for which we have neither precept nor example. I avow myself unable to judge of this, but is there no reason, dear friend, to suspect such a motion. As for Helmont, he has reason to follow the pressing of his conscience. I wish I might speak to him myself and question him about this matter. The Earl of Craven was the first that wrote this news. I believe he has also acquainted my sister of Osenbrugh with it, who has much affection for Gertrude[16] but the world and her husband do still possess her heart. God will in his due time touch us both; when your friends come they shall be willingly received and lodged by

Your true friend,
Elizabeth.

ELISABETH TO BENJAMIN FURLY

6/16 July 1677

Dear friend,

I see by your last your happy return out of England and your design to come hither with George Keith and his wife and L.S. They will be welcome but the great assembly you propose will find more difficulty, because many

---

16. It is not known who Gertrude is. "My sister of Osenbrugh" likely refers to one of Elisabeth's sisters, most likely Louise Hollandine, but it is not clear.

are not resolved to go that way. Though they seek God and approve many things, others are tied to relations as Ernestus and the most part have an aversion against all that relishes of a sect since the 24th of Matthew[17] makes them cautious. I have many servants in my house that seek God heartily but will run away from me at the name of Quaker. I wish God would put it into your heart how to deal with them. As to the [blank in source text] they will be well bestowed if they serve the friends. I should be glad to see Helmont after his change with all those whom you mention, to whom I pray deliver the greetings of

Your very loving friend,

Elizabeth.

ELISABETH TO ROBERT BARCLAY

1/11 March 1677

Dear friend,

We join in the aversion from much correspondence and agree also in this point that knowledge without light is uncertain and words without deeds are vain. Therefore my breathings unto the Lord are both for light and power to yield real obedience unto that light which he affords me, but I cannot submit unto the opinion or practice of any others though I grant that they have more light than myself. The Countess of Conoway[18] does well to go on the way which she thinks best, but I should not do well to follow her, unless I had the same conviction. Neither did it ever enter into my thoughts so to do. I love all that love God, and am ready to embrace all that is undoubtedly good. I am far from judging them or the rest, as being prohibited me by our saviour in the 7th of Matthew,[19] but I am not apt to believe anybody infallible though he be a true regenerated child of God. Only the Lord Jesus Christ had the spirit imparted without measure. Others have their measures and limits. You will say it is self-love and shunning the cross that breeds these thoughts. I will not disavow that great fault of self-love, which I find in many important occasions. I pray and strive against it, but the foresaid truths have another ground. The 24th of Matthew is a great bar to all conformity which comes by choice or persuasion. Nevertheless, I am really concerned in that deliverance of your father and friends out of prison and do love the Duke of

17. Matthew 24:4–5 warns: "Take heed that no man deceive you. For many shall come in my name, saying I am Christ; and shall deceive many."

18. Anne Finch, Viscountess Conway (1631–78/79), became a Quaker in 1677. She is most famous for her *Principles of the Most Ancient and Modern Philosophy,* first published in 1690.

19. Matthew 7:1: "Judge not, that ye be not judged."

York[20] the better for procuring it. Pray God multiply his light and his love among you, and give a true spiritual union among all those that truly love him, howsoever dispersed among all the sects in Christendom or elsewhere that the spouse of the Lamb may be fitted for her wedding. I hope that my free confession may not deprive me of your prayer who am really

Your affectionate friend,

Elizabeth.

ROBERT BARCLAY TO ELISABETH

Theobalds near London, 12 July 1677

Dear friend,

By thy letter of the last of the month past I understand of the friends being with thee and was refreshed by the account they gave me of thy kind and Christian entertainment of them (they having overtaken me in Holland). God will not be wanting to reward thy love as well as to increase the same. Finding no ready passage straight for Scotland I came over here, and albeit I had no great expectation of success, I resolved once more to try thy cousin the Duke of York. So I told him that I understood from Scotland that notwithstanding Lauderdale was there and had promised ere he went to do something, yet our friends' bonds were rather increased and that now there was only one thing to be done which I desired of him and that was to write effectually to the Duke of Lauderdale in that style wherein Lauderdale might understand that he was serious in the business and did really intend the thing he wrote concerning should take effect, which I knew he might do. I supposed the other would answer, which if he would do I must acknowledge as a great kindness, but if he did write and not in that manner so that the other might not suppose him to be serious, I would rather he should excuse himself the trouble, desiring withal to excuse my plain manner of dealing as being different from the court way of soliciting, all which he seemed to take in good part and said he would so write as I desired for my father and me, but not for the general. So he has given me a letter, whether it may prove effectual or not I cannot determine but of this thou may hear of hereafter. I am now entered into my journey and intend to pass by the way of Ragby. What thou writes of the councillor of the electors, and the other preacher is very acceptable to me to hear, whose joy it is to understand that the eyes

20. James Stuart, second son of Charles I, and Elisabeth's cousin. Upon his brother Charles II's death in 1685, he became James II of England and James VII of Scotland.

of any are opened to see the truth as it is in this day revealed. As it should be much more to hear that any came into that universal obedience which the life and power thereof leads to, which life and power as it is felt in the inward parts is more than all the words can be spoken of which I know thou has at sometimes not been insensible, and therefore my soul's desire for thee is that thou may more and more come out of all that which cumbers to feel this virtue of truth, to operate in and redeem thy soul from all the difficulties that do or may attend thee, which in the nature of it, it is powerful to do, albeit thy temptations were both greater and more numerous than they are, if received by thee in the love of it, and with a heart fully resigned to obey it in all its requirings without consulting with flesh and blood or turning by the plain and simple leadings thereof by wise and fleshly reasonings which will never admit of the government and rule of the cross of Christ as thou well knows and will not refuse to acknowledge. Therefore are the more concerned to watch against it in thy own particular as I hope in measure thou does, and my heart's desire is thou may make mention of my dear and tender love to Anna, whose servant as also the French woman I forget not. To Anna I thought to have written apart, but must now leave it until another opportunity. If thou sees meet to salute that councillor of the electors in my name you may do it. I shall add no more at present but that I am

Thy real and unfeigned friend,

Barclay.

ELISABETH TO ROBERT BARCLAY

Ruden, 25 November 1677

Dear friend,

I have now a true account touching Colonel Mollison's children.[21] He hath left two sons of which the youngest died a few days after him of the same disease. The other is likewise deceased upon the road as his mother was going for Duisburg in the land of Cleve where she is still. I am also informed that the said Colonel made his will before he went to the army, and that Colonel Melvil, a Scotch man that is governor of Cell in Lunenburg,[22] has a particular knowledge of it, to whom your brother-in-law may address himself. I hope that you are still in freedom and the Duke of York's interces-

---

21. Colonel Mollison might be a son of the prominent Scottish Quaker Gilber Molleson, whose daughter Christian Barclay married in 1669.

22. No further information on Colonel Melvil has been found.

sion has been effectual for you and your father. I also recommend to your prayers

Your loving friend,
Elizabeth.

ROBERT BARCLAY TO ELISABETH

Ury, 28 December 1677

Dear friend,

In the same love of our Lord Jesus Christ wherein I have once and again heretofore visited thee, do I now salute thee in the present sense of that divine love being moved so to do, which motion (for the love I bear thee and the earnest desire of my soul for thy establishment and advancement in the ways of truth and righteousness) I am always ready to follow, albeit I have no delight in any formal correspondences, nor am anyways inclinable to uphold them, having abundantly seen that to multiply the best of words whether by speech or writing where the life immediately moves not thereto is but vanity and doth but engender unto death. Therefore being at this present in a measure of the sense of that precious life (in which I have formerly been with thee and in which I have often remembered thee, when at a great outward distance, and observed by none so to do), I could not omit in the flowings of the same thus dearly to salute thee, earnestly desiring with my whole soul that thou maist always be kept in that inward tenderness and lowliness of mind, where thou may never forget the tender visitation of God's unutterable love to thee who hath so long waited to be gracious unto thee, and hath not ceased to call upon thee that thou may repent and be saved. Beware that thou do not content thyself with the sight of those things lest the secret workings of self therethrough betray thee from really feeding enough upon the life, which is more than talking of it, or from really being delivered from the spirit of this world in all its transformings, which is more than to confess its vanity and exclaim against it. Where the simplicity takes true place, there the things are more than the words of it; but where self is strong and the wise part prevails which yet remains uncrucified and is not brought down unto the obedience of Christ, there the thing is quickly comprehended but not so readily enjoyed, thus the truth is held in unrighteousness. It is a blessed place to dwell in that godly fear and simplicity where obedience to the least thing revealed is cheerfully rendered, and the mind is only willing to know that it may answer and obey. For there are not a few suffer themselves to be betrayed while they persuade themselves they would readily do anything if they were once but fully persuaded it were their duty, while they observe not yet somewhat of self that works more deeply and hiddenly to prejudicate them against that which is cross to a part yet alive in them. So that albeit they seem to wait only for clearness from the Lord to do accordingly, yet there is a desire from self and thence a hope that the Lord may determine according to their mind and not contrary to it, upon which proceedeth that profession of being so ready to obey, which prejudice of the mind often blinds the eye of the soul and if light break through makes obedience the more difficult. This I have often observed in my own experience, and in my way coming home did find it to have been the trial of that truly noble and virtuous lady, the vice Countess of Conoway, who told me she had looked upon some things practiced by us as so small and inconsiderable that she was apt to believe either that there was not that weight in them which we seemed to lay upon them, or if it should so appear to her, she could very easily yield to the practice. But when she came to find it her place so to do, then she saw there was a great deal more difficulty than she apprehended and could not have believed to have found in herself so strong wrestlings before she could give up to obey, especially considering her circumstances, who being constantly tied to her chamber was thereby delivered from many of those affronts whom the like case might make others liable to. From the same ground sometimes the mind gives way to or invents means to staff of a full obedience to what God is ready to call unto be doing things somewhat like it, whereby it pleases itself by reckoning it is out of the common road of the world. But all such imitations are but at best like Abraham's desiring Ishmael might live before the Lord, which show an unwillingness to wait until Isaac, the seed of promise, should be born, who alone was to inherit the blessing. Therefore this was a desiring to rejoice in the seed of the bondwoman who was to be cast out and not to inherit with the seed. This bondwoman is by the apostle Paul interpreted of this first birth, which is to be denied and crucified in all its motions that the true seed may arise to which the blessing is so that, however any may please themselves in the works thereof, yet experience will prove its inefficacy. The heavenly dew will not descend thereupon from above, nor the blessing will not accompany. Neither will the ground blossom and bring forth the blessed fruits which are acceptable to God and by which the soul receives power to be delivered from the bonds of death and is made partaker of the glorious liberty of the sons of God. The Lord who moves me thus to write unto thee gives the light and discerning to apply the same to thy good, that thou may be naked and simple before him. Laying aside all thy own workings and contrivances and all fig leaf coverings, which will be too narrow in the day of the Lord, thou may be passive in his hand and may suffer him to work thee according to his own mind unto a perfect conformity to the image of his son so that thou may not fall short of the glory of his chosen but may receive an inheritance among the saints in light forever. The salutation of my very dear love let these transmit to Anna, her maid, and the French woman. I was not a little refreshed to understand of the second visit given thee by the friends. I shall always be glad to hear of thy welfare, wishing the grace and peace of our Lord Jesus Christ to continue with thee and be multiplied unto thee. Amen.

Thy very affectionate friend,

Barclay.

P.S. Thine with the account of Colonel Molison's wife and children I have. Thy cousin's intercessions have taken place and are likely to prove successful, but in these things I desire over all to have an eye to the Lord, knowing the mountains may fall and the hills be removed out of their place but the Lord remains forever the sure rock and bulwark of his people.

ROBERT BARCLAY TO ELISABETH

Rotterdam, 6 May 1679

Dear friend,

Thou may think it strange that after so long a silence, I should now apply myself to answer thy last (which came to my hands at a time when I was under great bodily weakness) for which I will not trouble thee with any further apology than to assure thee that no want of respect or regard to thee but an unwillingness to work in mine own will, and a fear in so doing rather to hurt than help thee hath hindered me until now. Had I given way to my own inclinations and to the course of that love which without flattery I can say I have for thee so as to have exprest but the hundred part of that concern which frequently possessed me upon thy account, I have overcharged thee with my letters, but knowing it is not the will of man that bringeth about the work of God, I choosed rather to be silent than forward. But being through a singular occasion come to this country and not having access to make thee a visit, I found a true liberty from the Lord in my spirit thus to salute thee, which I hope will neither be unacceptable nor yet unprofitable unto thee. My soul's desire to God for thee is that thou may never forget the tender visitations of God's love unto thy soul but that by retaining always a living sense thereof, thou may answer them and not fall short of receiving the benefit thereof for the true redemption of thy soul, neither by despairing to receive from him that power and grace that's needful, nor yet by suffering the enemy to abuse thee through begetting a prejudice to some things as if God would never require them of thee. And so upon that supposition hedge up thy own way and cut out thy own path to thyself, and previously set bounds to thyself, thus far to go and no further. For it is hard so distinctly to understand that to be duty which the mind is unwilling should be so far more is resolved not to believe to be so upon a false supposition that it will not, which proceeds from an unwillingness it should, which prejudice makes the mind unapt to see. I would not hereby be understood as if I urged thee to do anything by imitation, for I know no such service can be acceptable, but only that thou may be so resigned to the will of God as to have the testimony of his spirit in thy heart that thou are ready to answer him in all his requirings, however much reproach it bring thee from the world as being cross to its ways and customs. And it was only to evidence to thee how far in this one may be deceived of the right understanding of their own hearts that I made mention in my last of the condition of that honourable Lady who is now gone to her place not as if I proposed her practice for thee to imitate (but only I signified her condition as an example). Therefore in judging so thou did mistake, for my design in all that which I have laboured towards thee is no other than that thou may really come to be acquainted with the mind and will of God and truly be found willing to answer it, so as by receiving the life and virtue of Christ in thy soul thou may feel redemption by it and know the justification thereof by passing from death to life. If thou really arrive here I have my end, if thou die daily to the world and spirit thereof and live to God and his kingdom, if thou feel thyself in truth daily converted, and that thy mind be redeemed from the vanity of its thoughts, and brought into stillness and unity with God, so that from wandering in the visible thou may be brought to be still in that which is invisible, then shall I greatly rejoice in thy behalf, for herein I have peace before God, that I never sought to gather thee nor others to myself but to the Lord. I pretend to be no sect master and disgust all such. My labour is only as an ambassador to instruct all to be reconciled to God, and I desire no more than to be manifest in the consciences of those to whom I come that I am such, by the answer of that of God there, to which therefore in thy conscience I recommend my testimony without seeking or desiring anything which for Christ and his truth's sake to deny is the daily labour by the grace of God of

 Thy sincere and truly affectionate friend,
  Barclay.

P.S. Make mention of my dear love to Anna if yet she is with thee

ELISABETH TO WILLIAM PENN

Herford, 2 May 1677

This, friend, will tell you that both of your letters were very acceptable, together with your wishes for my obtaining those virtues which may make me a worthy follower of our great king and saviour Jesus Christ. What I have done for his true disciples is not so much as a cup of cold water: it affords them no refreshment; neither did I expect any fruit of my letter to the Duchess of L.,[23] as I have expressed at the same time unto B.F.[24] But since R.B.[25] desired I should write it, I could not refuse him, nor omit to do anything that was judged conducing to his liberty, though it should expose me to the derision of the world. But this a mere moral man can reach at; the true inward graces are yet wanting in

Your affectionate friend,
Elizabeth.

WILLIAM PENN TO ELISABETH

A Salutation to Elizabeth Princess Palatine, and Anna Maria d'Hornes Countess of Hornes, at Herwerden in Germany.
My worthy friends,

Such as I have, such I give unto you, the dear and tender salutation of light, life, peace and salvation by Jesus Christ the blessed Lamb of God. With the unspeakable joy of which he has replenished my soul at this time, that my cup overflows, which is the reward of them that cheerfully drink his cup of tribulations, that love the cross, and triumph in all the shame, reproaches and contradictions of the world that do attend it. My God take you by the hand, and gently lead you through all the difficulties of regeneration, and, as you have begun to know and love his sweet and tender drawings, so resign the whole conduct of your lives to him.

Dispute not away the precious sense that you have of him, be it as small as a grain of mustard seed, which is the least of all seeds, there is power in it (if you do but believe) to remove the greatest mountains of opposition. O precious is this faith, yea more precious than the glory and honour of this world that perishes. It will give courage to go with Christ before Caiaphas and Pilate;

23. Duchess of Lauderdale.
24. Benjamin Furly.
25. Robert Barclay.

yea, to bear his cross without the camp, and to be crucified with him, knowing that the spirit of God and of glory shall rest upon them. To the inheritors of this faith is reserved the eternal kingdom of peace and joy in the Holy Ghost.

O be you of that little flock unto whom Jesus said, fear not, for it is my Father's good pleasure to give you a kingdom. And to be of this flock you must become as sheep, and to be as sheep you must become harmless, and to become harmless you must hear and follow the Lamb of God, as he is that blessed light which discovers and condemns all the unfruitful works of darkness, and makes harmless as a dove, which word all leaves not one piccadillo or circumstance undiscovered or unjudged. And the word "darkness" takes in the whole night of apostasy. And the word "unfruitful" is a plain judgement against all those dark works. Wherefore out of them all come and be you separated, and God will give you a crown of life which shall never fade away.

O the lowness and meanness of those spirits that despise or neglect the joys and glories of immortality, for the sake of the things which are seen that are but temporal, debasing the nobility of their souls, abandoning the government of the divine spirit, and embracing with all ardency of affection and sensual pleasures of this life. But such as persevere therein shall not enter into God's rest forever.

But this is not all that hinders and obstructs in the holy way of blessedness, for there is the world's fear as well as the world's joy that obstructs many, or else Christ had not said "Fear not!" to his little flock. The shame of the cross is a yoke too uneasy and a burden too heavy for flesh and blood to bear, 'tis true, but therefore shall flesh and blood never enter into the kingdom of God. And not to them that are born of the flesh, but to those that are born of the spirit through the word of regeneration, is appointed the kingdom, and that throne which shall judge the twelve tribes of Israel and all the world. The Lord perfect what he has begun in you, and give you dominion over the love and fear of this world.

And, my friends, if you would profit in the way of God, despise not the day of small things in yourselves. Know this: that to desire and sincerely to breathe after the Lord is a blessed state. You must seek before you find. Do you believe? Make not haste; extinguish not those small beginnings by an over-earnest or impatient desire of victory. God's time is the best time, be you faithful and your conflict shall end with glory to God, and the reward of peace to your own souls. Therefore love the judgement, and love the fire; start not aside, neither flinch from the scorching of it, for it will purify and refine you as gold seven times tried; then comes the stamp and seal of the Lord upon his own vessel, holiness to him forever, which he never gave, nor will give to reprobate silver, the state of the religious worshippers of the world. And herein be comforted, that Zion shall be redeemed through judgement, and her converts through righteousness, and after the appointed time of mourning is over, the Lord will give beauty for ashes, the oil of joy for mourning, and the garment of praise for the spirit of heaviness. Then shall you be able to say "Who is he that condemns us? God has justified us. There is no condemnation to us that are in Christ Jesus, who walk not after the flesh but after the spirit."

Wherefore, my dear friends, walk not only not after the fleshly lusts, but also not after the fleshly religions, and worships of the world: for that that is not born of the spirit, is flesh and all flesh shall wither as the grass, and the beauty of it shall fade away as the flower of the field before God's sun that is risen and rising. But the word of the Lord in which is life, and that life, the light of men, shall endure forever and give life eternal to them that love and walk in the light.

And I entreat you, by the love you have for Jesus, have a care how you touch with fleshly births, or say Amen, by word or practice, to that which is not born of the spirit. For God is not to be found of that, in yourselves or others, that calls him Father, and he has never begotten it in them, that latitude and conformity is not of God, but secretly grieves his spirit and obstructs the growth of the soul in its acquaintance, and intimate communion with the Lord. "Without me," says Jesus, "you can do nothing; and all that came before me are thieves and robbers." If so, O what are they that pray and preach and sing without Jesus, and follow not him in those duties, but even in them crucify him? O that I may find in you an ear to hear, and a heart to perceive, and embrace these truths of Jesus.

And I can say, I have great cause to hope, and patiently wait till the salvation of God be further revealed to you and the whole family, with whom (I may acknowledge) I was abundantly refreshed and comforted, in that God in measure made known the riches of his grace, and operation of his celestial power to you. And his witness shall dwell with you (if we never see you more) that God magnified his own strength in our weakness. With him we leave our travels, affectionately recommending you to his Holy Spirit of grace, that you may be conformed in the image of his own dear son, who is able and ready to preserve you. O stay your minds upon him and he will keep you in perfect peace, and abide with you forever. The Almighty take you into his holy protection now and forever. I am,

Your true friend ready to serve you with fervent love in the will of God,
William Penn.

My dear companions do, with me, give you the dear salutation of unfeigned love and those in the family that love and desire to follow the Lord Jesus in sincerity and truth without wavering.

P.S. We are this evening bound towards Manheim, the court of the Prince Palatine,[26] and travelled about twelve English miles on foot.

ELISABETH TO WILLIAM PENN

4/14 September 1677

Dear Friend,

I have received your greetings, good wishes and exhortations with much joy, and shall follow the latter as far as it will please our great God to give me light and strength. I can say little for myself, and can do nothing of myself, but I hope the Lord will conduct me in his time, by his way, to his end; and shall not shrink for his fire; I do long for it. And when he assures my ways, I hope he will give me power to bear the cross I meet therein. I am also glad to hear the journey back has been prosperous both in the constitutions of your bodies to withstand the badness of the weather, and in the reception you had in Cassel, Frankfort, and Crisheim. Nothing surprised me there but the good old Dury, in whom I did not expect so much ingenuity, having lately written a book, entitled *Le Veritable Chretien*,[27] that does speak, in another way. I wish to know what reception you have had at Fredericksbourg, and if this finds you at Cleve, I wish you might take an occasion to see the two pastors of Mulheim, which do really seek the Lord, but have some prejudice against your doctrine, as also the Countess there. It would be of much use for my family to have them disabused yet God's will be done in that, and all things else, concerning

Your loving friend in the Lord Jesus,
                    Elizabeth.

Let both your friends and companions receive my hearty commendations here.

WILLIAM PENN TO ELISABETH

To the Princess Elizabeth,
Salvation in the cross, Amen.
Dear and truly respected friend,

My soul most earnestly desires your temporal and eternal felicity, which stands in your doing the will of God now on earth, as tis done in heaven.

26. Elisabeth's brother Charles Louis.

27. Elisabeth here is alluding to Barclay (Robert Barclay of Ury or D'Ury) and his *Apology for the True Christian Religion*.

O dear Princess, do it! Say the word once in truth and righteousness, not my will, but yours be done, O God! Your days are few and then you must go to judgement. Then an account of your talent God will require from you. What improvement have you made? Let it prove and show its own excellency, that it is of God, and that it leads all that love it to God. O that you maybe able to give an account with joy!

I could not leave this country, and not testify the resentments I bear in my mind of that humble and tender entertainment you gave us at your court. The Lord Jesus reward you: and surely he has a blessing in store for you. Go on, be steadfast, overcome and you shall inherit. Do not despond, one that is mighty is near you, a present help in the needful time of trouble. O let the desire of your soul be to his name and to the remembrance of him. O wait upon the Lord, and you shall renew your strength! The youth shall faint, and the young men shall fail, but they that trust in the Lord shall never be confounded.

I wish you all true and solid felicity, with my whole soul. The Lord God of heaven and earth have you in his keeping, that you may not lose, but keep in that divine sense, which, by his eternal word, he has begotten in you. Receive, dear Princess, my sincere and Christian salutation. Grace, mercy, and peace be multiplied among you all that love the Lord Jesus.

Your business I shall follow, with all the diligence and discretion I can, and by the first give you an account, after it shall please the Lord to bring me safe to London. All my brethren are well, and present you with their dear love, and the rest with you that love Jesus, the light of the world, in your family. You have taught me to forget you are a Princess, and therefore I use this freedom, and to that of God, in you, am I manifest, and I know my integrity. Give if you please, the salutation of my dear love to A.M. de Hornes, with the enclosed. Dear Princess, do not hinder but help her. That may be required of her, which (considering your circumstances) may not yet be required of you. Let her stand free and her freedom will make the passage easier unto you. Accept what I say, I entreat you, in that pure and heavenly love and respect, in which I write so plainly to you. Farewell my dear friend, and the Lord be with you, I am more than I can say,

Your great lover and respectful friend,
William Penn.

I refer you to the enclosed for passages. We visited Gistall and Hooftman[28] and they us: they were at one or two of the meetings at Amsterdam. Vale in eternum.

---

28. The identities of Gistall and Hooftman are unknown.

ELISABETH TO WILLIAM PENN

Herford, 29 October 1677

Dear friend,

Your tender care of my eternal well-being does oblige me much, and I will weigh every article of your counsel to allow as much as lies in me, but God's grace must be assistant. As you say yourself, he accepts nothing that does not come from him. If I had made me bare of all worldly goods, and left undone what he requires most, I mean to do all, for and by his son, I shall be in no better condition than this present. Let me hold him first governing in my heart, learn to do what he requires of me, but I am not able to teach others, being not taught of God myself. Remember my love to G.F., B.F., G.K.[29] and dear Gertruick. If you write no words than your postscript, I can make a show to read it. Do not think I go from what I spoke to you that last evening. I only stay to do it in a way that is answerable before God and man. I can say no more now, but recommend to your prayers,

Your true friend,

Elizabeth.

I almost forgot to tell you that sister writes me word. She had been glad you had taken your journey by Osenbrugh to return to Amsterdam. There is a man, a Drossard of Limbourg near this place (to whom I gave an examplar of R.B.'s *Apology*) very desirous to speak with some of the friends.

ELISABETH TO WILLIAM PENN

17 November

Dear friend,

I have received a letter from you that seems to have been written at your passage into England, which I wish may be prosperous, without date, but not without virtue, to spur me on, to do and suffer the will of our God. I can say in sincerity and truth, your will be done. O God, because I wish it heartily, but I cannot speak in righteousness, until I possess that righteousness which is acceptable unto him. My house and my heart shall be always open to those that love him. Gichtel[30] has been well, satisfied with the conferences between you. As for my business, it will go as the Lord pleases, and remain in him.

Your affectionate friend,

Elizabeth.

29. George Fox, Benjamin Furly, and George Keith.
30. The identity of Gichtel is unclear.

SERIES EDITORS' BIBLIOGRAPHY

PRIMARY SOURCES

Alberti, Leon Battista (1404–72). *The Family in Renaissance Florence.* Trans. Renée Neu
Watkins. Columbia, SC: University of South Carolina Press, 1969.

Arenal, Electa, and Stacey Schlau, eds. *Untold Sisters: Hispanic Nuns in Their Own Works.*
Trans. Amanda Powell. Albuquerque, NM: University of New Mexico Press,
1989.

Astell, Mary (1666–1731). *The First English Feminist: Reflections on Marriage and Other
Writings.* Ed. and Introd. Bridget Hill. New York: St. Martin's Press, 1986.

Atherton, Margaret, ed. *Women Philosophers of the Early Modern Period.* Indianapolis, IN:
Hackett Publishing Co., 1994.

Aughterson, Kate, ed. *Renaissance Woman: Constructions of Femininity in England: A Source
Book.* London and New York: Routledge, 1995.

Barbaro, Francesco (1390–1454). *On Wifely Duties.* Trans. Benjamin Kohl in Kohl and
R. G. Witt, eds., *The Earthly Republic.* Philadelphia: University of Pennsylvania
Press, 1978, 179–228. Translation of the preface and book 2.

Behn, Aphra. *The Works of Aphra Behn.* 7 vols. Ed. Janet Todd. Columbus, OH: Ohio
State University Press, 1992–96.

Blamires, Alcuin, ed. *Woman Defamed and Woman Defended: An Anthology of Medieval Texts.*
Oxford: Clarendon Press, 1992.

Boccaccio, Giovanni (1313–75). *Famous Women.* Ed. and trans. Virginia Brown. The I
Tatti Renaissance Library. Cambridge, MA: Harvard University Press, 2001.

———. *Corbaccio or the Labyrinth of Love.* Trans. Anthony K. Cassell. Second revised edition. Binghamton, NY: Medieval and Renaissance Texts and Studies,
1993.

Booy, David, ed. *Autobiographical Writings by Early Quaker Women.* Aldershot and Brookfield: Ashgate Publishing Co., 2004.

Brown, Sylvia. *Women's Writing in Stuart England: The Mother's Legacies of Dorothy Leigh,
Elizabeth Joscelin and Elizabeth Richardson.* Thrupp, Stroud, Gloceter: Sutton, 1999.

Bruni, Leonardo (1370–1444). "On the Study of Literature (1405) to Lady Battista
Malatesta of Moltefeltro." In *The Humanism of Leonardo Bruni: Selected Texts.* Trans. and
Introd. Gordon Griffiths, James Hankins, and David Thompson. Binghamton,
NY: Medieval and Renaissance Studies and Texts, 1987, 240–51.

Castiglione, Baldassare (1478–1529). *The Book of the Courtier.* Trans. George Bull. New York: Penguin, 1967; *The Book of the Courtier.* Ed. Daniel Javitch. New York: W. W. Norton & Co., 2002.

Christine de Pizan (1365–1431). *The Book of the City of Ladies.* Trans. Earl Jeffrey Richards. Foreward Marina Warner. New York: Persea Books, 1982.

———. *The Treasure of the City of Ladies.* Trans. Sarah Lawson. New York: Viking Penguin, 1985. Also trans. and introd. Charity Cannon Willard. Ed. and introd. Madeleine P. Cosman. New York: Persea Books, 1989.

Clarke, Danielle, ed. *Isabella Whitney, Mary Sidney and Aemilia Lanyer: Renaissance Women Poets.* New York: Penguin Books, 2000.

Couchman, Jane, and Ann Crabb, eds. *Women's Letters Across Europe, 1400–1700.* Aldershot and Brookfield: Ashgate Publishing Co., 2005.

Crawford, Patricia and Laura Gowing, eds. *Women's Worlds in Seventeenth-Century England: A Source Book.* London and New York: Routledge, 2000.

"Custome Is an Idiot": Jcobean Pamphlet Literature on Women. Ed. Susan Gushee O'Malley. Afterword Ann Rosalind Jones. Chicago and Urbana: University of Illinois Press, 2004.

Daybell, James, ed. *Early Modern Women's Letter Writing, 1450–1700.* Houndmills, England and New York: Palgrave, 2001.

De Erauso, Catalina. *Lieutenant Nun: Memoir of a Basque Transvestite in the New World.* Trans. Michele Ttepto and Gabriel Stepto; foreword by Marjorie Garber. Boston: Beacon Press, 1995.

Elizabeth I: Collected Works. Ed. Leah S. Marcus, Janel Mueller, and Mary Beth Rose. Chicago: University of Chicago Press, 2000.

Elyot, Thomas (1490–1546). *Defence of Good Women: The Feminist Controversy of the Renaissance.* Facsimile Reproductions. Ed. Diane Bornstein. New York: Delmar, 1980.

Erasmus, Desiderius (1467–1536). *Erasmus on Women.* Ed. Erika Rummel. Toronto: University of Toronto Press, 1996.

Female and Male Voices in Early Modern England: An Anthology of Renaissance Writing. Ed. Betty S. Travitsky and Anne Lake Prescott. New York: Columbia University Press, 2000.

Ferguson, Moira, ed. *First Feminists: British Women Writers 1578–1799.* Bloomington, IN: Indiana University Press, 1985.

Galilei, Maria Celeste. *Sister Maria Celeste's Letters to her father, Galileo.* Ed. and trans. Rinaldina Russell. Lincoln, NE, and New York: Writers Club Press of Universe.com, 2000; *To Father: The Letters of Sister Maria Celeste to Galileo, 1623–1633.* Trans. Dava Sobel. London: Fourth Estate, 2001.

Gethner, Perry, ed. *The Lunatic Lover and Other Plays by French Women of the 17th and 18th Centuries.* Portsmouth, NH: Heinemann, 1994.

Glückel of Hameln (1646–1724). *The Memoirs of Glückel of Hameln.* Trans. Marvin Lowenthal. New Introd. Robert Rosen. New York: Schocken Books, 1977.

Harline, Craig, ed. *The Burdens of Sister Margaret: Inside a Seventeenth-Century Convent.* Abridged ed. New Haven: Yale University Press, 2000.

Henderson, Katherine Usher, and Barbara F. McManus, eds. *Half Humankind: Contexts and Texts of the Controversy about Women in England, 1540–1640.* Urbana: University of Illinois Press, 1985.

Hoby, Margaret. *The Private Life of an Elizabethan Lady: The Diary of Lady Margaret Hoby 1599–1605.* Phoenix Mill: Sutton Publishing, 1998.

Humanist Educational Treatises. Ed. and trans. Craig W. Kallendorf. The I Tatti Renaissance Library. Cambridge, MA: Harvard University Press, 2002.

Hunter, Lynette, ed. *The Letters of Dorothy Moore, 1612–64.* Aldershot and Brookfield: Ashgate Publishing Co., 2004.

Joscelin, Elizabeth. *The Mothers Legacy to her Unborn Childe.* Ed. Jean leDrew Metcalfe. Toronto: University of Toronto Press, 2000.

Kaminsky, Amy Katz, ed. *Water Lilies, Flores del agua: An Anthology of Spanish Women Writers from the Fifteenth Through the Nineteenth Century.* Minneapolis: University of Minnesota Press, 1996.

Kempe, Margery (1373–1439). *The Book of Margery Kempe.* Trans. and ed. Lynn Staley. A Norton Critical Edition. New York: W. W. Norton, 2001.

King, Margaret L., and Albert Rabil, Jr., eds. *Her Immaculate Hand: Selected Works by and about the Women Humanists of Quattrocento Italy.* Binghamton, NY: Medieval and Renaissance Texts and Studies, 1983; second revised paperback edition, 1991.

Klein, Joan Larsen, ed. *Daughters, Wives, and Widows: Writings by Men about Women and Marriage in England, 1500–1640.* Urbana, IL: University of Illinois Press, 1992.

Knox, John (1505–72). *The Political Writings of John Knox: The First Blast of the Trumpet against the Monstrous Regiment of Women and Other Selected Works.* Ed. Marvin A. Breslow. Washington: Folger Shakespeare Library, 1985.

Kors, Alan C., and Edward Peters, eds. *Witchcraft in Europe, 400-1700: A Documentary History.* Philadelphia: University of Pennsylvania Press, 2000.

Krämer, Heinrich, and Jacob Sprenger. *Malleus Maleficarum* (ca. 1487). Trans. Montague Summers. London: Pushkin Press, 1928; reprinted New York: Dover, 1971.

Larsen, Anne R., and Colette H. Winn, eds. *Writings by Pre-Revolutionary French Women: From Marie de France to Elizabeth Vigée-Le Brun.* New York and London: Garland Publishing Co., 2000.

de Lorris, William, and Jean de Meun. *The Romance of the Rose.* Trans. Charles Dahlbert. Princeton: Princeton University Press, 1971; reprinted University Press of New England, 1983.

Marcus, Leah S., Janel Mueller, and Mary Beth Rose, eds. *Elizabeth I: Collected Works.* Chicago: University of Chicago Press, 2000.

Marguerite d'Angoulême, Queen of Navarre (1492–1549). *The Heptameron.* Trans. P. A. Chilton. New York: Viking Penguin, 1984.

Mary of Agreda. *The Divine Life of the Most Holy Virgin.* Abridgment of *The Mystical City of God.* Abr. by Fr. Bonaventure Amedeo de Caesarea, M.C. Trans. from French by Abbé Joseph A. Boullan. Rockford, IL: Tan Books, 1997.

Mullan, David George. *Women's Life Writing in Early Modern Scotland: Writing the Evangelical Self, c. 1670–c. 1730.* Aldershot and Brookfield: Ashgate Publishing Co., 2003.

Myers, Kathleen A., and Amanda Powell, eds. *A Wild Country Out in the Garden: The Spiritual Journals of a Colonial Mexican Nun.* Bloomington: Indiana University Press, 1999.

Russell, Rinaldina, ed. *Sister Maria Celeste's Letters to Her Father, Galileo.* San Jose and New York: Writers Club Press, 2000.

Teresa of Avila, Saint (1515–82). *The Life of Saint Teresa of Avila by Herself.* Trans. J. M. Cohen. New York: Viking Penguin, 1957.

————. *The Collected Letters of St. Teresa of Avila. Volume One: 1546–1577,* trans. Kieran Kavanaugh. Washington, DC: Institute of Carmelite Studies, 2001.

Travitsky, Betty, ed. *The Paradise of Women: Writings by Entlishwomen of the Renaissance.* Westport, CT: Greenwood Press, 1981.

Weyer, Johann (1515–88). *Witches, Devils, and Doctors in the Renaissance: Johann Weyer, De praestigiis daemonum.* Ed. George Mora with Benjamin G. Kohl, Erik Midelfort, and Helen Bacon. Trans. John Shea. Binghamton, NY: Medieval and Renaissance Texts and Studies, 1991.

Wilson, Katharina M., ed. *Medieval Women Writers.* Athens: University of Georgia Press, 1984.

————, ed. *Women Writers of the Renaissance and Reformation.* Athens: University of Georgia Press, 1987.

————, and Frank J. Warnke, eds. *Women Writers of the Seventeenth Century.* Athens: University of Georgia Press, 1989.

Wollstonecraft, Mary. *A Vindication of the Rights of Men and a Vindication of the Rights of Women.* Ed. Sylvana Tomaselli. Cambridge: Cambridge University Press, 1995. Also *The Vindications of the Rights of Men, The Rights of Women.* Ed. D. L. Macdonald and Kathleen Scherf. Peterborough, Ontario, Canada: Broadview Press, 1997.

Woman Defamed and Woman Defended: An Anthology of Medieval Texts. Ed. Alcuin Blamires. Oxford: Clarendon Press, 1992.

Women Critics 1660–1820: An Anthology. Edited by the Folger Collective on Early Women Critics. Bloomington, IN: Indiana University Press, 1995.

Women Writers in English 1350–1850: 15 published through 1999 (projected 30-volume series suspended). Oxford University Press.

Women's Letters Across Europe, 1400–1700. Ed. Jane Couchman and Ann Crabb. Aldershot and Brookfield: Ashgate Publishing Co., 2005.

Wroth, Lady Mary. *The Countess of Montgomery's Urania.* 2 parts. Ed. Josephine A. Roberts. Tempe, AZ: MRTS, 1995, 1999.

————. *Lady Mary Wroth's "Love's Victory": The Penshurst Manuscript.* Ed. Michael G. Brennan. London: The Roxburghe Club, 1988.

————. *The Poems of Lady Mary Wroth.* Ed. Josephine A. Roberts. Baton Rouge: Louisiana State University Press, 1983.

de Zayas Maria. *The Disenchantments of Love.* Trans. H. Patsy Boyer. Albany: State University of New York Press, 1997.

————. *The Enchantments of Love: Amorous and Exemplary Novels.* Trans. H. Patsy Boyer. Berkeley: University of California Press, 1990.

SECONDARY SOURCES

Abate, Corinne S., ed. *Privacy, Domesticity, and Women in Early Modern England.* Aldershot and Brookfield: Ashgate Publishing Co., 2003.

Ahlgren, Gillian. *Teresa of Avila and the Politics of Sanctity.* Ithaca: Cornell University Press, 1996.

Akkerman, Tjitske, and Siep Sturman, eds. *Feminist Thought in European History, 1400–2000.* London and New York: Routledge, 1997.

Allen, Sister Prudence, R.S.M. *The Concept of Woman: The Aristotelian Revolution, 750 B.C. –
A.D. 1250.* Grand Rapids, MI: William B. Eerdmans Publishing Company, 1997.
———. *The Concept of Woman: Volume II: The early Humanist Reformation, 1250–1500.*
Grand Rapids, MI: William B. Eerdmans Publishing Company, 2002.

Altmann, Barbara K., and Deborah L. McGrady, eds. *Christine de Pizan: A Casebook.*
New York: Routledge, 2003.

Ambiguous Realities: Women in the Middle Ages and Renaissance. Ed. Carole Levin and Jeanie
Watson. Detroit: Wayne State University Press, 1987.

Amussen, Susan D, and Adele Seeff, eds. *Attending to Early Modern Women.* Newark:
University of Delaware Press, 1998.

Andreadis, Harriette. *Sappho in Early Modern England: Female Same-Sex Literary Erotics
1550–1714.* Chicago: University of Chicago Press, 2001.

Architecture and the Politics of Gender in Early Modern Europe. Ed. Helen Hills. Aldershot and
Brookfield: Ashgate Publishing Co., 2003.

Armon, Shifra. *Picking Wedlock: Women and the Courtship Novel in Spain.* New York: Rowman and Littlefield Publishers, Inc., 2002.

Attending to Early Modern Women. Ed. Susan D. Amussen and Adele Seeff. Newark: University of Delaware Press, 1998.

Backer, Anne Liot. *Precious Women.* New York: Basic Books, 1974.

Ballaster, Ros. *Seductive Forms.* New York: Oxford University Press, 1992.

Barash, Carol. *English Women's Poetry, 1649–1714: Politics, Community, and Linguistic Authority.* New York and Oxford: Oxford University Press, 1996.

Barker, Alele Marie, and Jehanne M. Gheith, eds. *A History of Women's Writing in Russia.*
Cambridge: Cambridge University Press, 2002.

Battigelli, Anna. *Margaret Cavendish and the Exiles of the Mind.* Lexington: University of
Kentucky Press, 1998.

Beasley, Faith. *Revising Memory: Women's Fiction and Memoirs in Seventeenth-Century France.*
New Brunswick: Rutgers University Press, 1990.

———. *Salons, History, and the Creation of Seventeenth-Century France.* Aldershot and
Brookfield: Ashgate Publishing Co., 2006.

Becker, Lucinda M. *Death and the Early Modern Englishwoman.* Aldershot and Brookfield:
Ashgate Publishing Co., 2003.

Beilin, Elaine V. *Redeeming Eve: Women Writers of the English Renaissance.* Princeton: Princeton University Press, 1987.

Bennett, Lyn. *Women Writing of Divinest Things: Rhetoric and the Poetry of Pembroke, Wroth,
and Lanyer.* Pittsburgh: Duquesne University Press, 2004.

Benson, Pamela Joseph. *The Invention of Renaissance Woman: The Challenge of Female Independence in the Literature and Thought of Italy and England.* University Park: Pennsylvania
State University Press, 1992.

——— and Victoria Kirkham, eds. *Strong Voices, Weak History? Medieval and Renaissance Women in their Literary Canons: England, France, Italy.* Ann Arbor: University of
Michigan Press, 2003.

Berry, Helen. *Gender, Society and Print Culture in Late-Stuart England.* Aldershot and Brookfield: Ashgate Publishing Co., 2003.

Beyond Isabella: Secular Women Patrons of Art in Renaissance Italy. Ed. Sheryl E. Reiss and
David G. Wilkins. Kirksville, MO: Turman State University Press, 2001.

Beyond Their Sex: Learned Women of the European Past. Ed. Patricia A. Labalme. New York: New York University Press, 1980.

Bicks, Caroline. *Midwiving Subjects in Shakespeare's England.* Aldershot and Brookfield: Ashgate Publishing Co., 2003.

Bilinkoff, Jodi. *The Avila of Saint Teresa: Religious Reform in a Sixteenth-Century City.* Ithaca: Cornell University Press, 1989.

———. *Related Lives: Confessors and Their Female Penitents, 1450–1750.* Ithaca, NY: Cornell University Press, 2005.

Bissell, R. Ward. *Artemisia Gentileschi and the Authority of Art.* University Park: Pennsylvania State University Press, 2000.

Blain, Virginia, Isobel Grundy, and Patricia Clements, eds. *The Feminist Companion to Literature in English: Women Writers from the Middle Ages to the Present.* New Haven: Yale University Press, 1990.

Blamires, Alcuin. *The Case for Women in Medieval Culture.* Oxford: Clarendon Press, 1997.

Bloch, R. Howard. *Medieval Misogyny and the Invention of Western Romantic Love.* Chicago: University of Chicago Press, 1991.

Bogucka, Maria. *Women in Early Modern Polish Society, Against the European Background.* Aldershot and Brookfield: Ashgate Publishing Co., 2004.

Bornstein, Daniel, and Roberto Rusconi, eds. *Women and Religion in Medieval and Renaissance Italy.* Trans. Margery J. Schneider. Chicago: University of Chicago Press, 1996.

Brant, Clare, and Diane Purkiss, eds. *Women, Texts and Histories, 1575–1760.* London and New York: Routledge, 1992.

Briggs, Robin. *Witches and Neighbours: The Social and Cultural Context of European Witchcraft.* New York: HarperCollins, 1995; Viking Penguin, 1996.

Brink, Jean R., ed. *Female Scholars: A Traditioin of Learned Women before 1800.* Montréal: Eden Press Women's Publications, 1980.

———, Allison Coudert, and Maryanne Cline Horowitz. *The Politics of Gender in Early Modern Europe.* Sixteenth Century Essays and Studies, 12. Kirksville, MO: Sixteenth Century Journal Publishers, 1989.

Broude, Norma, and Mary D. Garrard, eds. *The Expanding Discourse: Feminism and Art History.* New York: HarperCollins, 1992.

Brown, Judith C. *Immodest Acts: The Life of a Lesbian Nun in Renaissance Italy.* New York: Oxford University Press, 1986.

——— and Robert C. Davis, eds. *Gender and Society in Renaisance Italy.* London: Addison Wesley Longman, 1998.

Burke, Victoria E. Burke, ed. *Early Modern Women's Manuscript Writing.* Aldershot and Brookfield: Ashgate Publishing Co., 2004.

Burns, Jane E., ed. *Medieval Fabrications: Dress, Textiles, Cloth Work, and Other Cultural Imaginings.* New York: Palgrave Macmillan, 2004.

Bynum, Carolyn Walker. *Fragmentation and Redemption: Essays on Gender and the Human Body in Medieval Religion.* New York: Zone Books, 1992.

———. *Holy Feast and Holy Fast: The Religious Significance of Food to Medieval Women.* Berkeley: University of California Press, 1987.

Campbell, Julie DeLynn. "Renaissance Women Writers: The Beloved Speaks her Part." Ph.D diss., Texas A&M University, 1997.

Catling, Jo, ed. *A History of Women's Writing in Germany, Austria and Switzerland.* Cambridge: Cambridge University Press, 2000.

Cavallo, Sandra, and Lyndan Warner. *Widowhood in Medieval and Early Modern Europe.* New York: Longman, 1999.

Cavanagh, Sheila T. *Cherished Torment: The Emotional Geography of Lady Mary Wroth's Urania.* Pittsburgh: Duquesne University Press, 2001.

Cerasano, S. P., and Marion Wynne-Davies, eds. *Readings in Renaissance Women's Drama: Criticism, History, and Performance 1594–1998.* London and New York: Routledge, 1998.

Cervigni, Dino S., ed. *Women Mystic Writers. Annali d'Italianistica* 13 (1995) (entire issue).

——— and Rebecca West, eds. *Women's Voices in Italian Literature.* Special issue. *Annali d'Italianistica* 7 (1989).

Charlton, Kenneth. *Women, Religion and Education in Early Modern England.* London and New York: Routledge, 1999.

Chojnacka, Monica. *Working Women in Early Modern Venice.* Baltimore: Johns Hopkins University Press, 2001.

Chojnacki, Stanley. *Women and Men in Renaissance Venice: Twelve Essays on Patrician Society.* Baltimore: Johns Hopkins University Press, 2000.

Cholakian, Patricia Francis. *Rape and Writing in the* Heptameron *of Marguerite de Navarre.* Carbondale and Edwardsville: Southern Illinois University Press, 1991.

———. *Women and the Politics of Self-Representation in Seventeenth-Century France.* Newark: University of Delaware Press, 2000.

Christine de Pizan: A Casebook. Ed. Barbara K. Altmann and Deborah L. McGrady. New York: Routledge, 2003.

Clogan, Paul Maruice, ed. *Medievali et Humanistica: Literacy and the Lay Reader.* Lanham, MD: Rowman & Littlefield, 2000.

Clubb, Louise George (1989). *Italian Drama in Shakespeare's Time.* New Haven: Yale University Press

Clucas, Stephen, ed. *A Princely Brave Woman: Essays on Margaret Cavendish, Duchess of Newcastle.* Aldershot and Brookfield: Ashgate Publishing Co., 2003.

Conley, John J., S.J. *The Suspicion of Virtue: Women Philosophers in Neoclassical France.* Ithaca, NY: Cornell University Press, 2002.

Crabb, Ann. *The Strozzi of Florence: Widowhood and Family Solidarity in the Renaissance.* Ann Arbor: University of Michigan Press, 2000.

The Crannied Wall: Women, Religion, and the Arts in Early Modern Europe. Ed. Craig A. Monson. Ann Arbor: University of Michigan Press, 1992.

Creative Women in Medieval and Early Modern Italy. Ed. E. Ann Matter and John Coakley. Philadelphia: University of Pennsylvania Press, 1994.

Crowston, Clare Haru. *Fabricating Women: The Seamstresses of Old Regime France, 1675–1791.* Durham, NC: Duke University Press, 2001.

Cruz, Anne J. and Mary Elizabeth Perry, eds. *Culture and Control in Counter-Reformation Spain.* Minneapolis: University of Minnesota Press, 1992.

Datta, Satya. *Women and Men in Early Modern Venice.* Aldershot and Brookfield: Ashgate Publishing Co., 2003.

Davis, Natalie Zemon. *Society and Culture in Early Modern France.* Stanford: Stanford University Press, 1975.

————. *Women on the Margins: Three Seventeenth-Century Lives.* Cambridge, MA: Harvard University Press, 1995.

DeJean, Joan. *Ancients against Moderns: Culture Wars and the Making of a Fin de Siècle.* Chicago: University of Chicago Press, 1997.

————. *Fictions of Sappho, 1546–1937.* Chicago: University of Chicago Press, 1989.

————. *The Reinvention of Obscenity: Sex, Lies, and Tabloids in Early Modern France.* Chicago: University of Chicago Press, 2002.

————. *Tender Geographies: Women and the Origins of the Novel in France.* New York: Columbia University Press, 1991.

————. *The Reinvention of Obscenity: Sex, Lies, and Tabloids in Early Modern France.* Chicago: University of Chicago Press, 2002.

D'Elia, Anthony F. *The Renaissance of Marriage in Fifteenth-Century Italy.* Cambridge, MA: Harvard University Press, 2004.

Dictionary of Russian Women Writers. Ed. Marina Ledkovsky, Charlotte Rosenthal, and Mary Zirin. Westport, CT: Greenwood Press, 1994.

Dixon, Laurinda S. *Perilous Chastity: Women and Illness in Pre-Enlightenment Art and Medicine.* Ithaca: Cornell University Press, 1995.

Dolan, Frances, E. *Whores of Babylon: Catholicism, Gender and Seventeenth-Century Print Culture.* Ithaca: Cornell University Press, 1999.

Donovan, Josephine. *Women and the Rise of the Novel, 1405–1726.* New York: St. Martin's Press, 1999.

Early [English] Women Writers: 1600–1720. Ed. Anita Pacheco. New York and London: Longman, 1998.

Eigler, Friederike and Susanne Kord, eds. *The Feminist Encyclopedia of German Literature.* Westport, CT: Greenwood Press, 1997.

Engendering the Early Modern Stage: Women Playwrights in the Spanish Empire. Ed. Valeria (Oakey) Hegstrom and Amy R. Williamsen. New Orleans: University Press of the South, 1999.

Erdmann, Axel. *My Gracious Silence: Women in the Mirror of Sixteenth-Century Printing in Western Europe.* Luzern: Gilhofer and Rauschberg, 1999.

Erickson, Amy Louise. *Women and Property in Early Modern England.* London and New York: Routledge, 1993.

Extraordinary Women of the Medieval and Renaissance World: A Biographical Dictionary. Ed. Carole Levin, et al. Westport, CT: Greenwood Press, 2000.

Ezell, Margaret J. M. *The Patriarch's Wife: Literary Evidence and the History of the Family.* Chapel Hill: University of North Carolina Press, 1987.

————. *Social Authorship and the Advent of Print.* Baltimore: Johns Hopkins University Press, 1999.

————. *Writing Women's Literary History.* Baltimore: Johns Hopkins University Press, 1993.

Farrell, Michèle Longino. *Performing Motherhood: The Sévigné Correspondence.* Hanover, NH and London: University Press of New England, 1991.

Feminism and Renaissance Studies. Ed. Lorna Hutson. New York: Oxford University Press, 1999.

The Feminist Companion to Literature in English: Women Writers from the Middle Ages to the Present. Ed. Virginia Blain, Isobel Grundy, and Patricia Clements. New Haven: Yale University Press, 1990.

Feminist Encyclopedia of Italian Literature. Edited by Rinaldina Russell. Westport, CT: Greenwood Press, 1997.

Feminist Thought in European History, 1400–2000. Ed. Tjitske Akkerman and Siep Sturman. London and New York: Routledge, 1997.

Ferguson, Margaret W. *Dido's Daughters: Literacy, Gender, and Empire in Early Modern England and France.* Chicago: University of Chicago Press, 2003.

———, Maureen Quilligan, and Nancy J. Vickers, eds. *Rewriting the Renaissance: The Discourses of Sexual Difference in Early Modern Europe.* Chicago: University of Chicago Press, 1987.

Ferraro, Joanne M. *Marriage Wars in Late Renaissance Venice.* Oxford: Oxford University Press, 2001.

Fletcher, Anthony. *Gender, Sex and Subordination in England 1500–1800.* New Haven: Yale University Press, 1995.

Franklin, Margaret. *Boccaccio's Heroines.* Aldershot and Brookfield: Ashgate Publishing Co., 2006.

French Women Writers: A Bio-Bibliographical Source Book. Ed. Eva Martin Sartori and Dorothy Wynne Zimmerman. Westport, CT: Greenwood Press, 1991.

Frye, Susan and Karen Robertson, eds. *Maids and Mistresses, Cousins and Queens: Women's Alliances in Early Modern England.* Oxford: Oxford University Press, 1999.

Gallagher, Catherine. *Nobody's Story: The Vanishing Acts of Women Writers in the Marketplace, 1670–1820.* Berkeley: University of California Press, 1994.

Garrard, Mary D. *Artemisia Gentileschi: The Image of the Female Hero in Italian Baroque Art.* Princeton: Princeton University Press, 1989.

Gelbart, Nina Rattner. *The King's Midwife: A History and Mystery of Madame du Coudray.* Berkeley: University of California Press, 1998.

Giles, Mary E., ed. *Women in the Inquisition: Spain and the New World.* Baltimore: Johns Hopkins University Press, 1999.

Gill, Catie. *Women in the Seventeenth-Century Quaker Community.* Aldershot and Brookfield: Ashgate Publishing Co., 2005.

Glenn, Cheryl. *Rhetoric Retold: Regendering the Tradition from Antiquity Through the Renaissance.* Carbondale and Edwardsville, IL: Southern Illinois University Press, 1997.

Goffen, Rona. *Titian's Women.* New Haven: Yale University Press, 1997.

Going Public: Women and Publishing in Early Modern France. Ed. Elizabeth C. Goldsmith and Dena Goodman. Ithaca: Cornell University Press, 1995.

Goldberg, Jonathan. *Desiring Women Writing: English Renaissance Examples.* Stanford: Stanford University Press, 1997.

Goldsmith, Elizabeth C. *Exclusive Conversations: The Art of Interaction in Seventeenth-Century France.* Philadelphia: University of Pennsylvania Press, 1988.

———, ed. *Writing the Female Voice.* Boston: Northeastern University Press, 1989.

——— and Dena Goodman, eds. *Going Public: Women and Publishing in Early Modern France.* Ithaca: Cornell University Press, 1995.

Grafton, Anthony, and Lisa Jardine. *From Humanism to the Humanities: Education and the Liberal Arts in Fifteenth-and Sixteenth-Century Europe.* London: Duckworth, 1986.

The Graph of Sex and the German Text: Gendered Culture in Early Modern Germany 1500–1700. Ed. Lynne Tatlock and Christiane Bohnert. Amsterdam and Atlanta: Rodolphi, 1994.

Grassby, Richard. *Kinship and Capitalism: Marriage, Family, and Business in the English-Speaking World, 1580–1740.* Cambridge: Cambridge University Press, 2001.

Greer, Margaret Rich. *Maria de Zayas Tells Baroque Tales of Love and the Cruelty of Men.* University Park: Pennsylvania State University Press, 2000.

Grossman, Avraham. *Pious and Rebellious: Jewish Women in Medieval Europe.* Trans. Jonathan Chipman. Brandeis/University Press of New England, 2004.

Gutierrez, Nancy A. *"Shall She Famish Then?" Female Food Refusal in Early Modern England.* Aldershot and Brookfield: Ashgate Publishing Co., 2003.

Habermann, Ina. *Staging Slander and Gender in Early Modern England.* Aldershot and Brookfield: Ashgate Publishing Co., 2003.

Hacke, Daniela. *Women Sex and Marriage in Early Modern Venice.* Aldershot and Brookfield: Ashgate Publishing Co., 2004.

Hackel, Heidi Brayman. *Reading Material in Early Modern England: Print, Gender, Literacy.* Cambridge: Cambridge University Press, 2005.

Hackett, Helen. *Women and Romance Fiction in the English Renaissance.* Cambridge: Cambridge University Press, 2000.

Hall, Kim F. *Things of Darkness: Economies of Race and Gender in Early Modern England.* Ithaca, NY: Cornell University Press, 1995.

Hamburger, Jeffrey. *The Visual and the Visionary: Art and Female Spirituality in Late Medieval Germany.* New York: Zone Books, 1998.

Hampton, Timothy. *Literature and the Nation in the Sixteenth Century: Inventing Renaissance France.* Ithaca, NY: Cornell University Press, 2001.

Hannay, Margaret, ed. *Silent But for the Word.* Kent, OH: Kent State University Press, 1985.

Hardwick, Julie. *The Practice of Patriarchy: Gender and the Politics of Household Authority in Early Modern France.* University Park: Pennsylvania State University Press, 1998.

Harris, Barbara J. *English Aristocratic Women, 1450–1550: Marriage and Family, Property and Careers.* New York: Oxford University Press, 2002.

Harth, Erica. *Ideology and Culture in Seventeenth-Century France.* Ithaca: Cornell University Press, 1983.

————. *Cartesian Women. Versions and Subversions of Rational Discourse in the Old Regime.* Ithaca: Cornell University Press, 1992.

Harvey, Elizabeth D. *Ventriloquized Voices: Feminist Theory and English Renaissance Texts.* London and New York: Routledge, 1992.

Haselkorn, Anne M., and Betty Travitsky, eds. *The Renaissance Englishwoman in Print: Counterbalancing the Canon.* Amherst: University of Massachusetts Press, 1990.

Hawkesworth, Celia, ed. *A History of Central European Women's Writing.* New York: Palgrave Press, 2001.

Hegstrom (Oakey), Valerie, and Amy R. Williamsen, eds. *Engendering the Early Modern Stage: Women Playwrights in the Spanish Empire.* New Orleans: University Press of the South, 1999.

Hendricks, Margo, and Patricia Parker, eds. *Women, "Race," and Writing in the Early Modern Period.* London and New York: Routledge, 1994.

Herlihy, David. "Did Women Have a Renaissance? A Reconsideration." *Medievalia et Humanistica* 13 n.s. (1985): 1–22.

Hill, Bridget. *The Republican Virago: The Life and Times of Catharine Macaulay, Historian.* New York: Oxford University Press, 1992.

Hills, Helen, ed. *Architecture and the Politics of Gender in Early Modern Europe.* Aldershot and Brookfield: Ashgate Publishing Co., 2003.

A History of Central European Women's Writing. Ed. Celia Hawkesworth. New York: Palgrave Press, 2001.

A History of Women in the West.

    Volume 1: *From Ancient Goddesses to Christian Saints.* Ed. Pauline Schmitt Pantel. Cambridge, MA: Harvard University Press, 1992.

    Volume 2: *Silences of the Middle Ages.* Ed. Christiane Klapisch-Zuber. Cambridge, MA: ZHarvard University Press, 1992.

    Volume 3: *Renaissance and Enlightenment Paradoxes.* Ed. Natalie Zemon Davis and Arlette Farge. Cambridge, MA: Harvard University Press, 1993.

A History of Women Philosophers. Ed. Mary Ellen Waithe. 3 vols. Dordrecht: Martinus Nijhoff, 1987.

A History of Women's Writing in France. Ed. Sonya Stephens. Cambridge: Cambridge University Press, 2000.

A History of Women's Writing in Germany, Austria and Switzerland. Ed. Jo Catling. Cambridge: Cambridge University Press, 2000.

A History of Women's Writing in Italy. Ed. Letizia Panizza and Sharon Wood. Cambridge: University Press, 2000.

A History of Women's Writing in Russia. Edited by Alele Marie Barker and Jehanne M. Gheith. Cambridge: Cambridge University Press, 2002.

Hobby, Elaine. *Virtue of Necessity: English Women's Writing, 1646–1688.* London: Virago Press, 1988.

Horowitz, Maryanne Cline. "Aristotle and Women." *Journal of the History of Biology* 9 (1976): 183–213.

Howell, Martha. *The Marriage Exchange: Property, Social Place, and Gender in Cities of the Low Countries, 1300–1550.* Chicago: University of Chicago Press, 1998.

Hufton, Olwen H. *The Prospect defore Her: A History of Women in Western Europe, 1: 1500–1800.* New York: HarperCollins, 1996.

Hull, Suzanne W. *Chaste, Silent, and Obedient: English Books for Women, 1475–1640.* San Marino, CA: Huntington Library, 1982.

Hunt, Lynn, ed. *The Invention of Pornography: Obscenity and the Origins of Modernity, 1500–1800.* New York: Zone Books, 1996.

Hutner, Heidi, ed. *Rereading Aphra Behn: History, Theory, and Criticism.* Charlottesville: University Press of Virginia, 1993.

Hutson, Lorna, ed. *Feminism and Renaissance Studies.* New York: Oxford University Press, 1999.

The Invention of Pornography: Obscenity and the Origins of Modernity, 1500–1800. Ed. Lynn Hunt. New York: Zone Books, 1996.

Italian Women Writers: A Bio-Bibliographical Sourcebook. Edited by Rinaldina Russell. Westport, CT: Greenwood Press, 1994.

Jaffe, Irma B., with Gernando Colombardo. *Shining Eyes, Cruel Fortune: The Lives and Loves of Italian Renaissance Women Poets.* New York: Fordham University Press, 2002.

James, Susan E. *Kateryn Parr: The Making of a Queen.* Aldershot and Brookfield: Ashgate Publishing Co., 1999.

Jankowski, Theodora A. *Women in Power in the Early Modern Drama.* Urbana, IL: University of Illinois Press, 1992.

Jansen, Katherine Ludwig. *The Making of the Magdalen: Preaching and Popular Devotion in the Later Middle Ages.* Princeton: Princeton University Press, 2000.

Jed, Stephanie H. *Chaste Thinking: The Rape of Lucretia and the Birth of Humanism*. Bloomington: Indiana University Press, 1989.

Jones, Ann Rosalind and Peter Stallybrass. *Renaissance Clothing and the Materials of Memory*. Cambridge: Cambridge University Press, 2000.

Jordan, Constance. *Renaissance Feminism: Literary Texts and Political Models*. Ithaca: Cornell University Press, 1990.

Kagan, Richard L. *Lucrecia's Dreams: Politics and Prophecy in Sixteenth-Century Spain*. Berkeley: University of California Press, 1990.

Kehler, Dorothea and Laurel Amtower, eds. *The Single Woman in Medieval and Early Modern England: Her Life and Representation*. Tempe, AZ: MRTS, 2002.

Kelly, Joan. "Did Women Have a Renaissance?" In her *Women, History, and Theory*. Chicago: University of Chicago Press, 1984. Also in Renate Bridenthal, Claudia Koonz, and Susan M. Stuard, eds., *Becoming Visible: Women in European History*. Third edition. Boston: Houghton Mifflin, 1998.

———. "Early Feminist Theory and the *Querelle des Femmes*." In *Women, History, and Theory*.

Kelso, Ruth. *Doctrine for the Lady of the Renaissance*. Foreword by Katharine M. Rogers. Urbana: University of Illinois Press, 1956, 1978.

Kendrick, Robert L. *Celestical Sirens: Nuns and their Music in Early Modern Milan*. New York: Oxford University Press, 1996.

Kermode, Jenny, and Garthine Walker, eds. *Women, Crime and the Courts in Early Modern England*. Chapel Hill: University of North Carolina Press, 1994.

King, Catherine E. *Renaissance Women Patrons: Wives and Widows in Italy, c. 1300–1550*. New York and Manchester: Manchester University Press (distributed in the U.S. by St. Martin's Press), 1998.

King, Margaret L. *Women of the Renaissance*. Foreword by Catharine R. Stimpson. Chicago: University of Chicago Press, 1991.

Krontiris, Tina. *Oppositional Voices: Women as Writers and Translators of Literature in the English Renaissance*. London and New York: Routledge, 1992.

Kuehn, Thomas. *Law, Family, and Women: Toward a Legal Anthropology of Renaissance Italy*. Chicago: University of Chicago Press, 1991.

Kunze, Bonnelyn Young. *Margaret Fell and the Rise of Quakerism*. Stanford: Stanford University Press, 1994.

Labalme, Patricia A., ed. *Beyond Their Sex: Learned Women of the European Past*. New York: New York University Press, 1980.

Lalande, Roxanne Decker, ed. *A Labor of Love: Critical Reflections on the Writings of Marie-Catherine Desjardins (Mme de Villedieu)*. Madison, NJ: Fairleigh Dickinson University Press, 2000.

Lamb, Mary Ellen. *Gender and Authorship in the Sidney Circle*. Madison: University of Wisconsin Press, 1990.

Laqueur, Thomas. *Making Sex: Body and Gender from the Greeks to Freud*. Cambridge, MA: Harvard University Press, 1990.

Larsen, Anne R., and Colette H. Winn, eds. *Renaissance Women Writers: French Texts/American Contexts*. Detroit, MI: Wayne State University Press, 1994.

Laven, Mary. *Virgins of Venice: Enclosed Lives and Broken Vows in the Renaissance Convent*. London: Viking, 2002.

Ledkovsky, Marina, Charlotte Rosenthal, and Mary Zirin, eds. *Dictionary of Russian Women Writers*. Westport, CT: Greenwood Press, 1994.

Lehfeldt, Elizabeth A. *Religious Women in Golden Age Spain: The Permeable Cloister.* Aldershot and Brookfield: Ashgate Publishing Co., 2005.

Lerner, Gerda. *The Creation of Patriarchy* and *Creation of Feminist Consciousness, 1000–1870.* Two vols. New York: Oxford University Press, 1986, 1994.

Levack. Brian P. *The Witch Hunt in Early Modern Europe.* London: Longman, 1987.

Levin, Carole, and Jeanie Watson, eds. *Ambiguous Realities: Women in the Middle Ages and Renaissance.* Detroit: Wayne State University Press, 1987.

Levin, Carole, Jo Eldridge Carney, and Debra Barrett-Graves. *Elizabeth I: Always Her Own Free Woman.* Aldershot and Brookfield: Ashgate Publishing Co., 2003.

Levin, Carole, et al. *Extraordinary Women of the Medieval and Renaissance World: A Biographical Dictionary.* Westport, CT: Greenwood Press, 2000.

Levy, Allison, ed. *Widowhood and Visual Culture in Early Modern Europe.* Aldershot and Brookfield: Ashgate Publishing Co., 2003.

Lewalsky, Barbara Kiefer. *Writing Women in Jacobean England.* Cambridge, MA: Harvard University Press, 1993.

Lewis, Gertrud Jaron. *By Women for Women about Women: The Sister-Books of Fourteenth-Century Germany.* Toronto: University of Toronto Press, 1996.

Lewis, Jayne Elizabeth. *Mary Queen of Scots: Romance and Nation.* London: Routledge, 1998.

Lindenauer, Leslie J. *Piety and Power: Gender and Religious Culture in the American Colonies, 1630–1700.* London and New York: Routledge, 2002.

Lindsey, Karen. *Divorced Beheaded Survived: A Feminist Reinterpretation of the Wives of Henry VIII.* Reading, MA: Addison-Wesley Publishing Co., 1995.

Lochrie, Karma. *Margery Kempe and Translations of the Flesh.* Philadelphia: University of Pennsylvania Press, 1992.

Longino Farrell, Michèle. *Performing Motherhood: The Sévigné Correspondence.* Hanover, NH: University Press of New England, 1991.

Lougee, Carolyn C. *Le Paradis des Femmes: Women, Salons, and Social Stratification in Seventeenth-Century France.* Princeton: Princeton University Press, 1976.

Love, Harold. *The Culture and Commerce of Texts: Scribal Publication in Seventeenth-Century England.* Amherst: University of Massachusetts Press, 1993.

Lowe, K. J. P. *Nuns' Chronicles and Convent Culture in Renaissance and Counter-Reformation Italy.* Cambridge: Cambridge University Press, 2003.

Lux-Sterritt, Laurence. *Redefining Female Religious Life: French Ursulines and English Ladies in Seventeenth-Century Catholicism.* Aldershot and Brookfield: Ashgate Publishing Co., 2005.

MacCarthy, Bridget G. *The Female Pen: Women Writers and Novelists 1621–1818.* Preface by Janet Todd. New York: New York University Press, 1994. (Originally published by Cork University Press, 1946–47).

Mack, Phyllis. *Visionary Women: Ecstatic Prophecy in Seventeenth-Century England.* Berkeley: University of California Pres, 1992.

Maclean, Ian. *Woman Triumphant: Feminism in French Literature, 1610–1652.* Oxford: Clarendon Press, 1977.

———. *The Renaissance Notion of Woman: A Study of the Fortunes of Scholasticism and Medical Science in European Intellectual Life.* Cambridge: Cambridge University Press, 1980.

MacNeil, Anne. *Music and Women of the Commedia dell'Arte in the Late Sixteenth Century.* New York: Oxford University Press, 2003.

Maggi, Armando. *Uttering the Word: The Mystical Performances of Maria Maddalena de' Pazzi, a Renaissance Visionary.* Albany: State University of New York Press, 1998.

Maids and Mistresses, Cousins and Queens: Women's Alliances in Early Modern England. Ed. Susan Frye and Karen Robertson. Oxford: Oxford University Press, 1999.

Marshall, Sherrin, ed. *Women in Reformation and Counter-Reformation Europe: Public and Private Worlds.* Bloomington: Indiana University Press, 1989.

Masten, Jeffrey. *Textual Intercourse: Collaboration, Authorship, and Sexualities in Renaissance Drama.* Cambridge: Cambridge University Press, 1997.

Matter, E. Ann, and John Coakley, eds. *Creative Women in Medieval and Early Modern Italy.* Philadelphia: University of Pennsylvania Press, 1994.

McGrath, Lynette. *Subjectivity and Women's Poetry in Early Modern England.* Aldershot and Brookfield: Ashgate Publishing Co., 2002.

McIver, Katherine A. *Women, Art, and Architecture in Northern Italy, 1520–1580.* Aldershot and Brookfield: Ashgate Publishing Co., 2006.

McLeod, Glenda. *Virtue and Venom: Catalogs of Women from Antiquity to the Renaissance.* Ann Arbor: University of Michigan Press, 1991.

McTavish, Lianne. *Childbirth and the Display of Authority in Early Modern France.* Aldershot and Brookfield: Ashgate Publishing Co., 2005.

Medieval Women's Visionary Literature. Ed. Elizabeth A. Petroff. New York: Oxford University Press, 1986.

Medwick, Cathleen. *Teresa of Avila: The Progress of a Soul.* New York: Doubleday, 1999.

Meek, Christine, ed. *Women in Renaissance and Early Modern Europe.* Dublin and Portland: Four Courts Press, 2000.

Mendelson, Sara, and Patricia Crawford. *Women in Early Modern England, 1550–1720.* Oxford: Clarendon Press, 1998.

Merchant, Carolyn. *The Death of Nature: Women, Ecology and the Scientific Revolution.* New York: HarperCollins, 1980.

Merrim, Stephanie. *Early Modern Women's Writing and Sor Juana Inés de la Cruz.* Nashville, TN: Vanderbilt University Press, 1999.

Messbarger, Rebecca. *The Century of Women: The Representations of Women in Eighteenth-Century Italian Public Discourse.* Toronto: University of Toronto Press, 2002.

Miller, Nancy K. *The Heroine's Text: Readings in the French and English Novel, 1722–1782.* New York: Columbia University Press, 1980.

Miller, Naomi J. *Changing the Subject: Mary Wroth and Figurations of Gender in Early Modern England.* Lexington: University Press of Kentucky, 1996.

——— and Gary Waller, eds. *Reading Mary Wroth: Representing Alternatives in Early Modern England.* Knoxville: University of Tennessee Press, 1991.

Monson, Craig A. *Disembodied Voices: Music and Culture in an Early Modern Italian Convent.* Berkeley: University of California Press, 1995.

———., ed. *The Crannied Wall: Women, Religion, and the Arts in Early Modern Europe.* Ann Arbor: University of Michigan Press, 1992.

Moore, Cornelia Niekus. *The Maiden's Mirror: Reading Material for German Girls in the Sixteenth and Seventeenth Centuries.* Wiesbaden: Otto Harrassowitz, 1987.

Moore, Mary B. *Desiring Voices: Women Sonneteers and Petrarchism.* Carbondale: Southern Illinois University Press, 2000.

Mujica, Bárbara. *Women Writers of Early Modern Spain.* New Haven: Yale University Press, 2004.

Musacchio, Jacqueline Marie. *The Art and Ritual of Childbirth in Renaissance Italy.* New Haven: Yale University Press, 1999.

Newman, Barbara. *God and the Goddesses: Vision, Poetry, and Belief in the Middle Ages.* Philadelphia: University of Pennsylvania Press, 2003.

Newman, Karen. *Fashioning Femininity and English Renaissance Drama.* Chicago: University of Chicago Press, 1991.

O'Donnell, Mary Ann. *Aphra Behn: An Annotated Bibliography of Primary and Secondary Sources.* Aldershot and Brookfield: Ashgate Publishing Co., 2 nd ed., 2004.

Okin, Susan Moller. *Women in Western Political Thought.* Princeton: Princeton University Press, 1979.

Ozment, Steven. *The Bürgermeister's Daughter: Scandal in a Sixteenth-Century German Town.* New York: St. Martin's Press, 1995.

———. *Flesh and Spirit: Private Life in Early Modern Germany.* New York: Penguin Putnam, 1999.

———. *When Fathers Ruled: Family Life in Reformation Europe.* Cambridge, MA: Harvard University Press, 1983.

Pacheco, Anita, ed. *Early [English] Women Writers: 1600–1720.* New York and London: Longman, 1998.

Pagels, Elaine. *Adam, Eve, and the Serpent.* New York: Harper Collins, 1988.

Panizza, Letizia, and Sharon Wood, eds. *A History of Women's Writing in Italy.* Cambridge: University Press, 2000.

Panizza, Letizia, ed. *Women in Italian Renaissance Culture and Society.* Oxford: European Humanities Research Centre, 2000.

Parker, Patricia. *Literary Fat Ladies: Rhetoric, Gender and Property.* London and New York: Methuen, 1987.

Pernoud, Regine, and Marie-Veronique Clin. *Joan of Arc: Her Story.* Rev. and trans. Jeremy DuQuesnay Adams. New York: St. Martin's Press, 1998.

Perry, Mary Elizabeth. *Crime and Society in Early Modern Seville.* Hanover, NH: University Press of New England, 1980.

———. *Gender and Disorder in Early Modern Seville.* Princeton: Princeton University Press, 1990.

———. *The Handless Maiden: Moriscos and the Politics of Religion in Early Modern Spain.* Princeton: Princeton University Press, 2005.

Petroff, Elizabeth A., ed. *Medieval Women's Visionary Literature.* New York: Oxford University Press, 1986.

Perry, Ruth. *The Celebrated Mary Astell: An Early English Feminist.* Chicago: University of Chicago Press, 1986.

The Practice and Representation of Reading in England. Ed. James Raven, Helen Small, and Naomi Tadmor. Cambridge: University Press, 1996.

Quilligan, Maureen. *Incest and Agency in Elizabeth's England.* Philadelphia: University of Pennsylvania Press, 2005.

Rabil, Albert. *Laura Cereta: Quattrocento Humanist.* Binghamton, NY: MRTS, 1981.

Ranft, Patricia. *Women in Western Intellectual Culture, 600–1500.* New York: Palgrave, 2002.

Rapley, Elizabeth. *A Social History of the Cloister: Daily Life in the Teaching Monasteries of the Old Regime.* Montreal: McGill-Queen's University Press, 2001.

———. *The Devotés: Women and Church in Seventeenth-Century France.* Kingston, Ontario: Mc-Gill-Queen's University Press, 1989.

Raven, James, Helen Small, and Naomi Tadmor, eds. *The Practice and Representation of Reading in England.* Cambridge: University Press, 1996.

Reading Mary Wroth: Representing Alternatives in Early Modern England. Ed. Naomi Miller and Gary Waller. Knoxville: University of Tennessee Press, 1991.

Reardon, Colleen. *Holy Concord within Sacred Walls: Nuns and Music in Siena, 1575–1700.* Oxford: Oxford University Press, 2001.

Recovering Spain's Feminist Tradition. Ed. Lisa Vollendorf. New York: MLA, 2001.

Reid, Jonathan Andrew. "King's Sister — Queen of Dissent: Marguerite of Navarre (1492–1549) and Her Evangelical Network." Ph.D diss., University of Arizona, 2001.

Reiss, Sheryl E,. and David G. Wilkins, ed. *Beyond Isabella: Secular Women Patrons of Art in Renaissance Italy.* Kirksville, MO: Turman State University Press, 2001.

The Renaissance Englishwoman in Print: Counterbalancing the Canon. Ed. Anne M. Haselkorn and Betty Travitsky. Amherst: University of Massachusetts Press, 1990.

Renaissance Women Writers: French Texts/American Contexts. Ed. Anne R. Larsen and Colette H. Winn. Detroit, MI: Wayne State University Press, 1994.

Rereading Aphra Behn: History, Theory, and Criticism. Ed. Heidi Hutner. Charlottesville: University Press of Virginia, 1993.

Rheubottom, David. *Age, Marriage, and Politics in Fifteenth-Century Ragusa.* Oxford: Oxford University Press, 2000.

Richardson, Brian. *Printing, Writers and Readers in Renaissance Italy.* Cambridge: University Press, 1999.

Riddle, John M. *Contraception and Abortion from the Ancient World to the Renaissance.* Cambridge, MA: Harvard University Press, 1992.

—————. *Eve's Herbs: A History of Contraception and Abortion in the West.* Cambridge, MA: Harvard University Press, 1997.

Roper, Lyndal. *The Holy Household: Women and Morals in Reformation Augsburg.* New York: Oxford University Press, 1989.

Rose, Mary Beth. *The Expense of Spirit: Love and Sexuality in English Renaissance Drama.* Ithaca, NY: Cornell University Press, 1988.

—————. *Gender and Heroism in Early Modern English Literature.* Chicago: University of Chicago Press, 2002.

—————, ed. *Women in the Middle Ages and the Renaissance: Literary and Historical Perspectives.* Syracuse: Syracuse University Press, 1986.

Rosenthal, Margaret F. *The Honest Courtesan: Veronica Franco, Citizen and Writer in Sixteenth-Century Venice.* Foreword by Catharine R. Stimpson. Chicago: University of Chicago Press, 1992.

Rublack, Ulinka, ed. *Gender in Early Modern German History.* Cambridge: Cambridge University Press, 2002.

Russell, Rinaldina, ed. *Feminist Encyclopedia of Italian Literature.* Westport, CT: Greenwood Press, 1997.

—————. *Italian Women Writers: A Bio-Bibliographical Sourcebook.* Westport, CT: Greenwood Press, 1994.

Sackville-West, Vita. *Daughter of France: The Life of La Grande Mademoiselle.* Garden City, NY: Doubleday, 1959.

Sage, Lorna, ed. *Cambridge Guide to Women's Writing in English.* Cambridge: University Press, 1999.

Sánchez, Magdalena S. *The Empress, the Queen, and the Nun: Women and Power at the Court of Philip III of Spain.* Baltimore: Johns Hopkins University Press, 1998.

Sartori, Eva Martin, and Dorothy Wynne Zimmerman, eds. *French Women Writers: A Bio-Bibliographical Source Book.* Westport, CT: Greenwood Press, 1991.

Scaraffia, Lucetta, and Gabriella Zarri. *Women and Faith: Catholic Religious Life in Italy from Late Antiquity to the Present.* Cambridge, MA: Harvard University Press, 1999.

Scheepsma, Wybren. *Medieval Religious Women in the Low Countries: The 'Modern Devotion', the Canonesses of Windesheim, and Their Writings.* Rochester, NY: Boydell Press, 2004.

Schiebinger, Londa. *The Mind has no sex?: Women in the Origins of Modern Science.* Cambridge, MA: Harvard University Press, 1991.

———. *Nature's Body: Gender in the Making of Modern Science.* Boston: Beacon Press, 1993.

Schutte, Anne Jacobson, Thomas Kuehn, and Silvana Seidel Menchi, eds. *Time, Space, and Women's Lives in Early Modern Europe.* Kirksville, MO: Truman State University Press, 2001.

Schofield, Mary Anne, and Cecilia Macheski, eds. *Fetter'd or Free? British Women Novelists, 1670–1815.* Athens: Ohio University Press, 1986.

Schutte, Anne Jacobson. *Aspiring Saints: pretense of Holiness, Inquisition, and Gender in the Republic of Venice, 1618–1750.* Baltimore: Johns Hopkins University Press, 2001.

———, Thomas Kuehn, and Silvana Seidel Menchi, eds. *Time, Space, and Women's Lives in Early Modern Europe.* Kirksville, MO: Truman State University Press, 2001.

Seifert, Lewis C. *Fairy Tales, Sexuality and Gender in France 1690–1715: Nostalgic Utopias.* Cambridge, UK: Cambridge University Press, 1996.

Shannon, Laurie. *Sovereign Amity: Figures of Friendship in Shakespearean Contexts.* Chicago: University of Chicago Press, 2002.

Shemek, Deanna. *Ladies Errant: Wayward Women and Social Order in Early Modern Italy.* Durham, NC: Duke University Press, 1998.

Silent But for the Word. Ed. Margaret Hannay. Kent, OH: Kent State University Press, 1985.

The Single Woman in Medieval and Early Modern England: Her Life and Representation. Ed. Dorothea Kehler and Laurel Amtower. Tempe, AZ: MRTS, 2002.

Smarr, Janet L. *Joining the Conversation: Dialogues by Renaissance Women.* Ann Arbor: University of Michigan Press, 2005.

Smith, Hilda L. *Reason's Disciples: Seventeenth-Century English Feminists.* Urbana: University of Illinois Press, 1982.

———. *Women Writers and the Early Modern British Political Tradition.* Cambridge: Cambridge University Press, 1998.

Snook, Edith. *Women, Reading, and the Cultural Politics of Early Modern England.* Aldershot and Brookfield: Ashgate Publishing Co., 2005.

Sobel, Dava. *Galileo's Daughter: A Historical Memoir of Science, Faith, and Love.* New York: Penguin Books, 2000.

Sommerville, Margaret R. *Sex and Subjection: Attitudes to Women in Early-Modern Society.* London: Arnold, 1995.

Soufas, Teresa Scott. *Dramas of Distinction: A Study of Plays by Golden Age Women.* Lexington: The University Press of Kentucky, 1997.

Spencer, Jane. *The Rise of the Woman Novelist: From Aphra Behn to Jane Austen.* Oxford: Basil Blackwell, 1986.

Spender, Dale. *Mothers of the Novel: 100 Good Women Writers Before Jane Austen*. London and New York: Routledge, 1986.

Sperling, Jutta Gisela. *Convents and the Body Politic in Late Renaissance Venice*. Foreword by Catharine R. Stimpson. Chicago: University of Chicago Press, 1999.

Steinbrügge, Lieselotte. *The Moral Sex: Woman's Nature in the French Enlightenment*. Trans. Pamela E. Selwyn. New York: Oxford University Press, 1995.

Stephens, Sonya, ed. *A History of Women's Writing in France*. Cambridge: Cambridge University Press, 2000.

Stephenson, Barbara. *The Power and Patronage of Marguerite de Navarre*. Aldershot and Brookfield: Ashgate Publishing Co., 2004.

Stocker, Margarita. *Judith, Sexual Warrior: Women and Power in Western Culture*. New Haven: Yale University Press, 1998.

Straznacky, Marta. *Privacy, Playreading, and Women's Closet Drama, 1550–1700*. Cambridge: Cambridge University Press, 2004.

Stretton, Timothy. *Women Waging Law in Elizabethan England*. Cambridge: Cambridge University Press, 1998.

Strong Voices, Weak History: Early Women Writers and Canons in England, France, and Italy. Ed. Pamela J. Benson and Victoria Kirkham. Ann Arbor: University of Michigan Press, 2005.

Stuard, Susan M. "The Dominion of Gender: Women's Fortunes in the High Middle Ages." In Renate Bridenthal, Claudia Koonz, and Susan M. Stuard, eds. *Becoming Visible: Women in European History*. Third edition. Boston: Houghton Mifflin, 1998.

Summit, Jennifer. *Lost Property: The Woman Writer and English Literary History, 1380–1589*. Chicago: University of Chicago Press, 2000.

Surtz, Ronald E. *The Guitar of God: Gender, Power, and Authority in the Visionary World of Mother Juana de la Cruz (1481–1534)*. Philadelphia: University of Pennsylvania Press, 1991.

———. *Writing Women in Late Medieval and Early Modern Spain: The Mothers of Saint Teresa of Avila*. Philadelphia: University of Pennsylvania Press, 1995.

Suzuki, Mihoko. *Subordinate Subjects: Gender, the Political Nation, and Literary Form in England, 1588–1688*. Aldershot and Brookfield: Ashgate Publishing Co., 2003.

Tatlock, Lynne, and Christiane Bohnert, eds. *The Graph of Sex* (q.v.).

Teaching Tudor and Stuart Women Writers. Ed. Susanne Woods and Margaret P. Hannay. New York: MLA, 2000.

Teague, Frances. *Bathsua Makin, Woman of Learning*. Lewisburg, PA: Bucknell University Press, 1999.

Thomas, Anabel. *Art and Piety in the Female Religious Communities of Renaissance Italy: Iconography, Space, and the Religious Woman's Perspective*. New York: Cambridge University Press, 2003.

Tinagli, Paola. *Women in Italian Renaissance Art: Gender, Representation, Identity*. Manchester: Manchester University Press, 1997.

Todd, Janet. *The Secret Life of Aphra Behn*. London, New York, and Sydney: Pandora, 2000.

———. *The Sign of Angelica: Women, Writing and Fiction, 1660–1800*. New York: Columbia University Press, 1989.

Tomas, Natalie R. *The Medici Women: Gender and Power in Renaissance Florence*. Aldershot and Brookfield: Ashgate Publishing Co., 2004.

Traub, Valerie. *The Renaissance of Lesbianism in Early Modern England.* Cambridge: Cambridge University Press, 2002.

Valenze, Deborah. *The First Industrial Woman.* New York: Oxford University Press, 1995.

Van Dijk, Susan, Lia van Gemert, and Sheila Ottway, eds. *Writing the History of Women's Writing: Toward an International Approach.* Proceedings of the Colloquium, Amsterdam, 9–11 September. Amsterdam: Royal Netherlands Academy of Arts and Sciences, 2001.

Vickery, Amanda. *The Gentleman's Daughter: Women's Lives in Georgian England.* New Haven: Yale University Press, 1998.

Vollendorf, Lisa. *The Lives of Women: A New History of Inquisitional Spain.* Nashville, TN: Vanderbilt University Press, 2005.

Walker, Claire. *Gender and Politics in Early Modern Europe: English Convents in France and the Low Countries.* New York: Palgrave, 2003.

Wall, Wendy. *The Imprint of Gender: Authorship and Publication in the English Renaissance.* Ithaca, NY: Cornell University Press, 1993.

Walsh, William T. *St. Teresa of Avila: A Biography.* Rockford, IL: TAN Books & Publications, 1987.

Warner, Marina. *Alone of All Her Sex: The Myth and Cult of the Virgin Mary.* New York: Knopf, 1976.

Warnicke, Retha M. *The Marrying of Anne of Cleves: Royal Protocol in Tudor England.* Cambridge: Cambridge University Press, 2000.

Watt, Diane. *Secretaries of God: Women Prophets in Late Medieval and Early Modern England.* Cambridge, England: D. S. Brewer, 1997.

Weaver, Elissa. *Convent Theatre in Early Modern Italy: Spiritual Fun and Learning for Women.* New York: Cambridge University Press, 2002.

Weber, Alison. *Teresa of Avila and the Rhetoric of Femininity.* Princeton: Princeton University Press, 1990.

Welles, Marcia L. *Persephone's Girdle: Narratives of Rape in Seventeenth-Century Spanish Literature.* Nashville: Vanderbilt University Press, 2000.

Whitehead, Barbara J., ed. *Women's Education in Early Modern Europe: A History, 1500–1800.* New York and London: Garland Publishing Co., 1999.

Widowhood and Visual Culture in Early Modern Europe. Ed. Allison Levy. Aldershot and Brookfield: Ashgate Publishing Co., 2003.

Widowhood in Medieval and Early Modern Europe. Ed. Sandra Cavallo and Lydan Warner. New York: Longman, 1999.

Wiesner, Merry E. *Working Women in Renaissance Germany.* New Brunswick, NJ: Rutgers University Press, 1986.

Wiesner-Hanks, Merry E. *Christianity and Sexuality in the Early Modern World: Regulating Desire, Reforming Practice.* New York: Routledge, 2000.

———. *Gender, Church, and State in Early Modern Germany: Essays.* New York: Longman, 1998.

———. *Gender in History.* Malden, MA: Blackwell, 2001.

———. *Women and Gender in Early Modern Europe.* Cambridge: Cambridge University Press, 1993.

———. *Working Women in Renaissance Germany.* New Brunswick, NJ: Rutgers University Press, 1986.

Willard, Charity Cannon. *Christine de Pizan: Her Life and Works.* New York: Persea Books, 1984.

Wilson, Katharina, ed. *Encyclopedia of Continental Women Writers.* 2 vols. New York: Garland, 1991.

Winn, Colette, and Donna Kuizenga, eds. *Women Writers in Pre-Revolutionary France.* New York: Garland Publishing, 1997.

Winston-Allen, Anne. *Convent Chronicles: Women Writing about Women and Reform in the Late Middle Ages.* University Park: Pennsylvania State University Press, 2004.

Women and Monasticism in Medieval Europe: Sisters and Patrons of the Cistercian Reform, ed. Constance H. Berman. Kalamazoo: Western Michigan University Press, 2002.

Women, Crime and the Courts in Early Modern England. Ed. Jenny Kermode and Garthine Walker. Chapel Hill: University of North Carolina Press, 1994.

Women in Italian Renaissance Culture and Society. Ed. Letizia Panizza. Oxford: European Humanities Research Centre, 2000.

Women in Reformation and Counter-Reformation Europe: Public and Private Worlds. Ed. Sherrin Marshall. Bloomington, IN: Indiana University Press, 1989.

Women in Renaissance and Early Modern Europe. Ed. Christine Meek. Dublin-Portland: Four Courts Press, 2000.

Women in the Inquisition: Spain and the New World. Ed. Mary E. Giles. Baltimore: Johns Hopkins University Press, 1999.

Women in the Middle Ages and the Renaissance: Literary and Historical Perspectives. Ed. Mary Beth Rose. Syracuse: Syracuse University Press, 1986.

Women Players in England, 1500–1660: Beyond the All-Male Stage. Ed. Pamela Allen Brown and Peter Parolin. Aldershot and Brookfield: Ashgate Publishing Co., 2005.

Women, "Race," and Writing in the Early Modern Period. Ed. Margo Hendricks and Patricia Parker. London and New York: Routledge, 1994.

Woodbridge, Linda. *Women and the English Renaissance: Literature and the Nature of Womankind, 1540–1620.* Urbana: University of Illinois Press, 1984.

Woodford, Charlotte. *Nuns as Historians in Early Modern Germany.* Oxford: Clarendon Press, 2002.

Woods, Susanne. *Lanyer: A Renaissance Woman Poet.* New York: Oxford University Press, 1999.

——— and Margaret P. Hannay, eds. *Teaching Tudor and Stuart Women Writers.* New York: MLA, 2000.

Writing the Female Voice. Ed. Elizabeth C. Goldsmith. Boston: Northeastern University Press, 1989.

Writing the History of Women's Writing: Toward an International Approach. Ed. Susan Van Dijk, Lia van Gemert and Sheila Ottway Proceedings of the Colloquium, Amsterdam, 9–11 September. Amsterdam: Royal Netherlands Academy of Arts and Sciences, 2001.

INDEX